Also by *William J. Lederer*

OUR OWN
WORST ENEMY

William J. Lederer

W· W· NORTON & COMPANY · INC·

New York

Contents

Author's Note

Many people—some in Vietnam and some in the United States—have helped me write this book. Unfortunately I cannot thank my Vietnamese friends by name. If I did this they might receive a midnight visit from General Loan's men, or from Vice President Ky's secret police.

In some cases I dare not identify my American sources of information—especially if they are on active duty in the military. Therefore the names in this book will be fictional—unless the persons are historically known or when identification is unavoidable. When the names are real, there will be a note so stating.

William Sloane, Director of the Rutgers University Press, is a real name and a real person. This book could not have been written without Bill Sloane's perceptive editorial talents, generosity, and wide knowledge of many Asian problems. Despite a terribly busy schedule of his own, he spent weeks organizing the ever-changing material, tempering it, and breathing perspective into it. He encouraged me when I felt low. I felt low often, because writing *Our Own Worst Enemy* has been a traumatic experience. I felt like a physician who is forced to diagnose that a loved family member has cancer.

Eric Swenson, Executive Editor of W. W. Norton & Company, acted as father, mother, and author's hand-holder during the writing—which is the same thing he has done for almost every book I have written in the last twenty years.

And in the final crush, while we hovered over the printer's shoulder in Brattleboro, Miss Patricia Irving proved to be the Joan of Arc of southern Vermont.

W. J. L.

Dunster House,
Harvard University,
Cambridge, Massachusetts
March 14, 1968

I

OUR OWN
WORST ENEMY

———

"You have allowed your hysterical fear of Marxism to destroy your sense of political reality."

CHOU EN-LAI to the
author in Chungking,
China, July 1940

1 NOT LONG ago I returned from my thirty-fourth trip to Asia and my ninth tour of Vietnam. As I departed from Tan Son Nhut Airport, the U.S. Marines were reinforcing Khe Sanh in expectation of a massive North Vietnamese attack.

I had not gone to Vietnam to write an analytical book about that country. It was to have been merely an early stop on a tour of Southeast Asia to research for a book on global affairs. The Vietnamese situation would have been described in one section at most, and the volume I had in mind would have included a total of forty foreign countries.

After a month in Vietnam my mission changed. It changed violently. For me there was no choice. All my other activities had to be delayed. I was forced to drop everything and write about Vietnam; about Vietnam and nothing else. My entire background rose up and made my decision for me.

I have been a professional student and observer of Asian affairs since 1940, and a professional military man even longer. I have observed wars and political turmoil in almost every Southeast Asian nation. Death, destruction, and international power struggles have been my business for the greater part of my adult life.

I thought I had learned to control my reactions to bloodshed, havoc, ruthlessness, and national despair.

But what I saw in Vietnam taught me better. The practices I witnessed in Vietnam violated almost everything I had learned at military schools and as a combat officer.

American techniques in Vietnam profaned my experiences as a political activist and as a lifelong specialist in revolutionary warfare.

I beheld the United States being beaten—not by the strength of the enemy but by its own mistakes and incompetence.

I was embarrassed by U.S. officials who did not seem to realize that a catastrophe was exploding beneath them. Or, if the officials were conscious of America's foundering and bungling, they dissembled and spoke about the future as if success were assured. Time, they usually implied, was on our side, mistakes were being corrected, progress was certain, victory inevitable.

Perhaps. But it does not look that way from here—or there.

American defeats in Vietnam today are not slow. They are not even incremental. They are swift, absolute, and often deadly. Official double-talk, moralizing, exhortation, and slick public relations can no longer conceal them. The concrete facts are that the beatings we are taking, both politically and militarily, are painful, immediate, often bloody, and mostly unnecessary.

Our major efforts and commitments have been military, an area in which the United States always feels successful. We have never, we believe, lost a war. Therefore our failures and casualties in Vietnam have cost us much of our national confidence.

Our inability to win in Vietnam has patently humiliated the White House, the Department of State, and the Pentagon. There is a conviction held by many Americans that our leaders will do almost anything to salve their pride and protect their careers. It is held that militarily we are entering a stage of desperation. There is even a widely believed rumor that the Joint Chiefs of Staff has approved plans for the use of nuclear weapons and an invasion of North Vietnam.

What these leaders do not realize is that the concept of "there can be no substitute for victory" has been misapplied. Victory in Vietnam cannot come by devastating the land and the people we came to save. Victory cannot exist without a political victory. Certainly we should know this after more than two decades of defeat in Vietnam.

Most Americans do not realize that through our associations with the French and Ngo Dinh Diem the United States has been militarily engaged in Vietnam for over twenty-three years. The French were defeated. Ngo Dinh Diem was defeated. Today we are still losing. In 1968—after three years of hard fighting; 20,000 American deaths; 125,000 wounded; and the expenditure of $75 billion—the Vietcong still have the political and military initiative in about three-quarters of South Vietnam. And it is increasing.

In 1965 the United States held military offensives in four corps areas. In the spring of 1968 U.S. troops were on the defensive throughout all of South Vietnam.

The number of villages militarily or politically controlled by the Vietcong *increased* during 1967 and early 1968. This is confirmed by "Hamlet Estimates" made independently by both the United States and the Vietnamese governments. These estimates, incidentally, are classified as "confidential," and directly contradict U.S. government pronouncements—such as the Komer report of late 1967.

Vietcong control is not limited to peasants in isolated villages. It extends into American military complexes, including Danang, Saigon, and Hue. These bastions are guarded by billions of dollars of U.S. war equipment and thousands of U.S. and South Vietnamese troops. There are daily air reconnaissances of the surrounding areas. There are check points, patrols, and sentries. Yet an American cannot move about the outskirts of his own strongholds without armed protection. Ambulances going at night from one hospital to another within American and ARVN (South Vietnamese Army) districts have an armed man "riding shotgun" in the back.

The influence of the Vietcong even reaches into the U.S. Army units. The U.S. 25th Division (not far from Saigon) cannot have rifle practice at its own rifle range without sending a heavily armed patrol along with the soldier-marksmen. After six years of armed-combat involvement, we even have a problem protecting our own combat troops.

Since 1965 the number of armed enemy in South Vietnam has almost tripled to approximately 300,000. The U.S. bombings and "search and destroy" tactics seem to have the opposite effect from what was intended. No major unit of the enemy has been defeated or destroyed. In early 1968 the Vietcong assaulted and breached thirty-six major cities and towns in South Vietnam. They shelled or entered almost all major U.S. bases. Despite the heaviest bombing in the world's history, the flow of enemy supplies to the South has tripled during the last three years. The supplies which the Vietcong can't get from the North, they get from the United States.

With each year we have become more and more hated by the Vietnamese people, both North and South. That they dislike us (and hence resist the political paths we wish them to take) is natural. We have made beggars out of them. For example, the Vietnamese formerly exported rice. Today they are on rice rations. During 1968 America will have to send Vietnam at least 1,800,000 tons of rice or there will be starvation.

Not only is there hunger, but today there are approximately 4 million refugees and displaced persons in South Vietnam. To grasp the depth of this misery, on a map of the U.S.A. draw a line between Fargo, North Dakota, and Austin, Texas. If the United States had the same proportion of refugees as Vietnam, every family west of that line (50 million people) would be homeless refugees.

Every American west of Austin—from Mexico to Canada—would be sleeping in fields, in cemeteries, on roads, and begging for a handout. If the United States had the same proportion of citizens killed and wounded as South Vietnam has, there would be 25 million casualties in our country—about one out of every eight persons, the majority of them civilians.

The average Vietnamese blames the war casualties, the miseries, the loss of homes on the United States presence in South Vietnam and the government which we support there. This is the impression I received from peasants and intellectuals, both in Vietnam and in America. Whether or not the blame is properly assigned, the fact is that America and the South Vietnamese military-junta government is held responsible by the people. This has tainted every facet of Vietnamese life. For example, desertions from the South Vietnamese Army still are from 8,000 to 10,000 a month. It stimulates Vietnamese to resist—some directly by fighting, some by giving aid to those who oppose us, some by passiveness and desertion. The Vietnamese military success appears to be almost a miracle.

Today there are well over a million men fighting on our side in Vietnam. United States air firepower is about 1,000 to 1 over the enemy's. Our ground fire superiority is at least 10 to 1. Yet the enemy, the same which defeated the French and Ngo Dinh Diem (and hence also us), has few tanks, practically no planes, no warships, and only a fraction of the material resources available to the United States. Still, as in the past twenty-three years, the same lean enemy continues to thwart the United States, the most powerful and the richest country in the world. For a generation—since 1945—victory of any kind has been impossible for us.

Is it not obvious that we are doing something wrong?

We have botched up almost everything we have attempted in Vietnam. We haven't even been able to spend our billions efficiently or with dignity. The Vietnamese leaders we have supported were—and are—held in contempt by the people. And when we shook our steel fists and started military campaigns, we couldn't even find the enemy. On the average, out of every 1,000 "search and destroy missions" the U.S. Army has fired at the enemy less than twenty times.

One of the reasons we have been so impotent in Vietnam is that we have allowed two additional deadly enemies to enter the war. These two additional enemies give tremendous support to the North Vietnamese and to the Vietcong. These two enemies of the United States supply North Vietnam and the Vietcong with war materiel and food. They help maintain high morale. They assist in recruitment. They stimulate the determination to resist and defeat the United States.

Even though these two allies of our enemy are among America's most dangerous foes, we have been helpless against them. We are afraid to take action to thwart their deadly actions. We do not have the courage or integrity to confront them.

The two countries who are giving this support to North Vietnam and to the Vietcong are not Russia and Red China.

They are South Vietnam and the United States. We are our own worst enemy.

II

THE

DEAF AND DUMB AMERICAN

"So we're making a search and destroy sweep for VC in this here hamlet, and I go into a hut. There's an old woman there with several kids. She has black pajamas on and looks mean. I say to her, 'Where's your husband?' She shakes her head, and so I ask her again and she shakes her head again.

"I go outside after the interpreter, and when I'm outside I see the old woman in black pajamas running out of the house and toward the jungle. I holler for her to stop, but she keeps on. So I shot her. Why would she run if she weren't a VC? Sure, maybe she wasn't, but in war you can't take a chance. Maybe she was running for a rifle.

"If the old woman had spoken English, she might be alive today."

A GI telling about a hamlet near Saigon which was searched by the U.S. Army, June 1967

2   FIRST let us confront ourselves.

What is America attempting to accomplish in Vietnam?

From official speeches and papers, I conclude that our objective there is to help establish a free, autonomous, self-determined South Vietnam, which we hope will be non-Communist; a South Vietnam that will be economically and politically stable, and with at least the beginnings of democracy.

We hope to defeat the National Liberation Front in combat; or persuade them that they should join the U.S.-supported Saigon government instead of their revolutionary regime.

To have the people of South Vietnam voluntarily choose a non-Communist regime, it will be necessary to convince the South Vietnamese people that social justice will be a policy and practice of the regime which the United States advocates.

These objectives require communication between the United States and the Vietnamese people. They require a dialogue, person to person, face to face, which will convince the Vietnamese that America's motives and ideas are good and advantageous to the Vietnamese, and that the NLF rule and the North Vietnamese totalitarian ideas are disadvantageous.

So much for the political objectives. To gain our military objectives requires that the United States be able to identify and locate the NLF and North Vietnamese military units. It is impossible to defeat them militarily—or persuade them with reason—unless one can find them.

This requires, absolutely and unequivocally, communication between Americans and Vietnamese. However, this has been impossible. There are few Americans in the entire United States establishment in Vietnam who speak the language well enough to discuss the subtleties of politics, military tactics, intelligence, and economics with the Vietnamese on a local level. We are linguistically poor.[1] True, there are several thousand Americans who have had short courses in Vietnamese, lasting from three months to nine months. This is better than nothing; but it is not sufficient to exchange complex ideas and develop trust. It is enough to order a meal in a restaurant or tell somebody where to carry a bundle; but it is not enough to discuss the nuances of politics and security with the peasants, let alone the generals.

For Vietnamese people, the United States is mute except to the local, urban, French-speaking elite who don't communicate with the masses either. The NLF, however, has thousands of well-trained cadres who go into the villages and are persuasive about such complicated matters as absentee landlords, water rights, corruption, and other political and military subjects.

America doesn't even have enough people with adequate language capability to interrogate prisoners. We now turn North Vietnamese and Vietcong prisoners over to the South Vietnamese. The South Vietnamese treat the enemy prisoners with a cruelty which is beyond the imagination of a Westerner's mind.

The United States is blamed for the cruelty inflicted on the enemy prisoners. The blame is well deserved, be-

[1] In all the colleges and universities of the United States there are only about thirty Americans who are Vietnam specialists. Of these, only about a dozen have Vietnamese language capabilities.

cause the responsibility for the torture of enemy prisoners is ours. The United States signed the 1922 Geneva Agreement concerning the treatment of prisoners; the agreement states that the responsibility for good treatment rests with the nation which captures the prisoners. Therefore the inhuman way the North Vietnamese and the NLF prisoners of war are handled by the South Vietnamese is an American burden and responsibility. The North Vietnamese and the NLF know this, *as do we also*. It is absurd for us to complain about the bad treatment of captured Americans while we turn enemy prisoners over to the South Vietnamese knowing that they will be tortured, often to death, in the effort to get information.

We turn the prisoners over because we are incapable of interrogating them ourselves. We don't know enough of the language. Also we are ignorant of the culture and the history and the religion and the traditions of the Vietnamese—without which whatever they said could not be interpreted.

If several thousand of our own people were fluent in Vietnamese, we could get our own intelligence information. Today, as the Vietnamese government admits, approximately 30 per cent of the South Vietnamese Department of Intelligence is made up of North Vietnamese or Vietcong or enemy sympathizers. How can you run a war with intelligence obtained from such people?

Our entire war effort, both political and military, is dependent upon interpreters. It is estimated that we employ about 30,000 Vietnamese interpreters. Almost every U.S. adviser has one; almost every military unit, no matter how small, has one. God only knows how many are employed by the Embassy, USAID, USIS, CIA, and the various other U.S. agencies.

Even if these interpreters are sympathetic to our cause and are honest, still, most of them are incompetent. Associates of mine and I myself have tested interpreters throughout South Vietnam. The majority of them know only a few hundred words of English, if that many. Therefore, frequently they do not entirely understand what the American who employs them says. But they know just enough to say something in Vietnamese and then give a reply of sorts in English—even though often it gives the American the wrong answer to the wrong question; or they tell the Vietnamese to whom the American is speaking something different from what the American said.

It is no wonder that American leaders so often make false reports to the American public. Frequently official reports sent back are based on what has been told Americans by Vietnamese interpreters; and there is no knowing how many of them are Vietcong.[2]

Even if the interpreters are loyal, even if they have studied English hard, many of them are not very bright. There is a popular saying in Vietnam, "If you have been a failure at everything else, you can become an interpreter for the Americans."

In 1960 a coup was planned to depose Ngo Dinh Diem. The Vietnamese generals who maneuvered the coup asked the American general who was Chief of the U.S. Military Assistance and Advisory Group to meet with them. Also members of the American press. They wished to explain to the American general what they were doing. They wanted to say why they had organized the coup, and explain the reforms they felt were needed to make Vietnam a decent country.

The senior American general arrived at the meeting accompanied by his French interpreter. The rebel Vietnamese generals, through the French interpreter, started to explain events.

[2] It is a primary rule in Asian politics and war that if you want to get information about an enemy and if you wish to spread destructive information to the enemy, place your men as interpreters in the enemy's ranks. This has been practiced on the United States with great success for the enemy.

At this moment a representative of President Ngo Dinh Diem (who was hiding in his palace) came to the meeting place with a message. Ngo Dinh Diem's representative and the rebel generals began negotiating. They discussed what reforms Ngo Dinh Diem would have to make in Vietnam if he were to be allowed to remain president. These discussions were conducted in front of the Americans, in Vietnamese.

After over an hour of talk, the representative of President Ngo Dinh Diem accepted the demands of the rebel generals and promised that the president would put certain reforms into effect.[3]

The rebel generals were satisfied and rushed out to stop their troops from bombing the palace. The representative of Ngo Dinh Diem also rushed out. The coup was over. But none of the Americans had any idea of what the negotiations were about. They did not know until the account was published in French newspapers.

It so happened that once Ngo Dinh Diem was back in active power, he failed to keep his promises for reforms. The Americans in Vietnam did not know that reforms had been promised, even though the negotiations had been held in front of them. Had the United States known what reforms had been promised by President Ngo Dinh Diem at that time, the whole history of Vietnam and the United States might have been different. The reforms—if carried out —might have been enough to cause the Vietcong to go home and melt back into a normal society; and there might not be any war in Vietnam today. Once the immediate crisis was over it was impossible for American diplomats to get political leverage on Ngo Dinh Diem.

For the price of ten airplanes, $25 million, we could train a thousand people to be fluent in Vietnamese. It could

---

[3] (1) Land reforms were to take place immediately, (2) non-Catholics were to be in Ngo Dinh Diem's cabinet, (3) more Southerners were to be in the cabinet, (4) Nhu, Madame Nhu, and Archbishop Thuc were to be dismissed from power.

be done in two years. If we had a thousand men and women who were bilingual in Vietnamese, perhaps eventually the presence of the planes and their bombs would not be necessary.

Many people whom I have interviewed in Vietnam said that they had requested language training before being sent there. However, the Department of Defense and the Department of State had refused. Their reasons were that there was neither time nor funds.

In a public opinion survey which I held in Saigon, one of the people interviewed was a woman, twenty-five years old, married, a journalist and an editor.[4] What follows are the questions asked her (on the subject of interpreters) and her answers.[5]

QUESTION: What is the role of Vietnamese interpreters for the Americans here? Are they doing their work well? ANSWER: My country has been under foreign slavery— French—for eighty years. Generations of Vietnamese have acquired a stilted, biased attitude toward foreigners—they are big and they are white and they have had power and dominance over us. Even today this persists. Therefore, when a Vietnamese is in the position of doing something for the American, a foreigner, something at which the Vietnamese is obviously superior and on which the American must depend, then in what biased way will he do it? He will either do it with excessive, perhaps fearful respect—and in this instance he will tell the American what he believes the American wants to hear—or he will interpret with a cunning contempt, in which instance he will tell the American, with skillful subtleties, that which will confuse him or influence him to make a mistake. Also, remember, the Vietnamese is an Oriental. His total thinking pattern is

[4] This Vietnamese woman is a graduate of an American university. She holds a Master's degree in English.
[5] The survey was made of 113 people. It embraced all the social strata, including prostitutes, laborers, white collar workers, store clerks, soldiers, housewives, and intellectuals. The interviews were held in depth and were conducted by several Vietnamese, most of whom were graduates of U.S. colleges.

different from that of the American. "Yes," "No," and "Maybe" mean different things for us than they do for you. If I were an American I would trust only the interpreter who has been to school overseas for many years and has acquired the Western outlook and is treated as an equal; that is, one who is on the same pay level, gets the same courtesies, eats at the same table—in other words, an intimate friend.

The majority of interpreters I have heard do not have the skill to put into English what they hear in Vietnamese. Most of them have a limited English vocabulary and will change the meaning so that they can express things within the limits of their own very bad English.

QUESTION: Suppose there were ten thousand Americans here who spoke Vietnamese fluently?

ANSWER: They would be able to overhear conversations and thus learn much they do not know now. But as far as talking with Vietnamese, they would not get honest talk unless they lived on the same level, including eating with them. When an American leaves his air-conditioned suite after an expensive meal and talks with a Vietnamese who resides in a small, hot room and eats food which costs one-tenth that of the American, then the invisible communica tions bridge is destroyed before the conversation even starts. The American who speaks the language well and equalizes himself, he will learn a lot. If there were ten thousand of these, there would be no problems between Vietnamese and Americans. Under these circumstances the Americans could force the Vietnamese government to abolish corruption, to enforce justice; and the great leaders would come from hiding and work for their country. Now they must hide because they would be killed if they came out. Their time is not here until massive corruption and social injustice is reduced.

What this Vietnamese writer and editor said about interpreters is not unique. I have heard similar statements from many intelligent and patriotic Vietnamese over the last fifteen years.

In Vietnam the United States is dependent upon interpreters for *everything*. We cannot get supplies moved, get food or information, without interpreters. We cannot negotiate without interpreters. We cannot go into combat without interpreters. We are beggars; and because of this the South Vietnamese have contempt for us.

What the lady journalist said is worth repeating: "He [the interpreter] . . . will tell the American what he believes the American wants to hear—or he will interpret with cunning contempt, in which instance he will tell the American, with skillful subtleties, that which will confuse him or influence him to make a mistake. . . .

"The majority of interpreters I have heard do not have the skill to put into English what they hear in Vietnamese. Most of them have a limited English vocabulary and will change the meaning so that they can express things within the limits of their own very bad English."

Our lack of language capabilities in Vietnam defeats the very things for which we are fighting.

The United States is fighting in Vietnam so that the people of South Vietnam can, with freedom, without fear, determine and have the kind of government and life which they wish.

But the United States does not know what the people of South Vietnam want. The United States is isolated from the people of Vietnam. They can neither talk to them nor listen to them. We are unable to read their newspapers or listen to their radio programs. We are dependent on a few elite, mostly Northerners, who can speak English or French—and who control the interpreters who inform us.

Probably 90 per cent of the interpreters employed by the Americans in Vietnam are telling us either what the military junta, headed by President Thieu and Vice President Ky, want, or what the enemy wants.

This misinformation is debilitating the United States

not only in Vietnam but all over the world. I have seen it happen in Greece, in Indonesia, in China, in Thailand, even in France and Germany.

What the United States is attempting to do in Vietnam (and in other countries also) primarily concerns democracy and politics. We should not forget that "democracy" comes from a Greek word which means "popular government." Literally it means that people rule. The word "political" comes from the Greek word which means "pertaining to citizens."

The ugly and tragic fact is that in Vietnam the United States has no idea what is in the minds of the citizens; and Americans have no communication or dialogue of any kind with the Vietnamese people. Therefore it does not have the support of the people. And vice versa, the United States does not uphold and support the people of Vietnam. How can we? We don't even know what they want support in. We try to force them to do what we want, and what the Saigon government wants.

The United States is so dominated by its technologies and its wealth that it has lost touch with people. The United States believes it can spread democracy and maneuver politics by technology and money only. This may well be a fatal error in the life of our nation.

3   PSYCHOLOGICAL WARFARE is directed at the enemy's mind; it is techniques of persuading (or manipulating) the enemy to behave in a manner which is of advantage to one's own side. The desired behavior might be that of surrendering. It might cause the enemy to revolt against its own leadership, or to have self-doubts.

The first requirement of psychological warfare is the ability to communicate with the people you are trying to influence. You can communicate with them in two ways: (1) verbally, and (2) nonverbally.

Verbal communication means being able to communicate with them by words, either spoken or written.

Nonverbal communication concerns all other actions which will influence the enemy to do what you want him to do. These actions can either be violent or gentle. For example, if the presence of U.S. troops brings death and destruction to a South Vietnamese village; or if the presence of U.S. planes means the villages will be napalmed or wrecked with cluster-bomb units, then the villagers will reject the U.S.A. Instead they probably will support the Vietcong. This is nonverbal communication which defeats us. It is psychological warfare we are waging against ourselves.

When I was in Saigon I wanted to learn about American psychological warfare. I requested an interview with officers at psywar headquarters. Here is my experience.

The colonels at headquarters made a small speech about how many million leaflets had been dropped over North Vietnam, and also over the Vietcong-controlled areas of South Vietnam. The psywar experts showed me some of the leaflets. I asked the top U.S. expert present to tell me what the leaflet (printed in Vietnamese) said. The senior colonel reached for an English translation of the leaflet.

I told him I did not want the prepared translation. I wanted him to read the leaflet and translate it for me.

He said he did not speak or read Vietnamese; and neither was there any American in the psywar outfit who knew Vietnamese.

"Then," I asked, "how do you know for sure what's on the leaflets?"

He said the leaflets were prepared by trusted Vietnamese who were employed by the Psywar Division.

I told the colonel that at least 30 per cent of the Vietnamese in the South Vietnamese Department of Defense were either Vietcong or Vietcong sympathizers. Did the colonel know that the United States probably employed numbers of Vietcong?[6]

He shrugged.

It seemed crazy to me that the United States was dropping millions of leaflets all over the place and was not even sure what was on the leaflets.

I was told later that almost all of the leaflets dropped in North Vietnam went over the rural areas. I asked why they were not dumped over the highly populated cities, and I was told that it was too dangerous for the planes. There was too much flak.

The psywar officers told me that another example of their work is the *Chieu Hoy* program. This again involves the dropping of leaflets, leaflets intended for the Vietcong. The leaflet is a safe-conduct pass. With it the Vietcong can come into special South Vietnamese camps and be welcomed like long lost brothers. At these camps the *Chieu Hoys* will be treated kindly, they will receive medical care, good food, and also be taught a trade.

Later I investigated the *Chieu Hoy* program. The psywar people, the Vietnamese government, and just about every official U.S. spokesman had been saying that this is a very successful project; they give monthly figures as to how many Vietcong surrender via this route.

I learned that the *Chieu Hoy* program, like others equally highly praised, is a failure.

First, the South Vietnamese who administer these camps are incompetent to give the required political indoctrination (for which the camps were established). The *Chieu Hoys* are locked up like prisoners—even though they receive medical attention and better food than is available in the Vietcong areas.

Second, a large percentage of the *Chieu Hoys* escape after a month or two and return to the Vietcong. In short, the Vietcong come to the *Chieu Hoy* camps when they are ill

---

[6] The Vietcong who led the enemy attack into the U.S. Embassy during the Tet offensive in January 1968 were U.S. government employees.

or when they need rest and good food. When this has been obtained, they return to their regular Vietcong units, refreshed, rested, and ready to fight again. The United States and the South Vietnamese have been providing rest and recreation centers for the VC.

It was clear to me that the psywar efforts of the United States often backfired. Our presence, behavior, and plans usually proved to be psychologically helpful to the enemy.

I departed from psywar headquarters, where the psychological warfare people were using their energies the same way almost all other Americans in Saigon were: persuading America "that everything is going well in Vietnam." I had the feeling that our experts simply did not know enough to do otherwise.

4   EVER SINCE the United States became involved in Vietnam, in 1945, it seems that the majority of official reports on the situation there have been untrue. Reading over the twenty-three years' accumulation of misinformation is a staggering experience. False information has been used not only as a means of deceiving and persuading the public; it has also been the basis for foreign policy.

In contrasting official reports from Vietnam with the actual events, it would appear that many U.S. officials are either idiots or liars. Sometimes both.

I am convinced they fail to be truthful not because they are evil but because they simply do not have the intellectual equipment and training to work efficiently and honestly. They were and are incompetent. Sometimes, I believe, officials panic over their failures, and distort the facts to protect their own careers and reputations. Most of them are doomed from the start. In order for them to understand what Vietnam is all about, it is necessary to cast off certain prejudices of the Western mind. The Americans

involved in Vietnamese affairs, military, political, and economical, have been unable to cope with a situation which is
beyond their frame of reference. The problems of Vietnam
lay beyond their intellectual and moral fields. From the
very first they didn't know what was happening in Vietnam.

They never knew what was happening; therefore the
only thing left for them to do was to try to "look good."

The U.S. self-deception began in earnest in 1945
when we first started helping the French to regain their
Indochina colonies. As more and more Americans went to
Vietnam, the lies and self-deception increased in number
and magnitude. As early as 1951 the United States signed
an agreement with Vietnam for direct economic assistance.
That agreement was a farce. The Vietnamese did not receive the aid either directly or indirectly. It went to the
French.

One official statement after another was a forgery of
truth. Here is one example.

In the State Department Bulletin of 30 June 1952
there was a communiqué concerning France's military
efforts against the Vietminh: "There was unanimous satisfaction over the vigorous and successful course of military
operations. . . ."

This was a blatant falsehood. By June 1952 France
had lost control of almost all of Vietnam to the Vietminh.
France was desperate. During the previous six years she
had lost approximately 60,000 troops and had suffered
approximately 100,000 casualties. Yet the Department of
State referred to this as a "vigorous and successful course of
military operations."

In 1954 when the Vietminh finally defeated the
French, the affair was settled at an international meeting,
the Geneva Conference. The double-talk, and perhaps chi-
canery, which surrounded the Geneva Conference and sub-
sequent events is confusing. Perhaps that was the intent of
our spokesmen. I will not analyze the conference or what

happened after it. This is an issue the reader should think about for himself. I believe a résumé of the Geneva Conference would be revealing and helpful. The following condensation was prepared by the Committee of Foreign Relations of the U.S. Senate. It is from the committee's "Background Information Relating to Southeast Asia and Vietnam." I urge the reader to study this carefully, and then contrast it with U.S. actions which followed.

> May 8–July 21.—Geneva Conference on Indochina. The delegates are from Great Britain and the U.S.S.R. (joint chairmen), France, the United States, Communist China, Cambodia, Laos, and Vietnam, and the Vietminh regime. Agreements are signed on July 20 and 21 and the main provisions concerning Vietnam are that (1) Vietnam is to be partitioned along the 17th parallel into North and South Vietnam, (2) regulations are imposed on foreign military bases and personnel and on increased armaments, (3) countrywide elections, leading to the reunification of North and South Vietnam, are to be held by July 20, 1956, and (4) an International Control Commission (ICC) is to be established to supervise the implementation of the agreements. The United States and Vietnam are not signatories to the agreements. The United States issues a unilateral declaration stating that it (1) "will refrain from the threat of the use of force to disturb" the Geneva agreements, (2) "would view any renewal of the aggression in violation of the aforesaid agreements with grave concern and as seriously threatening international peace and security," and (3) "shall continue to seek to achieve unity through free elections, supervised by the U.N. to insure that they are conducted fairly."[7]

In October 1963, General Harkins, the senior U.S. Army officer in Vietnam said, ". . . victory in the sense that would apply to this kind of war is just months away. . . . I can safely say that the end of the war is in sight."

In February 1964, Secretary of State Dean Rusk

---

[7] The text of the Geneva Agreement is in Appendix C.

reported that there was no need for a greater involvement in Vietnam by the United States.

Today, four years later, we are involved in a major war.

In October 1965, McGeorge Bundy, who had been a presidential assistant, said that the initiative in the fighting had passed from the Communist insurgents to the United States and the South Vietnamese forces.

McGeorge Bundy is one of the smartest men I have ever met. I can't accept that he believed what he said unless he himself was badly informed.

In July 1966 Premier Nguyen Cao Ky predicted that U.S. air strikes would very soon force the enemy commanders to request a cease-fire. The following day he expressed confidence that North Vietnam's regime would fall within three months because of the U.S. raids against gasoline and oil storage depots near Hanoi and Haiphong.

Vice President Nguyen Cao Ky is not a fool. But an analysis of his statements indicates he is a liar. Yet this is the official the United States supports in South Vietnam.

On 1 June 1956, the Assistant Secretary of State for Eastern Affairs, Walter Robertson, made a public address. In it he said, ". . . And finally Vietnam today, in mid-1956, [is] progressing rapidly to the establishment of democratic institutions by elective processes, its people resuming peaceful pursuits, its army growing in effectiveness, sense of mission, and morale, the puppet Vietnamese politicians discredited, the refugees well on the way to permanent settlement, the countryside generally orderly and calm. . . .

"Perhaps no more eloquent testimony to the new state of affairs in Vietnam could be cited than the voice of the people themselves as expressed in their free election of last March. At that time the last possible question as to the feeling of the people was erased by an overwhelming majority for President Diem's leadership. . . ."

There is not one single true statement in this excerpt from Assistant Secretary of State Walter Robertson's address. I do not know of a single living historian or student of Vietnamese affairs, official or otherwise, who would disagree with me. In mid-1956, under President Ngo Dinh Diem, there was no democratic institution. The president was ruling the nation like a tyrant. The army was not growing in effectiveness. The so-called discrediting of puppet Vietnamese politicians simply meant that President Ngo Dinh Diem was murdering or jailing everyone who disagreed with him. The free election which Walter Robertson speaks of was a total fraud. The Vietnamese government reported a 95 per cent majority of votes for Ngo Dinh Diem even in areas which the Vietcong controlled and in which there were no voting booths. The "free elections" of Ngo Dinh Diem were completely rigged. That an Assistant Secretary of State should make such an untruthful statement is something I cannot understand. I knew Walter Robertson and he was an honorable man. The fact that he gave such misinformation to the public is something for all of us to ponder—because there are hundreds of other honorable Americans who have been doing the same thing. Was Walter Robertson a complete fool or was he forced to be? Or was he just covering up State Department failures? Or, as seems most likely, was the information being fed him by our observers on the spot totally false—deriving from men who had no knowledge of the land they were observing and no means of communicating with its people except through those who would profit by deceiving them?

In April and May of 1962, Secretary of Defense McNamara made a trip to Vietnam and reported, "There is no plan for introducing combat troops in South Vietnam."

He added that he was "tremendously encouraged" by progress in the war, and saw no reasons for a major increase in military aid to South Vietnam.

If a man as competent as McNamara can be so wrong, then something is grossly wrong with the intelligence-gathering systems of Defense and State.

In October 1963 the White House issued a statement following a trip to Vietnam by Mr. McNamara and General Maxwell Taylor, then Chairman of the Joint Chiefs of Staff: "Secretary McNamara and General Taylor reported their judgment that the major part of the U.S. military task can be completed by the end of 1965, although there may be a continuing requirement for a limited number of . . . training personnel."

Comment: About 20,000 Americans have died in Vietnam since McNamara and Maxwell Taylor said the above foolishness.

U.S. officials not only give bad information to the public, but they also are dishonest to each other. In June 1967, U.S. officials in JUSPAO (Joint United States Public Affairs Office) held a meeting in Saigon. It was a tense and serious affair. They were making plans for Secretary McNamara's inspection tour of Vietnam. For three hours these public officials—whose job it was to help Secretary McNamara know the truth—discussed what they should let McNamara see, and who and what he should not see during his tour. An eyewitness told me that members of the United States Embassy, the U.S. military, and AID wanted to let McNamara learn *only about things which would persuade him to approve their requests and policies,* and withhold from him those things which might result in disadvantage.

One of the frauds perpetrated on the American people concerns the South Vietnamese elections of September 1967.

The elections were rigged and distorted from the beginning. In May of 1967, for example, General Ky and

General Loan (Ky's hatchet man) had a meeting with all province representatives. Their purpose was to decide how to rig the elections. I have seen the transcribed minutes of the meetings. The part which interested me was their plans for fooling the Americans. It was decided, for example, that when the presidential campaign was well underway Ky would hold a public rally in Saigon, at a time and place and under circumstances which would guarantee the presence of American press and observers.

Ky's instructions were that at this rally some of Ky's men would be placed in the audience and would boo Ky. The purpose of this was to persuade the Americans that there was freedom of speech and demonstration, and that the election was being run in an environment of true democracy.

If anyone but Ky's own men booed him in public, General Loan's National Policemen were to identify him and "take care of him" later.

During the summer of 1967, General Thieu was afraid that General Ky would have General Loan assassinate him. He was so terrified that he told several American newsmen about this and requested that they "keep him in the news" as a means of protecting him. (Today Thieu is President and Ky is Vice President.)

About this time Thieu again called in some newsmen and, in a rage, reported that General Westmoreland had called on him and had tried to persuade him not to run for president.

When I queried JUSPAO about the incident, I was assured, "Oh, we know that Westy would never do a thing like that."

After double-checking the story, I again queried JUSPAO, and said I knew that Westmoreland had called on Thieu and had tried to talk him out of running for the presidency.

This time I was told that maybe Westmoreland had called on Thieu, but that whatever he said, Thieu must have misunderstood him.

Everything concerning the elections had a phony ring to it. Whether the elections did any good or not (I believe they did much harm because they "legitimatized" a military junta which had seized power by force), the way the elections were represented to the American people was distorted.

In the first place, both General Ky and General Thieu were ineligible for the elections. Their candidacy was illegal. The electoral law of South Vietnam states: "Government employees and military men, to run for elections, must file and take a leave of absence without pay beginning the closing date of application for the candidacy until the end of election day."

Vice Air Marshal Ky and General Thieu did not take a leave of absence. They wore their uniforms and stayed in office. By staying in office, Thieu and Ky maintained control of the National Police (now upped to 90,000), the South Vietnamese military forces, all official means of communication such as television stations, radio. They controlled the newspapers and transport (and denied these to their opponents) throughout the entire campaign.

There was much hullaballoo and self-congratulation about the number of voters who went to the polls. It was claimed that there was nearly total participation in the election by those who were eligible. Actually, however, only about one-third of the adult population was permitted to register. The remainder was disqualified as being Communist, anti-government, or living under the control of the Vietcong. And the one-third who did vote (the majority of them illiterate) voted under circumstances which made honest balloting impossible. Tran Van Dinh, who was the Chargé d'Affairs of South Vietnam to the United States in 1963, described the election in the 22 September issue of *Commonweal*. Part of it reads as follows:

> The Sept. voter . . . was handed 11 ballots—one for each presidential ticket (two names on each, President and Vice President); then he was given 48 other ballots—one for each senatorial slate (10 names on each). Thus he

had to go over 502 names and scrutinize 59 symbols (11 presidential; 48 senatorial). Many Vietnamese are illiterate; those who do read would have had to have taken a speed-reading course to fulfill their duty. Consider Kien Hoa province in the Delta, with 120,000 registered voters and 161 polling stations: voters there would have had to have been processed at the rate of 82 per hour, or 42 seconds per voter.

The voter did not care. His attention was directed at the familiar face of the policeman who controlled the polling booth. General Nguyen Ngoc Loan, head of the national police force and close associate of Nguyen Cao Ky had declared in a press conference in Saigon on Aug. 22: "National policemen will be stationed inside and outside booths all over the country. As the national police are the people in closest contact with the lowest echelon, there will be police telling them where to vote, how to vote and when to vote." The policemen also stamped the voter's registration card and anyone subsequently searched (a routine in South Vietnam) and found without the election day stamp on his card would be in danger of prison or even death. Finally no matter for whom he voted, the voter knew from past experience that the government candidates always win.

President Johnson sent a team of twenty-two men to Saigon to observe and report on the elections. This was another fraud. The members of the team did not speak Vietnamese, they knew nothing of Vietnamese politics or history or culture. They were incompetent to judge the elections; and their favorable report reflected their incompetence. They certainly did not know of the illegality of the two major candidates; or that opposition newspapers had been shut down by them; or that the only two other candidates who might have caused a sufficient upheaval to throw Thieu and Ky out were barred from the election: Dr. Au Truong Van Minh and General Duong Van Minh—a very popular man and a Southerner. Any candidate who had Buddhist backing found himself disqualified; and it was common knowledge that soldiers had been instructed to vote several times. Even General Thieu admitted this.

The presidential observation team certainly did not seem to take into consideration the fact that voting irregularities were pointed up in one-third of the polling places—and this in a nation where there is almost no free speech, and where there were members of the Gestapo-like National Police controlling everything. Nor did the president's team seem to consider that almost half of the Constitutional Assembly voted to throw out the election results.

It would be unfair to say that no good came from the election; and perhaps it was only a small bit of good which Washington hoped for when it forced the election down the throat of the Saigon government. But the nature of the "good" that resulted surely could not have been what was hoped for.

The election showed us that the Thieu-Ky regime does not have the backing of the people, and that the regime had to resort to bribery, terror, and disqualification of unfriendly voters (all of which are no less true for being customary attributes of elections in nations not ready for democracy) to stay in power. It showed that the Thieu-Ky regime will not listen to the people, that it is afraid of the democratic process.

The election was so completely rigged that it demonstrated the failure of our efforts to influence the Saigon government to make reforms.

The election was so highly publicized that it forced Western newsmen to focus away from military actions and toward political problems. Because of this, many people in the United States learned for the first time that some people in South Vietnam disagree with their government. There were, in fact, some anti-war candidates who did remarkably well at the polls, considering the nature of the controls imposed on voting. It is notable that a number of these anti-war candidates are now in jail.

These results are good, in a perverse sort of way. They expose facts of which many of us were previously unaware. If the President's committee had spelled out the results in this manner, it would have done a service to the country and enhanced its prestige. But it did not. It gave the American public the impression that the Vietnamese election was "as honest as possible" (which may be true), and that the democratic process in Vietnam had made progress.

Thus, the good results of the election came in spite of the election, and perhaps we should be thankful for them.

The Vietnamese falsehoods poured onto the American public are endless.

During the summer of 1967 the Marines were using the M-16 rifle for assault purposes. Under this heavy use, the rifle malfunctioned. It was not designed for that kind of work. Because of the malfunctioning of the M-16, many Marines died.

I was in Vietnam at the time.

When the stories of the M-16 were made public, the first thing the administration did was to make announcements that the M-16 rifle was the best one the United States had and, if it were cleaned properly, it would function properly.

The blame was placed on the Marines who were getting killed. Giving the public such an impression is criminal. We can criticize the Marines in many ways if we wish, but no one can ever be critical of them for failing to look after their equipment. At this they are the world's best professionals. The Marines who complained about the M-16 were justified in so doing. Since then both the M-16 rifle and its ammunition has been modified.

Actually the Marines do not wish to use the M-16 for assault purposes. They prefer the M-14 along with one automatic weapon per squad.

Even General Westmoreland once took notice of the distortion of events which the public receives. When he assumed command in Saigon, he said, "From 1960 to 1964 the United States was misinformed on the deterioration in Vietnam."

The implication in his statement was that under Westmoreland's leadership, the people of the United States would soon know the true state of affairs in Vietnam. Unfortunately matters have gotten worse since the general took command—despite his good intentions. When he and Ambassador Bunker came to Washington in December 1967, they gave America a progress report on Vietnam via television, meetings with the press, and briefings for Congress. The progress reports were filled with optimism and statistics which told how well everything else was going. One thing mentioned by Westmoreland and Bunker was that about 67 per cent of South Vietnam is under government control. The events of the now famous Tet offensive of January and February 1968 indicated quite the opposite. The Vietcong were able to enter and paralyze all the biggest cities in Vietnam. They breached almost every major American base.

Even information concerning deaths is falsified. The public generally is being told untruths regarding the number of enemy who are killed. Our government assures us the numbers are based on "body counts." Almost all newsmen I know believe that this body count business is a hokum. I do not know of any newsman who has been taken along to count bodies. Many have asked.

William Tuohy of the *Los Angeles Times* wrote, "Any man who's ever been in the field . . . knows there is no such thing as a body count. A platoon commander fighting for his life, trying to maneuver his platoon, simply doesn't have time to count enemy dead . . . Therefore, what this is is merely a battlefield estimate. Everyone knows this in the field. In Saigon, however, there are general officers who really believe that a body count literally consists of individual bodies counted."

It seems that the body count business has not

changed much since the French Indochinese war. I once heard a young French press officer ask General Navarre what he should tell the reporters about the number of Vietminh killed. General Navarre asked how many dead bodies had been counted. The press officer said about three hundred.

"Very well," said General Navarre. "We know that the Vietminh drag almost all of their dead away. That means if you have three hundred bodies, probably three thousand of the enemy were killed. Then we must allow a ten per cent for error . . . So tell the press that about thirty-three hundred Vietminh were killed . . ."

"By body count, sir?"

"How else?" said General Navarre, turning away.

An Army medical officer told me that even the U.S. Killed in Action numbers are not accurate. He said that a soldier who is wounded in battle but who dies the next day in the hospital is not listed as Killed in Action.

III

VIETNAM NOW IS ALSO THEN

"If you Americans had known even a little bit about my nation, you could have solved the Vietnamese problem in 1945. Just a little history. Just a little culture. . . ."

PROFESSOR VO VAN KIM in his discussion of U.S. failures and U.S. self-deception

5 FUTURE HISTORY is not always easy to recognize when you first come upon its portents. That was true for me a long time ago, in 1940. At that moment I was a young lieutenant, jg, not long out of Annapolis and serving in the Navy on USS *Tutuila*. The *Tutuila* was an elderly gunboat assigned to a station 1,500 miles up the Yangtze River. Our port at the time was Chungking, the wartime capital of the Chiang Kai-shek government of China.

Chungking was then under daily air bombardment from the Japanese, and had been for some time. There were many shelters from the frequent raids, most of them caves dug into the rock of the plateau on which much of the city stood. An elaborate system of air-raid warnings had been developed by the Chinese, and usually there was ample notice of an attack, but on this morning in late August of 1940, the system failed to give me adequate time to return to my ship. So I found myself in a dugout shelter on the heights above the Yangtze River, waiting out the raid.

In the cave, several hundred people milled around, perspiring and grumbling. Among them were three Jesuit priests whom I recognized. With them was a short, pudgy Caucasian, about sixty years old. His skin was red, perhaps from recent exposure to the sun; he was wearing a sleeveless brown shirt, khaki shorts, and sandals cut from old auto tires. Next to him was a small, fragile Chinese who appeared to weigh about ninety pounds. He was darker than most Chinese, and his face had enormous pores, perhaps pock marks. His small mouth was tight; around his head he had bound a blue sweatband. Looking at him, I guessed that he was a Southerner, perhaps a Yunnan tribesman, or possibly from Kwangsi Province or Hainan Island.

The pudgy Caucasian held out his hand. "I am Pierre Cogny."

One of the three priests said, "Father Pierre is from Saigon."

"You're a Jesuit?"

Father Pierre nodded. Then he pointed to his Chinese companion. "This is Mister Win."

My face must have implied a question.

"His name," said Father Pierre, "is spelled N-G-U-Y-E-N. It is pronounced Win. He is an Annamite from Vinh Long—just south of Saigon. He speaks Chinese, French, and Vietnamese, but no English."

"A priest?"

"No," said Father Pierre, inclining his head forward on his short, thick neck. "No. Nguyen is a patriot—in the original meaning of the word, of course. . . ."

A stick of Japanese bombs exploded near the shelter. Everyone flinched and ducked. Dirt fell from overhead. A blast of smoke and hot air slammed into the entrance tunnel. Women screamed. Babies began crying. Men started edging and crowding toward the entrance. There had been rumors that the Japs were putting poison gas into their bombs. All of us knew also that if a big one dropped too close, the entrance would collapse and everyone inside would be suffocated unless a digging crew arrived quickly.

Eventually the air cleared; no more bombs came close. Gradually the tenseness subsided.

Father Pierre turned to me and said, "Do you, by any chance, have a copy of the Declaration of Independence on your ship?"

"Yes, we do."

"Nguyen wants to know if we may make a copy of your Declaration of Independence."

"Of course."

Father Pierre came closer to me and said, in a low voice, "Nguyen is writing the declaration of independence for Indochina."

"Independence from France?"

"It will come sooner than you think. The Japanese have broken the backs of the French. In a few years Indochina will be able to free itself."

One of the other priests said, "Father Pierre feels strongly about this. He has served in Indochina most of his life. He has had legal training and has been defending the Annamites who have been arrested by the French."

"But it has done no good," said Father Pierre. "However, World War II is giving the Indochinese the opportunity they've been waiting for."

The sirens signaled that the air raid was over. The shelter disgorged its several hundred people. Father Pierre, Nguyen-the-Annamite, and I walked two miles downstream to where the *Tutuila* was moored. After we had eaten, I showed them a facsimile of the Declaration of Independence. Father Pierre put on his steel-rimmed glasses. He began to translate the Declaration into French, writing it down in a bent, dirty notebook. Nguyen looked over his shoulder—making a series of remarks in a South China dialect which I did not understand. Father Pierre interpreted: "Ah, yes, that preamble we must use . . . right after that, in here, we will state our complaints and reasons for independence . . . no, that does not apply to us . . . ah, this we must use exactly as the Americans wrote it. . . ."

For about an hour, Nguyen talked about the declaration of independence he was writing for his country—which was not yet independent and still a French colony.

I invited the two men to stay overnight.

"We must go," said Father Pierre. "Already we are several days late."

"Where are you going?"

"To Liuchow, to meet with Tong Van So."

"Who is Tong Van So?"

"An independence organizer. He and General Yeh[1] are training Vietnamese guerrilla units. . . ." He smiled. "They are being trained to fight the Japanese in Vietnam . . . and we have Chiang Kai-shek's blessing."

Just before dark the two men boarded a southbound junk. That was the last I ever saw of them, but I learned some years later that Father Pierre had been caught by the Japanese near Lao Cai and had been executed as a spy. As far as Nguyen was concerned, of course it was impossible to check up. Nguyen was his family name—and in Vietnam it is as common as Smith or Jones.

But Nguyen's declaration of independence is another matter. It was promulgated in Hanoi on 2 September 1945 as the Declaration of Independence of the Republic of Viet Nam;[2] and when I saw it in translation, it read very much like the one he had discussed with me on board USS *Tutuila* some five years before. Of the fifteen names signed at the bottom of the declaration, three are Nguyens. I have often wondered which, if any, of them, is the Nguyen I remember—the dark, small Annamite who had pock marks on his face and was wearing a blue sweatband.

The "independence organizer" whom Father Pierre and Nguyen were traveling to see in Liuchow—Tong Van So—of him we have all heard much. "Tong Van So" was one of his many aliases. In May 1941 he changed his name again, this time to Ho Chi Minh, and he has been known as Ho Chi Minh ever since. When I asked about him in later years, some people said he was a Communist devil. Others thought he was a nationalist saint.

Even though the very name, Ho Chi Minh, is an alias, it probably is the one by which the man will be

[1] Yeh Chien-ying, a Red Chinese general who was training troops for guerrilla work against the Japanese.

[2] See Appendix B.

remembered. For centuries people in Asia will recall him as the leader-of-peasants who, for twenty-odd years, defeated the massed power and force of the West. Even today the majority of the people of South Vietnam—both pro-Communist and anti-Communist—refer to him as "Uncle Ho," a term of respect and even of affection.

When Nguyen and Father Pierre departed Chungking for their meeting with "Tong Van So," Pearl Harbor was about a year in the future. The war in Europe had gone badly for the French, and I wondered if they would give sovereignty to the Indochinese. I asked this of a Chinese intellectual whom I knew, Chou En-lai, now Red China's Foreign Minister.

Chou shook his head very slightly and paused to consider. "No," he finally said, "the French colonial imperialists and their troops are still in Indochina. They are there now as Japanese puppets. Eventually Japan will be defeated, and then the Indochinese people will become free. It will not be easy. The French will send their armies to Indochina to hold on to their colonies. There will be a long, bloody war. It may last ten or twenty years. But in the end the Indochinese will defeat France and will become independent."

I said, "Roosevelt would not permit the French to send armies to Vietnam. He will insist on self-determination for the Indochinese."

"How do you know that?"

"I am informed about President Roosevelt's attitude on this subject."

"Nonsense!" said Chou En-lai. "Your United States will support the French imperialists. You have allowed your fear of Marxism to destroy your sense of political reality."

When Laughlin Curry, President Roosevelt's personal representative, came to Chungking, I reported to him all the conversations I had had with foreigners concerning Indochina. When I mentioned Chou En-lai's skepticism about American integrity in Indochina, Curry said, in effect, "He is wrong. I've heard President Roosevelt say he wants Indochina to be independent after the war. The President is sick to anger over the way the French have exploited those people. He believes self-determination in Asia is the key to future peace. He has said this should be obvious to anyone who has a sense of historical perspective."

6   ROOSEVELT'S STATEMENT, "This should be obvious to anyone who has a sense of historical perspective," is especially relevant to affairs in Vietnam. For years it caused me to dig into the subject, to save clippings, to interview people who had been to Indochina. But it was not until later that things fell into perspective for me.

The political and military behavior of the Vietnamese has been consistent for over a thousand years. The Vietnamese may quarrel among themselves, but they consider themselves one people. They may refer to each other as "people from the North," or "people from the South," but not as North Vietnamese or South Vietnamese. They consider themselves a single community; and they will band together to fight any foreign nation which invades them. This is a dominant tradition.

Every Vietnamese knows this and feels it deeply. Even illiterate peasants discuss events of the past, especially their ancestors' struggles for freedom from foreign domination. But the average Vietnamese generally does not learn history the way students learn it in the West. They learn their history by word of mouth. It is told by fathers to sons in over 13,000 hamlets. Sometimes it may deviate a little from what actually happened. The Vietnamese heroes may appear more heroic than life. The enemy may appear more villainous than life. Nevertheless, history the way the Vietnamese know it is what motivates their behavior today. For this reason I feel it is important that we briefly examine Vietnam's history *from the Vietnamese point of view*.

In March 1945, Japan eliminated French power in Indochina and turned a sovereign Vietnam over to the Vietnamese.

Despite the state of hostilities between Japan and the United States, the Japanese action was not out of harmony with U.S. foreign policy. President Roosevelt vehemently and often had insisted that France be prevented from getting her colonies back. Roosevelt gave orders that American forces in Southeast Asia would not in any way assist the French. General Wedemeyer wrote in his memoirs: "He [Roosevelt] evinced considerable interest in French Indochina and stated he was going to do everything possible to give the people in that area their independence. . . . He admonished me not to give any supplies to the French forces operating in that area. . . ."

But when World War II ended, U.S. foreign policy changed abruptly and without explanation. The United States became a partner in France's military effort to reconquer her Indochinese colonies. The billion dollars of American diplomatic, economic, and military aid continued for nine years—until France (and the United States) was humiliated and defeated at Dien Bien Phu in March of 1954.

Several months later, on October 9, 1954, the defeated French troops marched out of Hanoi and out of Vietnam. But not without suitable pomp and circumstance.

The pomp, at least, was all French and in the best official French military tradition. A moment in history, in which the vanquished recorded their pride. Cameras caught most of it—the tall white men in their battalions; the paratroopers with shined and glistening boots; the lanky, loose, black African mercenaries; the tight-lipped men of the Foreign Legion. They marched west out of Hanoi and out of their moment in history, defeated and symbolic. Young graduates of France's West Point, St. Cyr, led the companies. Older graduates led the battalions. But many of

France's corps of professional officers remained behind. They were dead, buried in the hot, moist earth of Vietnam.

All the morning of October 9 the vanquished made their way out of Hanoi. The cameras recorded the French divisions, with their gaily colored, well-pressed uniforms, their impressive and modern equipment (which included American tanks, American half-tracks, American trucks, and good jungle rifles), and their military bands. The music was lively, martial music. It was a scene not unlike an earlier one, when the British, under Lord Cornwallis, marched out of Yorktown in 1781. Then, the well-disciplined British veterans (also defeated by a rabble) paraded with their fifes merrily whistling a popular eighteenth-century tune, "The World Turned Upside Down."

The French marched out of Hanoi with the élan of victors. Some Legionnaires waved at people peeking from windows. (No one waved back.) Overhead, squadrons of French planes roared low and waggled their wings in tight formation.

On the same day, October 9, 1954, and at the same time, Ho Chi Minh's Vietnamese farmers and fishermen came into Hanoi from the other side of the city. These were the men who had beaten the parading French. Silently they straggled in, small brown men in torn clothes and dirty sneakers. Their hollow cheeks and sharp cheekbones testified to years of hunger and jungle sicknesses, and a desperate passion to throw out the men they judged to be their oppressors. Their appearance was deceptive. This was not a rag-tag outfit but a highly disciplined one.

They looked to left and right at the capital which most of them had never seen before. They appeared sure of themselves as warriors; still, they acted as if they did not know what to do next. These slender, brown men for years had been the rabble, the hunted and the exploited, and they seemed surprised at their own strength and their military victory. Although many had American weapons, a large number of the short, frail-looking men had homemade guns wrought from pipes fastened to hand-whittled wooden stocks. Some even had spears. Some pushed bicycles loaded with six hundred pounds of rice and ammunition. They certainly did not look like troops which could be victorious in twentieth-century combat, especially against a European army equipped with the latest weapons.

These were the tattered people of the People's Army. They were the muscle on the bone of Ho Chi Minh's organization. From hamlets they came, from the Mekong Delta, from the Red River Delta, from the Plateau of Tiger Teeth—all the way from the Gulf of Thailand to the Chinese border a thousand miles to the north.

Behind the gaunt militiamen, with their deeply muscled legs often knotted with varicose veins, came the hard core of Ho Chi Minh's military and political forces—the tough, organized cadres. They too had ragged clothes and the look of jungle fatigue and sickness; but most of them carried modern rifles and automatic weapons. Some had American walkie-talkies strapped to their backs. A few ate food from U.S. Army ration kits. Some had Russian equipment.

All morning the skinny, malaria-ridden peasant-victors with wispy beards slowly straggled in. Their unhurried gait, their apparently leisurely entrance may have been planned as proof of confidence. And all morning—on the other side of the city—the well-fed, well-shaved, abundantly equipped, defeated and depleted French Army paraded from Hanoi. Marching to the west, they went to the trucks, trains, planes, and ships which would return them to Paris and Marseilles, to Toulon and North Africa (there to fight another losing war against forces of "national liberation").

The Vietnamese peasants who entered Hanoi went immediately to police stations, public-utility buildings, communication centers, and warehouses. Their task was to take over and organize what was now their sovereign and independent nation, guaranteed by the Geneva Agreement. The crowds cheered them. Copies of the Declaration of

Independence of the Republic of Viet Nam—issued nine years earlier on 2 September—were posted on wall bulletins.

There are several remarkable documentary films of the defeat of France, films which make the viewer an eye-witness to France's and America's debacle, and to Ho Chi Minh's victory. The best was filmed by a U.S. Army photographic unit, and it is currently in the possession of the Department of Defense. I used it as a training film when, as a Navy captain, I was special assistant to the Commander in Chief, Pacific. In those days (the late 1950's) the film was unclassified. I used it to show how it is possible, and probable, that a small number of well-trained and highly motivated guerrilla forces in Asia could, and did, defeat a modern Western army equipped with all the latest technological weapons. That modern Western army had been badly led for the war it was fighting; its leaders were ignorant of local needs, of Asian culture and traditions, and could not grasp what it meant when a total revolutionary effort voluntarily was made by the majority of people.

In 1963 I tried to get a copy of this film. I was refused. The documentary has been classified as confidential; ordinary American citizens are now not allowed to look at it.

However, there are similar news clips available to the public, documentaries which show almost the same thing. They can be found in both French and American news-film libraries. There is, for example, a film clip of Ho Chi Minh. Robert Shaplen (who also saw the film of Ho Chi Minh) describes it in *The Lost Revolution*:

> Late in October, 1954, in the wake of the Geneva Conference, Ho triumphantly emerged from his forest hide-out, ending rumors that he had died there, and re-entered Hanoi with his victorious Vietminh troops. A film I witnessed at the time showed him to be the same frail, stooped wisp of a

man whose classic endurance of body and soul were almost visible aspects of his being, in contrast to the submerged shrewdness and guile that had marked his long career as one of the cleverest performers on the stage of world revolution. With typical humility, Ho rejected a gala public ceremony. He arrived in a captured three quarter ton French Army truck . . .[3]

The viewing of a series of old film clips (many of which are illogically optimistic) of the French-Indochina war—with the Hanoi scenes last—gives some insights into why the French were so completely defeated. A deceived nation cannot win wars! The French officials deceived both themselves and their nation. They deceived themselves and their nation exactly as the United States officials are doing.

If one reads the accounts of the war as reported by some of the news media, and if one studies the statements made by important officials, one is staggered at the distortions and lies which we, the public, were given as truth. Some of the older statements seem absurd now—but they were accepted as truth when first spoken! They may seem repetitious, but I believe they are worth emphasizing.

On 28 October, 1951, *The New York Times* reported: "General J. Lawton Collins [of the U.S.A.] said today his recent visits to the Southeast Asian countries had convinced him that there is 'no question' that the Communist menace in French Indo-China had been stopped."

On 2 January, 1954 (a few months before Dien Bien Phu), General Navarre told his French Union Forces in Indochina that he fully expected victory . . . after six more months of hard fighting.

On 21 March, 1954 (days before the Dien Bien Phu defeat), General Ely said that the crushing Vietminh loss in the battle for Dien Bien Phu gave rise to a hope for a major French victory.

On 23 March, 1954 (days before the end at Dien Bien Phu), Admiral Arthur W. Radford, USN, Chairman of

---

[3] Robert Shaplen, *The Lost Revolution,* p. 98. Harper Colophon edition, Harper and Row, Publishers, Inc., New York, 1966.

the Joint Chiefs of Staff, said: "The French are going to win. . . ."

But these statements are no more absurd than the ones the United States has been getting from national leaders and some press accounts of the last few years.

Professor Vo Van Kim, an authority on Vietnamese military history, has pointed out that U.S. failures in Vietnam and U.S. self-deception come from ignorance, not lack of national capabilities.

"If you people had known even a little bit about my nation, you could have solved the Vietnamese problem in 1945. Just a little history. Just a little culture."

7   THE VIETNAMESE have a history and traditions which are several thousand years older than is the United States. These small, stubborn people have fought for freedom more times than the United States has had wars; and they ultimately have won all their struggles against domination by foreigners.

Anyone who successfully deals with Vietnamese must know their history—because it controls and stimulates their current actions. The Vietnamese consider the past as part of today. Some actions of the Vietnamese appear strange—perhaps incredible—to outsiders who are unfamiliar with the country and its past. For example, the Vietnamese, both in the North and in the South, regard themselves as a nation; and Ho Chi Minh's victorious entry into Vietnam was a national triumph as well as a popular one. The victory was consistent with thousands of years of history—there were precedents for it—and to the Vietnamese it seemed once again to affirm centuries-old tradition. America's ignorance of this fact is one of the major reasons why the United States has, for twenty-three years, been militarily and politically frustrated in Vietnam. We knew nothing about Vietnam when we started; and we were unwilling to make the effort required to listen and learn.

Anyone who has come to understand how the Vietnamese feel about their country has learned that their traditions are oral ones. A Vietnamese tends to believe what he hears—when he hears it spoken in his own language and his own dialect, and by someone he knows from his own community. Even if he can read, he is likely to be suspicious of printed materials. A great part of the printed material to which he has been exposed in the past has been propaganda—untruthful, official, and unreliable. What he hears in talk may be merely rumor, but it is very Vietnamese to convert rumor into fact. Historical analysts and intelligence officers who rely on documents and papers for their conclusions will never arrive at the truth as a Vietnamese sees, hears—knows—it to be.

The people of Vietnam, intellectuals as well as workers and farmers, see what is happening to them today with a different means of perception than does a Westerner. Their present behavior grows from the Vietnamese view of history, especially the version told within their own community by village elders. I believe it is possible for an American to understand the history of Vietnam and its people from this indigenous point of view. But, to date, no one whose voice is influential has made the effort.

Attempting to view the present crisis through Vietnamese eyes, I have questioned many citizens, some in country villages, others in cities. During the past twenty-five years I have sought counsel and guidance from three old friends: Professor Vo Van Kim, Dr. (Mrs.) Huu Te Ton, and Ngo Duc Lieu. The Appendix contains biographical information on all three.

All Vietnamese come from the same ethnic stock and have a common linguistic and cultural heritage. They experience a feeling of national coherence, yet their relationship to the war is in contrast to the national crisis. Every Vietnamese, Northern, Central, or Southern, knows this is so. They understand why a South Vietnamese hamlet family living on dole in a refugee camp after having been evicted from ancestral land will disbelieve the leaflets showered upon them by American planes, and will scoff at the speeches or promises made by South Vietnamese officials who talk with Northern accents. Yet the same family will enthusiastically accept arguments from the National Liberation Front—because these arguments have cultural validity. All Vietnamese understand, too, why so many of their countrymen resisted France with determination, sacrifice, and efficiency, and why Vietcong guerrillas and North Vietnamese troops have continued their struggle with the same dedication, efficiency, and success. Also, they understand why the South Vietnamese military forces are usually corrupt, inefficient, and avoid combat. The United States pretense that this corruption does not exist or does not matter results in incredulous contempt from all Vietnamese. Americans do not appear to know what is possible in Vietnam and what is impossible, what is true and what is false.

The ancient Chinese, at least, observed the Vietnamese. Sometime near the year 200 B.C. the Chinese invaded the area which is now Vietnam and conquered it. Even then, the people were old in the land; the evidence indicates a settlement as far back as 2500 B.C. by people of an Indonesian stock; and there are archaeological sites in Tonkin which indicate that these settlers developed a complex and sophisticated civilization. But Chinese domination and occupation of Vietnam lasted, on and off, about a thousand years. In that millennium the Vietnamese elite adopted the culture, ethics, and administrative methods of the patient, observant Chinese.

In 939 A.D. the Vietnamese defeated and threw out the Chinese, and became independent. After that, they were twice invaded from the north: by the Mongols in 1278 and by the Ming Chinese in about 1400. The Vietnamese defeated both invaders by using the same type of guerrilla tactics as modern Vietnamese used against the French and now use against the United States. It is significant that the

Vietnamese techniques have been effective in various wars where weapons and combat methods were vastly different.

Marshal Tran Hung Dao, the Vietnamese general who defeated the Mongols almost seven hundred years ago, described his successful strategy: "The enemy must fight his battles far from home for a long time. . . . We must weaken him by drawing him into protected campaigns. Once his initial dash is broken, it will be easier to destroy him."

According to Professor Vo Van Kim there are a few other writings of that period which Vietnamese scholars attribute to Marshal Tran Hung Dao (in 1280) or members of his staff: "When the enemy is away from home for a long time and produces no victories and families learn of their dead, then the enemy population at home becomes dissatisfied and considers it a Mandate from Heaven that the armies be recalled. Time is always in our favor. Our climate, mountains, and jungles discourage the enemy; but for us they offer both sanctuary and a place from which to attack."

Later, from the time of the expulsion of the Ming Chinese in 1400 A.D. onward, the Vietnamese had a para doxical relationship with China. They have constantly been alert to keep China physically and militarily out of Vietnam;[4] yet they have had the conviction that China was the greatest nation on earth. In this spirit the Vietnamese guarded themselves against a recurrence of Chinese invasion; but they continued to model their state, their governors, their ethics, their culture, their war techniques, and their system of international relations along Chinese lines.

For about two thousand years there have been two main political structures in Vietnam. The first, the basic one, comprised the villages—about 95 per cent of the people. The villages were almost autonomous and governed by a locally elected council of leaders and elders. Generally, except for the matter of taxes, the villagers and the state

---

[4] A historical fact of which those who fear the spread of China's millions seem to be ignorant.

had little association. An old Vietnamese folk saying goes: "The authority of the emperor stops at the village gate." So it was. The representatives of the emperor recieved taxes outside the village gate. They did not enter.

Before the French conquered Vietnam in the mid-nineteenth century, the majority of the Vietnamese were living a relatively satisfying life, even though communities often moved to new frontiers. The Vietnamese expanded from the Red River to the Mekong Delta in eight centuries. They were a vigorous people, well organized on a tribal and village basis. The hub of national power belonged to the emperor. But the throne was not always hereditary. If the emperor violated the citizens, they—in accordance with a thousand years of practice—had the right to replace him. The Vietnamese have a firm tradition of revolution against an oppressive or unsuccessful administration. The Vietnamese also embrace the Mandate of Heaven concept. This belief defined the emperor as the chief national religious leader, an intermediary between the people and Heaven. If bad times came to the nation, the people interpreted the misfortune as an indication that the emperor had fallen out of favor with Heaven. Therefore the people considered it proper to replace the reigning emperor with a new one.

This relationship between an emperor and the people had great significance both practically and philosophically. If an emperor continued on the throne, he had both the Mandate of Heaven and the consent of those he governed. If he lost the latter, he was considered devoid of Heaven's assent as well. Thus, any government demonstrably had the consent of the governed up to the moment of revolution. But the power of government rested, pragmatically, in the people.

To illustrate with a modern example, there was popular rejoicing when Ngo Dinh Diem was assassinated in 1963. Diem, the people considered, had brought bad times to the people of Vietnam and had therefore forfeited the Mandate of Heaven. But today, in 1968, conditions in South Vietnam are worse than they were in Diem's time. Because

most South Vietnamese are convinced that the government officials in Saigon are the creatures of United States
policy, and that our policy has brought bad times upon the
people, there is dissatisfaction with us. A restaurant owner
in Gia Dinh put it to me: "The Americans have lost their
Mandate of Heaven."

For at least a thousand years, the highest administrative officers in Vietnam, the mandarins, were selected by
public examination. These examinations, Confucian in nature, were open to all citizens from beggars to royalty, even
though it was usually members of the elite who competed.
Whoever achieved the highest grade became a mandarin.
Thus, for centuries, the most honored citizens in Vietnam
were scholars. This tradition continues in full force today.
At the other end of the social scale came those men who
failed at all other professions and activities and became
soldiers. Theirs was the least respected stratum of society.
This tradition, too, lives on. The generals who administer
Vietnam today have power, but they do not have social
respect. They do not have the trust of the people.

To facilitate a centralized administration for national
affairs, the ancient Vietnamese empire was divided into
provinces which were administered by appointed governors. Under them (in size) was the canton, the equivalent
of a county in the United States. The directors of the
cantons were elected by village leaders. In turn, the local
people chose the village leaders. Within each village was a
certain amount of common property cultivated by all villagers. The profits from the common property supplied
money for schools and other local public needs. In domestic
affairs, the major political power was at the village level.
Anyone who opposed or attempted to destroy this pattern, as did the French, ultimately was thrown out of
power. Today, in North Vietnam, the villages have their
cadres and committees. This system gives the people a
feeling of the traditional culture, even if the real power is
elsewhere.

In historical Vietnam the villagers seldom traveled or

worked beyond easy walking distance from home. But with the ruling class—the aristocracy, the mandarins, the governors, the members of the royal court—this was not so. They traveled up and down the 1,300 miles of Vietnam. Often they intrigued or fought, usually in power struggles of the North against the South. There also were other drives to the west, into the highlands, and even into Cambodia, Laos, and Thailand.

Despite the political turbulences of the aristocracy, the Vietnamese, in a way peculiar to themselves, constantly and strongly felt a national unity. This attitude must still be taken into account by anyone involved in Vietnamese politics. The upper class has always indulged in coups d'etat and the exiling of political opponents—all the while also trying to maintain national coherence and unity. For example, the people who live in the South do not look at Ho Chi Minh as a foreigner. He is a Vietnamese like themselves.

Toward the end of the eighteenth century, the pressures of European expansion and colonialism began to impinge on Vietnam, as they did in many other parts of Asia. A long period of missionary penetration and adventurous trade preceded the first official French foothold in the area, which was signalized by a treaty between the King of Annam and Louis XVI. Under this treaty, in 1787, France secured possession of Quang Nam Province, and with it a base for naval operations.

In the following seven decades the Annamese attempted to throw the French out of their country, but from 1858 onward the French, strongly led and determined upon colonial conquest, made increasing territorial and military gains. It was not until almost the end of the century that French domination of what we now call Vietnam was complete, along with most of Laos and Cambodia.

Peace, however, did not follow. For seven years a series of complicated guerrilla wars and terrorist actions scratched away at the French control; this resulted in such

a series of French setbacks that the Vietnamese were burning villages in sight of the political capitals, even Hanoi.
Order was not restored until the French negotiated with the
court at Hue. The agreement recognized, in principle, the
Vietnamese right to independence under a protectorate. In
reality French-Indochina was a French colony over which
the colonials placed an ever-harsher and more profit-hungry
hand; and native officials were gradually controlled and
corrupted. Since then, in spite of a complexity of political
and military events, the Vietnamese have remained a village-
oriented people. They have never wavered from their inherent obsession to be independent. They have continued
to believe in their own national continuity. Authority above
the village level still is subject to the presence—or absence
—of the Mandate of Heaven, regardless of who wears the
crown of power.

At a seminar discussion of the present situation in
terms of past history, Philippe Devillers, the noted French
authority on Vietnam, said, "So, everyone of today is disturbed by this spectacle we are seeing in Saigon. But when
you are looking at a thousand years of history, you see that
it has been like this all the time. The very fabric of
Vietnamese history is made of this continuous fight between
people. There are strong kings and strong lords who sometimes succeed in establishing a very strong authority over
the turbulent aristocracy.

Philippe Devillers also had something to say about
the social patterns and ethics of the Vietnamese. The Vietnamese, like the Chinese, believe in ancestor and spirit
worship. Today this is still true. Spirits and ancestors are
associated with home and village; and one of the reasons
that families lived on the same piece of land for generation
after generation was to maintain this spiritual continuity
with the past. For the Buddhist and the Catholic alike, a
relocation into a refugee camp violates a deep and sacred
area of individual and spiritual adherence, one tied to a
long-familiar piece of land.

"I think," Devillers said, "that for eighty years [under the French] the Vietnamese have been in search of a new system of social values in which everyone can find his place without any discussion. They need a secure place in a secure system." He had been discussing the impact of European culture, largely the French impact, on Vietnam, and the extent to which it had disrupted immemorial values. "Marxism," he went on, "at least in the Vietnamese context, is one of the systems in which a given place can easily be found. It is not as difficult as a democratic system in which every individual has to struggle to find out what his place is."

Certainly, the decades of French colonialism failed to prepare the Vietnamese for the twentieth century. French policy destroyed native leadership. Well-organized village groups were weakened and stripped of responsibility. The election of important officials was forbidden. The emperor became a figurehead and virtually a prisoner.

Along with a systematic denigration of Vietnamese tradition and institutions, the French steadily insisted that the people themselves were inferior to their conquerors. Any reluctance on the part of a Vietnamese to accept the status of an inferior was punished by humiliation, prison, or death. There was no self-respecting relationship left open between a Vietnamese of any class or rank and the Westerner. Three generations of accumulated frustration for the Vietnamese has afflicted a deep excruciating suffering, a violation of personal and national pride. For them, the Americans have simply replaced the French. The average peasant believes today that the American is another version of the hated Frenchman. The French napalmed and machine-gunned villages. We do this also, only more efficiently and far more often.

From 1884 onward, as France possessed Vietnam more and more completely, the anger and emotional turbulence of the people became always more intense and restless. The French replaced the familiar Vietnamese legal system with the Napoleonic Code, which was not only foreign but confusing. Under it, no matter what crime a Frenchman committed against a Vietnamese—rape, theft, murder, or brutality—he was tried by a French judge and seldom, seldom convicted. But, under the same jurisdiction, a Vietnamese could be—and often was—severely punished for nothing worse than questioning the order of a Frenchman.

For the better part of a century, the Vietnamese lived a life of serfdom under French imperialism. The average national income for a full-time worker was ten dollars a year.

The French casualties of World War I placed strains on French manpower resources. Therefore, about 100,000 Vietnamese were shipped to France to support soldiers and to work as laborers. These Vietnamese got a brief taste of European life and of a comparative equality contrasted to the serf-like situation back home. They began to wonder why they could not have an existence in Vietnam similar to that of the common people of Europe, and they brought the question back with them when they returned.

The Vietnamese intellectuals began planning revolution. A few of them, including Ho Chi Minh, realized that to defeat the foreigners, foreign techniques would have to be studied and countered. The most successful revolutionary techniques appeared to be those of the Communists, who were building a new kind of society with some dimensions which appeared assimilable in an Asian setting. The revolutionary movement in Vietnam did not grow rapidly, but by 1930 the seeds planted in Europe had begun to grow. A few young intellectuals held clandestine meetings to discuss freedom. Some small demonstrations resulted; but the Vietnamese still remember how the French squelched most of them by machine-gunning the dissenters, beating them up, or putting them into jail. Philippe Devillers estimated that by 1945 there were 20,000 Vietnamese political offenders in French prisons.

8   DURING THE 1930's nationalism increased in Vietnam. The primary interest of the nationalists was to throw the French out and once more become a sovereign state. At that time, although Indochina consisted of five different countries (Annam, Tonkin, Cochin China, Laos, and Cambodia) and although there were various degrees of nationalism in each of these states, three-fourths of the people today call themselves Vietnamese, and a majority of them did so thirty years ago.

But the Vietnamese still were helpless. The French had fragmented their nation, controlled the press, controlled transport, communications, finances, and the military. Those Vietnamese who aspired to freedom did not know, under the circumstances, how to organize a revolution. They had no arms, no money, no system of attack. The French had a vast system of secret police and informers. Anyone suspected of nationalistic activities was brutally and swiftly eliminated. Ho Chi Minh's brother and sister were each sentenced to nine years of hard labor by the French for having "freedom tendencies." General Vo Nguyen Giap's wife died in a French prison, and his sister was executed by the French.

The few Vietnamese nationalists who were able to do so went abroad to study. They went wherever they would be welcomed and could learn revolutionary techniques. So they attended Chiang Kai-shek's Kuomintang Academy, which in the 1930's was a revolutionary organization. Or, in France, they were embraced by members of the French Communist cells. Others were invited to Russia. If America, Britain, or other democratic nations had welcomed the Vietnamese, they probably would have studied in the United States or Britain. But the Western nations did not want to openly assist a few unknown young Vietnamese radicals in planning the expulsion of the

French. Quite the opposite. Officially the Western powers—
with the exception of the Soviet Union—cooperated closely
in keeping the radical leaders of Asia under control.

So, all over the world, no one but the Communists
offered help to people who felt they had reasons for revolt.
In consequence, it was natural for all revolutionaries, Vietnamese included, to gravitate toward Communism. Where
else could they go for assistance and encouragement? Also,
the Communist programs in Russia seemed to be accomplishing for the people what the Vietnamese wanted to do
at home.

Europe and America of the 1930's were unable to
understand that a surge of nationalism was sweeping Asia.
The colonies were smoldering to be free. They did not wish
to be ruled by foreigners, and they turned to Communism
in desperation and by invitation.

Over the years, the Vietnamese had observed that
most Western nations had double political and moral standards of "freedom." For example, as Ngo Duc Lieu once
remarked to me, the Belgians and the French and the
British who defended themselves against Hitler's armies
were called Freedom Fighters. The Hungarians and the
Finns who defended themselves against Russia were called
Freedom Fighters. But Asians and Africans who tried to
gain freedom from foreign domination were called tools of
the Communists. By labeling native rebellions Communistic,
Western nations had an excuse to put the rebellions down
by force. To a Confucian culture, this double standard is
confusing. It is one of the reasons why, today, the North
Vietnamese are suspicious of American offers to negotiate.

Vietnamese scholars have reminded me that a similar
principle cropped up in the American labor movement of
the late nineteenth and early twentieth centuries. In such
industries as mining and steel, and the garment industry,
the workers lived an untenable existence. When leaders
organized the workers to improve their lot they were described as "dirty Bolsheviks," "un-American," and "a danger
to the society."

American management, which had economic and political power, used the allegation of Communism— whether it was a factor or not—as an excuse for maintaining the status quo by force. Sometimes Communists were involved, true; but the anger of the workers was stimulated by social injustices, not whipped up by Communist propaganda.

The Vietnamese who are aware of the social history of the United States cannot understand why Americans are unable to see the similarity between the labor struggle against economic tyranny in the United States and the Vietnamese people's aspirations. The struggle in Vietnam— as far as the common people are concerned—is civil and nationalistic, and such Communist dimensions as it may have are secondary. American political hysteria has distorted Communism as the major issue.

For most Vietnamese, the collapse of France in 1940 meant a chance for Vietnamese independence and freedom. The Vietnamese did not care in what political framework or ideology independence came, as long as it came, and as long as France and colonialism were eliminated.

In 1940 hardly any Americans were aware that the 27 million Vietnamese were hungry for independence from foreigners, and that they aspired for it with passion and desperation. Few Americans seem to be aware of it today.

9   IN 1940, soon after the Nazi conquest of France, the Japanese and the Vichy French governments signed an agreement which permitted the Japanese to station troops in Indochina. On paper, the Japanese recognized French colonial sovereignty; but in practice, the Japanese held the real power, and occupied Indochina as behind-the-scenes rulers.

For four long years the colonial French in Vietnam collaborated with their Japanese masters. The adjustment to the new status, indeed, took scarcely more than a month. The French even managed a kind of good cheer in the process, which was well-nigh incredible to anyone who remembered them from earlier years, when Vietnamese and foreign businessmen alike were treated as something resembling dung.

The cooperation of the French brought new hardships upon the Vietnamese. One of the chores undertaken by France was helping to collect food from the peasants for Japanese consumption. Sources in Hanoi have claimed that this ruthless program resulted in 2 million Vietnamese deaths from starvation. More conservative estimates put the figure closer to 1 million lives. Also the French assisted in organizing the Vietnamese people into slave labor corps which worked for the Japanese.

The United States was affected by France's cooperation with the Japanese. The French police organization and its section of secret informers assisted the Japanese. French police were used for the tracking down and capture of Vietnamese suspected of agitating for freedom, or even of sympathy with the Allied cause. And among the targets of this police program were American OSS personnel.

Perhaps the French did not regard the bargain as a bad one. Sixty thousand French colonials went on living much as before. Little of the old, grand manner had to be forgone. Even business went on more or less as usual. Huu Te Ton (who lived in Saigon in 1940 and 1941) quoted a French banker as saying, "The only thing I really object to is that the Japanese have diminished our profits."

In the long, bitter years from 1940 to late 1944, it developed that the Japanese had wangled a real bargain out of the Vichy French. They had the overt collaboration of a colonial administration and of a captive police, Army, Navy, and Air Force, or what remained of them. The colonial French, under Vichy instruction, were in fact supporting an enemy which was allied to the armies which were occupying their homeland and attempting to destroy Britain, the Allied nations, and eventually the United

States. In all Asia, French Indochina was the one efficient Japanese political success. In the other conquered areas—and conquest had not been required in the case of Vietnam—the Japanese were forced to throw out the colonials they found and to turn over the captured areas to puppet native regimes for administration. In Vietnam, the French did their work for them.

Meantime, the Vietnamese intellectuals who had access to radios listened to the Allied broadcasts and repeated them to their followers. They heard the promises of the Atlantic Charter meeting. Their radios brought them the "freedom" speeches of Allied orators and leaders, including Franklin Roosevelt on self-determination and the Four Freedoms. And later, after Roosevelt's death, they heard his successor declare that the foreign policy of the United States was founded on the concept of the freedom of all peoples, regardless of politics or religion.

As World War II continued and grew to global proportions, small revolutionary groups began to form all over Vietnam. At first there was little they could do beyond sporadic harassment of the Japanese; this kind of limited guerrilla warfare was too small to be significant. Meanwhile, in China, Ho Chi Minh was training agents and sending them home to stations all over Vietnam in readiness for a future which he apparently foresaw.

Late in 1944 the Vietnamese drive toward national freedom began to become effective. After half a lifetime of exile, intrigue, and propaganda, Ho Chi Minh returned to his native country. On December 22, 1944, near the mountain town of Cao Bang, Ho and Vo Nguyen Giap organized and created the first "official" unit of the Vietminh Army.[5] The two leaders were a scant ten miles south of the Chinese border, and the total strength of their unit was thirty-four

[5] "Vietminh" is a contraction of Vietnam Doc Lap Dong Minh which means The League for the Independence of Vietnam. It was first organized as a combination of Communists, Socialists, nationalists, and other groups which wanted independence from the Japanese and the French.

men. Giap named the new force the Vietnam Propaganda
and Liberation Unit.

In this miniscule beginning Ho Chi Minh and Giap
had had support from the United States. Experts of the
Office of Strategic Services had helped with the organization and with the formulation of its first objectives. These
were to supply intelligence information for the United
States, to develop an underground movement against the
Japanese, and to train more Vietnamese in anti-Japanese
guerrilla warfare.

Wherever it went in Vietnam, the new Propaganda
and Liberation Unit attracted popular support. The people
greeted Ho and Giap as national messiahs. By March of
1945, only three months later, Vietnamese popular histor-
ians assert that there were large Vietminh units in every
province of Vietnam and that there were approximately
100,000 Vietnamese participating in some way in the liberation program.

The Vietnamese began arming themselves. From the
OSS and from Vietnamese secret caches came several hundred rifles, automatic weapons, and the ammunition for
them. The United States supplied radio transmitters and
receivers. Primarily, these were to be used for relaying intelligence and helping the OSS to rescue American aviators
who had been shot down over Vietnam. However, the
radios also served as communication arteries for the Vietminh, permitting them to give orders and information to
Vietminh units all over the country. Soon, the Vietminh
began ambushing Japanese units, killing French informers,
and raiding military-supply depots.

The French were no longer able to control the scattered but mounting Vietnamese attacks. The Japanese became angry at their puppets and alarmed at rumors of an
imminent Allied launching on the Vietnam coast. Also, they
observed that many French colonials seemed to be deserting the Vichy establishment and turning their coats
toward the ever more-victorious Allies. On March 9, 1945,
the Japanese moved into this deteriorating situation and

took over the country and its administration from their French collaborators. The French Army was disarmed and held under guard. The French civilian administrators were relieved of their duties and confined.

On the eleventh of March, 1945, the Japanese had Bao Dai—the ruler of Vietnam under the French—announce the independence of Vietnam (with Bao Dai as emperor). Bao Dai proclaimed that all of the unequal treaties with the French were eliminated, that there were no more connections with France, and that Vietnam was again, as it had been before the arrival of the French, a sovereign nation.

For the Vietnamese people this declaration of independence of 11 March 1945 was the most important event in their modern history until that time. The Vietnamese had severed ties with France, and the French never could return. The occasion seemed enormous to the Vietnamese, but the Western nations did not take it seriously. In the French papers the event received almost no notice. *Le Figaro* gave only two lines of space on the back page. Almost all Western accounts of Vietnam history speak only of the declaration of independence proclaimed by Ho Chi Minh in September, six months later. But independence was first declared in March 1945, even if the auspices were Japanese.

Half a world away, in Paris, French colonial experts saw what had happened, but they refused to acknowledge the real situation. The idea of an independent Vietnam (and Laos and Cambodia) seemed absurd. As quickly as possible the Paris government issued a statement entitled, "The Declaration of 23 March, 1945."[6] This document stated that France granted limited autonomy to the states of Indochina. There were to be elections by which the Indochinese states would select their own administrators for internal affairs. All of these matters were to be under the "guidance" of a French governor general. For the rest, France would be responsible for foreign affairs, customs, trade, and defense.

[6] See Appendix B.

To the Vietnamese people, this French proclamation was ridiculous. In their eyes Vietnam had been an independent and sovereign country from March 11. This new country had severed all associations with a France which hadn't even been able to protect them against the Japanese.

The French proved no better than the rest of us at recognizing a historical movement. They had never understood that the Vietnamese burned with a national passion for freedom. The French failed to grasp that the Vietnamese believed they already had achieved much more than a French-supervised autonomy and that, in fact, they were now totally free and completely independent. Perhaps times do not change very fast.

(Some non-Communist Vietnamese have told me that they believe the Americans of today have an ignorance of Vietnamese feelings equal to that of the French in 1945. They contend that it would have been in the American self-interest to learn what the Vietnamese wanted and to have supported them. These informants suggested that, in shaping policy, the United States had listened only to a few fluent Northerners rather than to the people as a whole, and that the North Vietnamese to whom we did listen were men who had been kicked out of Hanoi and come south, "like carpetbaggers," to retrieve their fortunes and power.)

It took Bao Dai about a month and a half to form his cabinet. The new Vietnamese government worked toward one principal goal: to have Vietnam unified and stable before the French tried to return at the end of the war. The new government wanted a united North Vietnam (Tonkin) and South Vietnam (Cochin China), with the capital at the traditional city of Hue. This structural unification was accomplished by the eighth of August, 1945. The Vietnamese political structure was once more the same as it had been before the French came. Under the emperor, Bao Dai, a completely Vietnamese government controlled civil affairs throughout the nation.

The new unification was more geographical than political. The League for the Independence of Vietnam (the Vietminh) was daily becoming more vigorous. It was working, furthermore, at cross-purposes with the Bao Dai regime. A Vietnamese who served as Ho Chi Minh's speechwriter and secretary at Versailles in 1946 told me that he remembers Ho's declaring, "We must take over the government from Bao Dai. He will give our country back to France. He has neither the dedication nor the organization to resist France's seduction."

Vietnamese history dates the Japanese surrender as August 14, 1945, though our own VJ Day is officially September 2. Commencing then, in mid-August, the Vietminh began to take over the administration of some villages and small cities. Wherever it went, the people rallied to its support. People identified the Vietminh with resistance to the Japanese and the French, while they regarded Bao Dai less as their emperor than as a French puppet. At last the hated French were out of power, politically, economically, and administratively. Furthermore, Allied broadcasts were indicating that peace would soon be complete.

As the complete withdrawal of Japan now was inevitable, the Vietminh began working intensively for a takeover of the nation. Ho Chi Minh is quoted as having said in those weeks, "When the Allies land, Vietnamese must be in power. There must be a well-run state. Our leaders must be able to greet the Allies in the status of leaders of a sovereign country." Vietminh representatives went into Hanoi and south to Saigon. Ho Chi Minh was elected, by the Vietminh, to the presidency of the National Liberation Committee. Vo Nguyen Giap became commanding officer of the combined Vietminh guerrillas, and this organization was renamed the Vietnam Liberation Army.

Ho Chi Minh sent out an order, "The hour has struck for an offensive on all fronts."

On 13 August 1945, the day before Japan announced her surrender, the Indochinese Communist Party met in a National Congress, and:

. . . decreed the general uprising, and put into place the Vietnamese democratic republican regime . . . the ICP proposed a clear-cut program: guide the rebels so as to disarm the Japanese before the arrival of the Allies in Indochina; to take over the power that was in the hands of the Japanese and their puppets; and to receive, as the authority in control of the country, the Allied Forces coming to demobilize the Japanese.[7]

The Communists, who controlled the Vietminh, were attempting two things. The first was to lead the nationalist movement to undertake Vietnam's independence and prevent the return of French colonialism. The French might trick Bao Dai into something less than complete independence. Their second objective was to take charge of the Vietnamese power structure and prevent other Vietnamese political groups from controlling it.

The day after Japan surrendered, Emperor Bao Dai again proclaimed Vietnamese independence. He sent letters to China, the United States, France, and Great Britain requesting that Vietnam be recognized as a sovereign nation. The Big Four failed to reply, and in the following three weeks the entire history of Vietnam was to be changed.

Meantime, the defeated Japanese Army was standing by, waiting for orders from the victorious Allies. It is estimated by Vietnamese that about 5,000 Japanese deserted, with arms, and joined the Vietminh. These Japanese brought many weapons, and taught the Vietminh how to manufacture hand grenades and similar equipment.

In July 1945, at Potsdam, the Big Three—Britain, the United States, and China—made a decision concerning Vietnam. Britain would land a small force at Saigon to disarm and supervise repatriation of Japanese troops in the South at Saigon; and Nationlist China, at Hanoi, would disarm and supervise the repatriation of Japanese troops in the northern sectors of Vietnam.

On 19 August 1945 sections of Ho Chi Minh's Liber-

_____
[7] *La révolution d'août,* by Truong Chinh, Hanoi, 1946.

ation Army took over Hanoi. But Ho Chi Minh knew that, to take over the entire nation, he must have the advantage of political legitimacy. This could be obtained only from Emperor Bao Dai. A committee called on Bao Dai in Hue. Their instructions were to persuade him to abdicate. Part of their argument (according to Vietnamese sources) was that the Vietminh had the backing of the United States. Indeed, starting in 1944 the United States had armed the Vietminh, the OSS experts had gone on raids with them, and some were even officers of Vietminh units. Whatever the weight of the arguments may have been, Bao Dai abdicated and turned the imperial seal of authority over to Ho Chi Minh.

After Bao Dai's abdication[8] he became the chief adviser for the Vietminh. To what degree Bao Dai's actions were sincere, we do not know. There are many accounts. His life was such a chaos that one is inclined to believe he would do many things on whim—or agree to almost anything to save his life or maintain his fortune.

The Vietminh government, with Ho Chi Minh as head of state, took charge of the nation. Both in the North around Hanoi and in the South around Saigon there was relative peace and order. During this period—even though the machinery of government operated well—the Vietminh took brutally harsh steps to eliminate competition. Any and all leaders—were they nationalists, Trotskyites, or any other brand of Communist who opposed the Ho Chi Minh movement—were killed. Vo Van Kim estimates that as many as five hundred were murdered.

On the second of September 1945, the Vietminh issued the Declaration of Independence of the Republic of Viet Nam. Vietnam now was a republic, not a monarchy.

When the first small British contingent entered Saigon in September 1945, the city celebrated and was gay with Allied flags. There were more American flags than

[8] See Appendix B for Bao Dai's statement.

those of any other foreign nation; later the same display of American flags appeared in Hanoi. The Vietnamese populace believed at first that the arrival of the British marked the beginning of recognition of their independence. Hundreds of thousands of people turned out and paraded. America and England, the Vietnamese believed, would guarantee their independence.

There were reasons for this optimism. Had not the United States sent in American military teams to work with the Vietnamese against the Japanese? Had not the Vietnamese people had a spontaneous and popular uprising, and determined their own form of government? Had not the people of Vietnam fought the Japanese alongside the Allies? Had not President Roosevelt made many statements that the U.S. would never let the French return?

That afternoon, when the parades and the speeches were over in Saigon, there was a fracas and some shooting in one section of the city. The Vietnamese whom I have since interviewed have charged that the scuffle was provoked by the French, and reported that Vietnamese records have the names of the paid provocateurs. Two Vietnamese and one Frenchman were killed. Yet the French and British claimed at once that the Vietnamese crowd had gone berserk and murdered over a hundred Europeans.[9] The press, with access only to official news sources which they could quickly reach, reported this episode as described by French spokesmen.

On September 12 the main British surrender force landed near Saigon. It was a contingent of Gurkha troops. The commanding officer, General Douglas Davis Gracey, had received his orders from Admiral Louis Mountbatten, commander of the Southeast Asian theater, to concern himself with only his assigned tasks. These were to disarm the Japanese and to take care of the liberated Allied prisoners. The two assignments were expected to take five weeks.

[9] Harold Isaacs, *No Peace for Asia*, p. 152. The Macmillan Company, New York, 1947.

General Gracey interpreted his orders otherwise. He refused to speak with the Vietnamese officials of the new regime—the only existing government which he could have found. Instead, he spoke exclusively to the French, who were at this moment of history some two regimes back of the fact, having been replaced first by the Japanese and later by the Vietnamese. Under General Gracey's orders, perhaps at the suggestion of the French, a fatal political mistake was committed. The British jailed certain members of the Vietnamese government, and systematically began to make their administration powerless. All the imprisoned administrators were South Vietnamese. The significance of this was understood by their fellow Southerners.

It took five or six months for those Southern leaders who had not been consigned to jail to make their slow and painful escape northward, but they did. They all knew that if they went by open road they would be arrested. So they traveled the byways, via swamps and mountain trails. Most of them reached Hanoi. Among their number was Phen Ngoc Thach, the new government's Minister of Health.

General Gracey's next major action was to rearm 5,000 French troops and to give guns back to the defeated Japanese. He simultaneously ordered both these military units to duty on a wartime footing to help throw out the Vietnamese administrators. The British troops, with the assistance of the French and the rearmed Japanese units, proceeded to evict the Vietnamese from all government buildings.

These actions by the British drew a harsh comment from Douglas MacArthur: "If there is anything that makes my blood boil, it is to see our allies in Indochina and Java deploying Japanese troops to reconquer the little people we have promised to liberate. It is the most ignoble kind of betrayal."[10]

During those crucial weeks the Vietnamese learned

[10] Edgar Snow, *The Other Side of the River*, p. 686. Random House, New York, 1962.

that the United States had turned over to France war equipment worth $160 million. Soon French troops began to arrive at their traditional bases, wearing American uniforms. Their equipment included American tanks, vehicles, and airplanes. The French forces began to use this modern equipment—with American markings still in evidence—against the Vietminh.

A year or so ago I was talking to a fat and middle-aged woman in Saigon who owns a bar frequented by American servicemen. Twenty years earlier, she had commanded a guerrilla unit in the period when the rearmed French forces began to move against the Vietminh. She remembered clearly that her unit had been armed with bows and arrows made by the Vietnamese mountain tribes. She was philosophical about the problems she had confronted in those bitter days.

"Sure," she said, "bows and arrows are clumsy, and slow to load, and they do not have an effective range beyond forty yards. But at least we could manufacture our own ammunition, and arrows don't make any noise. Of course, we would rather have had automatic rifles, but we had to do the best we could with what we had. Only our regular cadres had American rifles—besides about a thousand Japanese rifles which the Hanoi groups had.

"I can tell you it made our anger big to be in the rice fields with bows and arrows, being shot at by Frenchmen using American automatic rifles and by Japanese using Japanese rifles, and being strafed by American planes flown by Frenchmen."

The British and the French, in an effort to make their actions appear reasonable, began a barrage of propaganda. The Vietminh, they said, not only were Communists, but also they were hated by the Vietnamese people. I have asked many Vietnamese about this claim. Without exception they replied that almost everyone knew of the Communist leaders; but the people did not hate them. Except for some political leaders who opposed the Communists and usually wanted the power for themselves, almost everyone supported the Vietminh voluntarily. This was a struggle against foreigners, a struggle for Vietnamese independence. The people, in fact, rallied to the Vietminh.

In northern Vietnam, shortly after the Vietminh had taken over from the Japanese, Hanoi was bedecked with flags. Next to the Vietnamese flags, again, as in Saigon, American flags were flying in the greatest numbers. Again, the Vietnamese hoped that America would guarantee their independence, and the Ho Chi Minh government tried to identify itself with the United States.

While the British, French, and Japanese were attempting to subdue the Vietminh government in the southern part of Vietnam, Nationalist Chinese had moved into the northern areas. Here, as in the South, the Japanese had stacked their arms and were ready to be evacuated to Japan. The problem was not one of organization but mostly of transport. To accomplish this relatively easy job, Chiang Kai-shek sent down his troops, armed with American rifles, airplanes, and tanks. Instead of merely taking care of the Japanese, the Chinese set about a business of their own. They systematically looted North Vietnam. Like locusts they worked over the countryside, taking food, money, equipment, deeds to property, and even bridges, which they sold as scrap iron. While they were about this liquidation of other people's assets, they sold much of the American military equipment to the Vietminh.

However, the Chinese did not disturb the Vietnamese administration. They permitted the Ho Chi Minh government to run the country, a fact which worried the French. The longer the Chinese occupied the Hanoi area, the more stable and popular the Ho Chi Minh government would surely appear. The French might lose the opportunity to complete their reconquest. Indeed, Chiang Kai-shek might go so far as to recognize the Hanoi government.

Before the Chinese and even before Ho Chi Minh had arrived in Hanoi, various American missions had reached the city. The Americans assured the Vietminh leaders (identifying them as nationalists and knowing nothing of their Marxist training) that the United States would assist them in preventing the French from returning. A Vietnamese-American Friendship Association soon became active and the Vietminh frequently were seen in public with Americans.

This Vietminh-American rapport was disturbing to the French. So also was that apparent recognition by the Chinese of the newly formed Vietnam government. To put a stop to these developments the French made a deal with the Chinese. Officially ratified on February 26, 1946, the agreement provided for a Chinese withdrawal from northern Vietnam in return for the cession by the French of certain rights and privileges which France had long held in China. While the Vietnamese may not have known of this development at once, they did know that French troops were constantly arriving in their country and that they were being ferried into Saigon and other points of debarkation in American ships manned by American sailors.

The Vietminh government, in the meantime, had been sending radio messages and letters almost daily to the Pope, President Truman, Stalin, the British government, and the Chinese government, requesting that attacks on their personnel and establishments by British, French, and Japanese forces be forbidden; and that, if necessary, the Great Powers send representatives to Vietnam to inspect conditions, talk to the people, and put the question of the future up for international arbitration. In their pleas to the Great Powers, the Vietnamese even suggested that Vietnam be put under an international trusteeship. No one answered the messages.

In 1946, after futile negotiations between France and Ho Chi Minh (in which France promised elections to the Vietnamese but later refused to allow them), the Vietminh decided the only way to get rid of France, unify Vietnam over French objections, and become a truly independent nation was by fighting.

The Vietminh decision to fight commenced the first of the two wars in Vietnam with which most of us are so bitterly familiar. It was a traditional decision in terms of Vietnamese history—a determination to drive out the foreign usurpers of the country's land and the people's life. The fact that the Vietminh proposed to pit a nation of pauperized Asian farmers, fishermen, and city dwellers against the massive resources of the West did not deter Ho and his colleagues.

The United States decision to supply the French with massive amounts of materiel, including vast quantities of sophisticated weaponry, is perhaps less easy to understand. The French record in Vietnam was inglorious. Colonialism was, and is, a repugnant concept to Americans, whose heritage is one of armed insurrection against it. Whatever conceptions of world politics may have operated in Washington ran counter to our national faith in the self-determination of peoples, to the spirit of Roosevelt's Four Freedoms, to promises made previously, and to the whole American style.

An almost hysterical fear of Communism had something to do with the United States willingness to aid and abet the French. So, perhaps, did our strategy of containment, by which the Communist continent of Asia was to be ringed with American bastions. There were reasons and reasons and reasons. But, as history was to prove, they added up to the wrong answer.

After eight years of bloody fighting, the French lost the war, climaxed by the siege of Dien Bien Phu, and, in October of 1954, marched out of Hanoi. They have not been back since. However, within a year the Americans slowly had begun to take their place in the Vietnamese puzzle.

The Geneva Conference of 1954[11] resulted in an armistice agreement between the French Union and the Vietminh. Vietnam was to be temporarily partitioned into two independent states, the line of demarcation being ap-

[11] See Appendix C.

proximately the 17th parallel North. Ho Chi Minh and the Vietminh were to govern the northern state. The southern half was to be governed by a regime which, for the time being, was arranged by France. The Geneva Agreement provided that two years later, in 1956, there would be general elections. The issue was, did the people want the two Vietnams to be continued, or were they to unify?

During this period Ngo Dinh Diem took over the active leadership of South Vietnam although he was not yet the head of state. There was an extensive publicity campaign to make him known to the people, and at the start he had much popular support.

The task which Ngo Dinh Diem faced was staggering. South Vietnam had been fragmented by the war. But the majority of people, both the common people and the elite, were behind him. However, he adopted a policy of running the nation single-handedly—with the help of his family. For the next eight years anyone who disagreed with his policies was labeled a Communist and was either jailed or shot. There was no freedom of the press. Diem eliminated most of the courageous, capable people who might have formed the nucleus of a leadership corps. He tolerated no criticism, and alienated almost all of the talented people of his nation.

Once when I was in Saigon, I sent out invitations to Vietnamese journalists for a party I wanted to have for the editor of a Saigon newspaper. The editor was a talented anti-Communist who actually supported Ngo Dinh Diem. When I got to the hotel where the party was scheduled, I found the vestibule filled with police. The police informed me that the public was so angry at my friend the editor that if the party were held a mob might invade the hotel and run amok. They could not guarantee *my* safety if I insisted on having the party. Therefore they recommended that I cancel the affair.

At that time, neither I nor the guests knew that the editor already was in jail. What had happened was that the editor had run a small editorial suggesting that there be more freedom in South Vietnam. He said it was necessary to have more freedom in the South than in the North. His paper had hardly been printed when soldiers invaded his printing plant, destroyed the equipment, and burned the newsprint.

Late in 1955 Ngo Dinh Diem had held an election which was handled entirely by his brother Nhu. It was a rigged election. Even the returns from Communist-controlled areas were reported as being 98 per cent for Ngo Dinh Diem. This was a blatant fraud and everyone knew it, including the Americans. But the election made Ngo Dinh Diem the "elected" legal president of South Vietnam. Rigged or not, he announced it as a Mandate from Heaven. From then on, Diem ruled like an absolute emperor.

Ngo Dinh Diem ignored the peasantry of his country —about 90 per cent of the population. Because he was receiving money and materials from the United States, he had no need of the taxes and backing which normally would have come from the countryside. He turned the reform of rural affairs over to his brother Nhu, who exploited the peasants so mercilessly that the common people came to feel even closer to the Vietminh than they had during the French war. Another of Ngo Dinh Diem's brothers, Thuc, was the Bishop of Vinh Long and later the Archbishop of Hue. He was known as "the viceroy" because he controlled the administration of the provinces. Anyone wanting anything had to get permission from Archbishop Thuc. Woodcutters wishing to cut wood had to get Thuc's permission; the men who made the logs into charcoal had to get Thuc's permission; and so on for all activities. The people hated and ridiculed Thuc. He was famous for his sexual promiscuities. The people referred to him sarcastically as "father for the pelvic thrust in the sexual movement." In short, the entire Ngo Dinh Diem family was hated.

The land reforms which the Vietminh had effected for the peasants were soon negated by Nhu. The United States did nothing to correct this shift away from popular hopes and general American policy.

In 1956 two important things happened.

The first was Ngo Dinh Diem's refusal to hold elections on the question of unification of the two Vietnams, as contemplated in the Geneva Agreement. This refusal had the backing and tacit approval of the United States. The Geneva treaty had stipulated that the elections were to be held in 1956. France, the defeated nation, had signed the treaty, and it was to be France's responsibility to see that the elections were carried out. But in 1955 France pulled out of Vietnam abruptly. She said she had too many other troubles and that it was impossible for her to execute her Geneva treaty responsibility for the election.

In 1956, Ngo Dinh Diem pointed out that France, not his government of South Vietnam, had signed the Geneva treaty. Therefore, said Ngo, he did not have to abide by that treaty; there would be no elections. He further argued that the Vietminh organization which was spread throughout South Vietnam would influence the elections in North Vietnam's favor. It was the consensus of political observers at that time that if there had been an election in 1956, Ho Chi Minh would have defeated Ngo Dinh Diem. Ho Chi Minh requested international supervision of the election to guarantee fairness. Ngo Dinh Diem, again with U.S. backing, refused. Blocking the promised election virtually brought on the war between the North and the South—because the North felt betrayed.

The second important, or rather tragic, development in 1956 was that the United States, under Lieutenant General Samuel ("Hanging Sam") Williams, began inten-

sive training of the South Vietnamese Army. The South
Vietnamese Army was developed as a conventional, Euro-
pean-type combat organization. Its cadres learned nothing
about guerrilla warfare. And, small wonder, even its weapons were unsuited to guerrilla warfare. This military mistake was the best gift the United States could have given to
the North Vietnamese and to the National Liberation Front.
Yet how could the U.S. Army teach revolutionary guerrilla
warfare? Our Army had little or no knowledge of its
techniques. Even today, a decade later, American soldiers
in Vietnam are untrained and incompetent in revolutionary
war techniques.

By 1957 the politicians and the press of the United
States considered Ngo Dinh Diem the "Miracle Man of
Vietnam." Ngo Dinh Diem had a high-powered American
public relations outfit to manage his affairs in America.
Ngo also was assisted by Joseph Buttinger, a "friend of
Vietnam." Buttinger's assistance operated at many levels,
including working with the Department of State and with
at least one senator. America was being deluged with
propaganda praising Ngo Dinh Diem—when in reality he
was reigning as a tyrant and sowing the seeds for a National Liberation Front victory, driving South Vietnam into
civil war and defeat.

While Ngo Dinh Diem's secret police were rounding
up everyone who dissented and putting thousands of them
in jail—and while the nation was going more and more
bankrupt, both politically and economically, despite the
rising level of American help—Americans were listening
to more and more praise of Ngo Dinh Diem. Ernest K.
Lindley wrote in *Newsweek* of 29 June 1959: "South Vietnam has made more striking progress in more ways than
any nation I have visited so far. . . . Diem . . . is one of
the ablest free Asian leaders."

Michigan State University had a project in South
Vietnam, paid for by the CIA. In the Autumn 1959 *Yale
Review*, the head of the project, Wesley Fishel, wrote:

On October 26, 1959, South Vietnam will celebrate its fourth anniversary of the Republic of Vietnam. The anticipated elections of 1956 have never been held, and the Communist capability in Vietnam, south of the 17th parallel, has been reduced to one of sheer nuisance activity. . . . It is one Asian area where Communism has been rolled back, and rolled back without war . . . There is little likelihood of a revolution against the regime.

Wesley Fishel could not have been more wrong; but almost everybody in the United States seemed to believe him. Ernest K. Lindley couldn't have been more wrong. The official cables and reports from Saigon agreed that Ngo Dinh Diem and his family were great and successful people. They had rolled back Communism.

Even our professional military men were wrong. Admiral Arthur Radford and Admiral Felix B. Stump (the Commander in Chief, Pacific) agreed that "President Ngo Dinh Diem was the most brilliant and successful Asian leader of democracy since Chiang Kai-shek."

In reality, almost everything in Vietnam was going opposite to United States hopes. The land-reform measures went from bad to worse, or failed to materialize. The peasants were becoming more and more frustrated. The Catholic minority was abusing the non-Catholic majority. The mountain tribes had lost their autonomy. Ngo Dinh Diem was more and more dictatorial through his secret police, and the high-handedness of Nhu and Madame Nhu was past the point of endurance. In April of 1960, a group of distinguished Vietnamese published a document in which they said that the power of the nation had been concentrated in the hands of an irresponsible member of the family from whom emanated all orders, and that there were unreasonable arrests and false elections. The distinguished group requested reforms.

Almost all of the signers of this paper were arrested.

In November 1960 the South Vietnamese Army rebelled, and there was an attempted coup.

It was in the late 1950's when people living in South Vietnam began churning with discontent against Ngo Dinh Diem. Of the many Vietnamese I interviewed at that time, almost everyone openly told me he wanted a change of government. It was this discontent which fostered the growth of the National Liberation Front. Outside of official circles I have never met a Vietnamese who considered the present civil war to have begun as an act of North Vietnamese aggression.

United States policy in Vietnam has been founded on a belief in North Vietnamese aggression. There may be other good reasons of self-interest which cause U.S. actions in Vietnam; and it is the responsibility of the President to tell us about them. But the two-Vietnam concept will not hold up.

To many Americans the Vietnamese appear to be a divided people, but they do not appear that way to the Vietnamese themselves. The way in which the peasants support the Vietcong and the North Vietnamese armies should make this self-evident. It is true that many Southerners received guerrilla training and political training in the North. But most of them went to the North voluntarily —for refuge and safety. They were fleeing from the French and, later, from Ngo Dinh Diem. When they returned South, it was not to commit aggression, but to help their relatives, neighbors, and countrymen dispose of what, in their opinion, were bad and oppressive governments. This was consistent with the Mandate of Heaven tradition.

The uprising of the National Liberation Front would have been improbable, perhaps impossible, had it not been for the tyranny of Ngo Dinh Diem and the ineptitude of the United States, which allowed Ngo Dinh Diem and his family to misrule. The argument that we could not interfere in the internal affairs of Vietnam was hogwash then as it is hogwash now. We put Ngo Dinh Diem into power; and we held him there.

By early 1959 the National Liberation Front had taken effective charge of much of the countryside. They had brought in well-armed, well-trained South Vietnamese who had gone to North Vietnam in 1954 and were now returning as efficient cadres. They now were skilled organizers who were welcomed back to their home villages by the people of the villages.

In February 1961, President Kennedy decided that a strong American was needed to take charge in Vietnam. Kennedy wanted someone who was a political activist and who also was familiar with revolutionary warfare tactics. He proposed to have Edward Lansdale as the new ambassador. He even had the papers made out for this appointment. But it was blocked by Secretary of State Dean Rusk, who said that if Lansdale went as ambassador, he, Rusk, would resign. Lansdale, an Air Force officer who worked for the CIA, was a bold activist who sometimes disagreed with State Department methods. He was the "Colonel Landslide" who had manipulated the election of a Philippine president in 1953. So, in March, Frederick Nolting was sent to Saigon as ambassador. The instructions he had from the Department of State were "to get along" with Ngo Dinh Diem and his family. Nolting, a polished diplomat, did just that. He "got along" with Ngo Dinh Diem.

By 1962 the United States had given Vietnam more than $2 billion in aid, plus a lot of bad military advice.

In 1963, when President Ngo Dinh Diem was murdered, the people responded with relief and gladness. His incumbency had been characterized by the worst features of a Communist tyrannical rule, and compounded by the worst features of a corrupt democracy.

The people of the South believed that the U.S.A., which had maintained Ngo Dinh Diem in power, had now got rid of him because he had lost his Mandate from Heaven.

The South Vietnamese people approved of the ending of Ngo Dinh Diem's rule, and they looked forward to the United States putting competent South Vietnamese leadership into power.

That did not happen.

IV

THE

GENEROUS
AMERICAN

"Without American money, guns, food, medicine, and supplies, we of the National Liberation Front would have a hard time surviving. . . ."

MAJOR PHAM VAN-LINH, logistics officer
for the National Liberation Front
(Vietcong)—in an interview
in Saigon, June 1967

10   EVERY GOVERNMENT we have helped into power in Vietnam has been inadequate; and all of them have been rejected by the Vietnamese people. First it was the French; next Ngo Dinh Diem; and then, after a period of coups and counter-coups, the military junta headed by General Thieu and Marshal Ky.

One of the measures of inadequacy is the degree of governmental corruption. We are speaking of excessive corruption, not the accepted Asian tradition of reasonable "cumshaw" for services rendered, which grew from a condition of low salaries for government officials. No one familiar with Asia would quarrel with reasonable cumshaw, but in Vietnam it has gone far, far beyond the traditional. It has, for example, become the usual method of acquiring government positions and the usual reason for wanting them—from top to bottom, from cop to general or province chief.

We cannot accept corruption on the scale that now exists in Vietnam. It is costing us American lives, battles, an enormous drain in gold and materiel; it can cost us the war.

My first experience with the Vietnamese black market occurred in Saigon. I told the Army public relations officer at JUSPAO (Joint United States Public Affairs

Office)[1] that I planned to go out with troops, and asked where I could buy jungle fatigues and jungle boots.

"We have lots of goodies for reporters if they have the right papers," he said, handing me an authorization to buy Army uniforms.

A friend took me, on the back of his scooter, to the big PX in Cholon, where the Army uniform shop is. Outside the compound, with its sandbags and U.S. armed guards, was a place for customers to park their vehicles. As the vehicles were parked, small Vietnamese boys ran up, their hands outstretched, demanding "watch-your-jeep [or scooter] money." They wanted money to stop "someone" from cutting ignition wires or letting air from tires. These miniature gangsters shook down American customers almost directly in front of the U.S. Army guards.

I angrily told a PX officer about the situation. He replied, "The street is Vietnamese territory. We are guests in this country. We have no jurisdiction over anything that happens in the street. Those kids can sell stolen PX merchandise out there and we can't touch them. Only the Vietnamese police can do anything."

"There was a Vietnamese policeman standing twenty feet away . . ."

"I assure you there's nothing we can do. We are guests in this country . . . and that's the way General Westmoreland has ordered it."

I made the obvious remark that it was a strange way to treat guests who were dying by the thousands to protect their hosts.

The major shrugged and said, "This is their country. We are fighting and dying in combat *because we have permission from the Vietnamese to be on those battlefields.* Parking scooters on their streets is something else."

A sergeant entered. "Major, the old woman is selling

---

[1] JUSPAO is the public relations office which handles all U.S. public affairs in Vietnam. The top man in it is a U.S. Embassy official.

soft drinks and cigarettes—it's all our merchandise—right in front of the PX entrance."

The major sighed wearily. He had to play the same phonograph record again. "Our hands are tied unless we catch her stealing the stuff from the PX. Forget about it." Then he asked the sergeant to take me to the uniform shop.

When I gave the clerk my authorization he shook his head. "We haven't had fatigues or jungle boots for months."

"When are you expecting them?"

He held up his hands and shrugged.

We returned to the street, mended the cut ignition wire on the scooter, and returned to JUSPAO. There I told the colonel that the store did not have jungle uniforms.

He laughed and said that I would have to find them where he and his men did—on the black market. "They may charge you a couple of bucks more, but the gear is always available and in all sizes. . . ."

I walked down the street past the USO and the flower markets and the sidewalk restaurants. It took about five minutes; and there was the "Tiny Black Market" (the name implying that there were bigger places elsewhere).

Stalls crowded and leaned against each other, as in any Oriental bazaar. Hundreds of customers milled about, pushing and inspecting the merchandise. Among them were four U.S. Army noncommissioned officers, one Army captain, and a U.S. Navy yeoman. Four Vietnamese policemen stood about, keeping order.

In the stalls were what must have been all the most desirable items from the PX. Among other things I noted were transistor radios, blankets, toasters, electric blenders, watches, clocks, cigarettes, tobacco, pens, shirts, televisions, cameras, film, toilet articles, patent medicines, shirts, lingerie, socks, and a variety of the best-advertised American liquors, as well as cans of just about every kind of food available in the Army commissary.

I asked a Vietnamese official if it were not against the law to sell merchandise stolen from the PX. He replied that it was, but that there was no proof it was stolen. When I pointed out that almost every item still carried the PX label and that the PX was the only local importer of this sort of merchandise, he spoke in the manner of a Supreme Court judge.

"That is true," he said, "but in this country for goods to be declared stolen, we must catch someone in the act of stealing them. One must be very careful in making charges. Perhaps the 'PX' stamped on that bottle of brandy is a brand name, eh?"

When I asked the U.S. Army captain if there wasn't a regulation forbidding military personnel from buying things on the black market, he grinned. "Who's kidding whom?" he said. "I want some Edgeworth tobacco. The PX doesn't have any. It's all down here. It costs five times as much—but it's here." He handed the proprietor a hundred piasters, put the small blue package in his pocket, and walked off.

I continued up and down the stalls looking for uniforms and jungle boots. There were none visible. Then one of the black market operators came up and, speaking in English, asked me what I wanted. When I told her, she said, "All complete uniform. Everything. Helmet. Pants. Boots. Shirt. Everything. Forty-five hundred piasters or thirty dollars. You want?"

"Are they new?"

"New. You want?"

"I want to see them."

"You buy them if new and right size?"

"Yes."

The woman turned to a boy, spoke to him in Vietnamese and gave him a piece of paper, then turned to me.

"Go with boy."

"Do I pay you?"

"Pay when you get clothes."

The boy took me several blocks along the street of

the hardware stores. After a while we entered a store that had copper pots in the window. The boy went to an old man who was clacking an abacus. Without speaking, the old man led me out the back of the store, across a yard, into an alley which stank of rotten vegetables, and then up two flights of dark stairs into the loft of another building.

The place looked like a U.S. Army ordnance ammunition depot. Everything seemed to be painted brown and to smell either of oil or fresh paint. Ordnance equipment was arranged in orderly lines, and neatly printed price tags hung from everything. Automatic rifles were $250. A 105-mm. mortar, sample only (if a customer wanted one, he could pick it up at the Cholon godown) was priced at $400. (*I wondered if the mortar which blew off my friend Clint Moreau's legs was purchased here.*)[2] There were about a thousand American rifles of different kinds standing neatly in racks. M-16's cost $80. On one side of the loft were uniforms of all services, including the U.S. Air Force. There was even U.S. Navy diving equipment.

The old man inquired as to my sizes, and brought me the uniform and boots. After I had tried them on, he said, "That will be thirty-five dollars in U.S. money."

I told him I had no U.S. money.[3]

"Your personal check is okay."

"No, I have only piasters."

"Okay, okay," he grumbled, "five thousand piasters."

"Later that evening I talked about the black market to an old friend whom I shall call Tran Trong Hoc (and of whom I'll speak more later).[4]

[2] Clint Moreau was a six-foot-four U.S. Marine who had had both legs blown off when a Vietcong mortar exploded near him. When the Marines over-ran the VC position, they found that the VC had been firing U.S. mortars and using U.S. ammunition.

[3] All dealings with Vietnamese must be done in piasters.

[4] Tran Trong Hoc formerly was a policeman in Hanoi. I met him in about 1955. In 1953 he had been imprisoned by the French for having attended an anti-French meeting. Later, in 1958, the Communists tried to kill him for refusing to inform on a friend.

He said, "What you saw is nothing. Go down to the
waterfront some day and see how the big operators work.
The whole South Vietnamese government—from Ky down
—is involved."

"Any Americans in on it?"

"Plenty are becoming millionaires—exactly as happened when the U.S. Army occupied Japan and Germany."

"How do you know?"

"The black market in Vietnam is about ten billion
dollars a year—all in American goods and monies. This
could not exist without American collusion. It would be
impossible. For example, everyone in Saigon talks about
how La Thanh Nghe of Ky's cabinet has gotten about a
million dollars in kickbacks from American pharmaceutical
firms. There has to be American collusion. You couldn't lose
ten billion dollars a year without it."

I did not answer.

"We'll go to the waterfront in a few days," said Tran
Trong Hoc, "and watch the big operations."

"Let's go now."

"We have to plan it well. I need a few days. If we
are not careful, neither of us will be alive to tell what we
saw."

11   THE "Little Black Market," which does business
openly near the U.S. Embassy and JUSPAO in Saigon, is
small stuff. It is only one bit of crookedness in the vast cesspool of cupidity. It is so small—by contrast to others—
that both the South Vietnamese and United States governments tacitly consider it semi-legitimate. The Little Black
Market is one of the showplaces of Saigon. Visitors on
official tours are shown the Little Black Market as they are
shown the U.S. Embassy, the railway station, the public
market, and so forth. Americans, as well as Vietnamese, buy

things at the Little Black Market because sometimes it has a better selection than the legitimate U.S. government stores from which the merchandise has been stolen. There is nothing disguised about the Little Black Market. Everyone—even the officials in charge—knows how its goods are sneaked out of the PX and the U.S. commissary and by whom, and who gets paid off. If either the U.S. government or the South Vietnamese government wished, the retail black market in Saigon could be eliminated within a week.

"We aren't too strict about it," said Tom McAlliffe, one of the U.S. police instructors in Saigon, "because in the first place we don't want to antagonize the Koreans or the Filipinos [both deeply involved in black market operations, both allies of the U.S.]; the black market helps stop inflation. I don't know how, but that's what our economists say."

Lieutenant Vo of the Vietnamese National Police said, "The Little Black Market is permitted to continue because it is useful to everyone. When the American press —or perhaps a visiting senator—complains about corruption we close the Little Black Market for a few days. That's it. Immediate action has been taken. The stalls have been closed. Sometimes the merchandise is burned in the street. Photographs are taken. A few people are arrested. The Americans are satisfied. Action against corruption has been taken. It takes pressure off the U.S. Embassy. It takes pressure off my government. Do you see how useful the Little Market is?"

I wanted to learn how the black market got its luxury items, so I went to its main Saigon supplier—the PX. When I arrived at the big PX in Cholon (Saigon) the store had not yet opened, and a line of people had formed. At the end of the line were two GI's who appeared to have come from the combat area. Their jungle clothes were mud-splattered, and their helmets were covered with camouflage netting. I was curious what two combat soldiers would buy in the PX, so I got behind them in line. The two GI's were from an isolated Signal Corps station beyond Pleiku, and the occasion of their being at the PX was to buy a refrigerator. Within the last few days their electrical supply had been converted from battery to generator. The men had chipped in to get a refrigerator so that they could have cold drinks, sandwiches, and so forth.

They told me how they had special arrangements to get the refrigerator on the airplane; and how the Special Services officer in Pleiku had found out that the refrigerators had arrived in Saigon the day before.

The doors of the PX opened, and the people went in.

When the GI's got to the counter, they learned that there were no more refrigerators. The shipment had arrived at noon the day before, and all refrigerators had been sold by closing time.

I began asking questions and learned that of the entire shipment of sixteen refrigerators twelve had been sold to Filipino and Korean soldiers.

How did the Filipinos and Koreans know about the refrigerators in order to buy them so quickly?

Here, again, the answer was simple.

The U.S. Army, which runs the PX in Saigon, had brought Filipinos and Koreans into the store at a managerial level. When there is a shipment of some desirable article, they call up their Korean and Filipino friends to tell them when the articles can be purchased.

The two disappointed GI's left the refrigerator counter. They went to the record player department. The record players also were sold out.

As the unhappy GI's walked out of the PX, one said, "You remember the Vietcong supply dump that was raided last month . . . ?"

"Yeh, I know. It had a refrigerator in it . . . with the PX tag on the back. And with U.S. antibiotics in the refrigerator. . . ."

"And they also had two record players."

"Goddammit. We get shot at while these Saigon commandos collaborate with the VC."

The PX in Vietnam is a $300 million a year business, according to the officer in charge, and it demonstrates in miniature why the United States is in deep trouble in Vietnam—and in foreign affairs in general.

The clerks in the PX's are Vietnamese women. There are over 5,000 of them. They speak little, if any, English. They do not know the merchandise and, on the average, they are uninterested and discourteous. Also, the Vietnamese women clerks steal from the PX's. In the month of May 1967, the small headquarters PX in Saigon lost $65,000 in petty pilferage alone. This is the *small* PX. At one time the PX management had the Vietnamese salesgirls searched as they left the store. The clerks objected to the search procedure and said they would go on strike unless the searching was stopped. The searching was stopped. The Americans who operate the PX (the U.S. Army, with a colonel in charge) would rather have things stolen from the exchange than "not look good" to the Vietnamese.

I personally have seen clerks standing on the main highway outside a PX removing PX merchandise from their bodices. They dropped the items into a basket while a Vietnamese man made notes of the amount and type of merchandise which each girl had contributed.

All purchases in the PX must be made with MPC (Military Payment Currency, which is sort of a Mickey Mouse money printed in order to stop the black-market exchange in currency). It is a crime for an American in Vietnam to use any currency except piasters in Vietnamese stores and MPC in U.S. establishments. Yet I have seen Americans pay a clerk (who was either Vietnamese or Filipino) with American dollars in the Saigon PX. I saw it for three days in a row.

Much of the merchandise in the PX's couldn't possibly have been chosen with the welfare of the GI's in mind. In the Saigon PX, for example, there were no alarm clocks. They hadn't had any for two months. There were no pipes. There was a shortage of film. The PX was "temporarily out" of good razor blades and Edgeworth tobacco. There was no mosquito repellent.[5] Nevertheless, the whole rear of the store was used for selling diamonds. It is simple to buy a $1,500 diamond or a fur coat in a PX. But often it is difficult to get those things which are needed in Vietnam.

The ration allowance is a standing joke—unenforced by the clerks and ignored by the black marketeers. I saw a Korean officer buy six bottles of brandy and six cartons of cigarettes. I followed him. He went to the black-market area, disappeared into one of the buildings there, and came out later without his packages. He went directly back to the PX, where he purchased six more bottles of liquor and six more cartons of cigarettes, and then went to the black-market area again.

The liquor in PX's and other government stores is tax-free. In Vietnam one can buy whiskey at approximately one-third the price that he can in the United States. Same for cigarettes.

Merchandise headed for the PX—and also for the commissary—is stolen before it gets to the PX and commissary as well as after it is on the shelves. But the corruptions involve more than the black market. For example, some time ago, the PX liquor-purchasing agent, an American civilian, shared an apartment in Saigon with another American, the representative of the company which sold a nationally famous bourbon whiskey. The PX purchasing agent had his rent paid for, he had his food paid for, and his "home entertainment" paid for. The PX liquor-purchasing agent overbought the salesman's product, and six months later the PX in Vietnam still was overstocked with it.

[5] Later I found the "temporarily out" items for sale on the black market which is adjacent to the U.S. Public Affairs Office building. There (at three times the PX price) I found alarm clocks, pipes, film, insect repellent, good razor blades, and American tobacco.

The PX purchasing agent involved was caught at his unethical activities. At this writing he is working for the PX in Germany and at a higher position than he held in Vietnam. This entire story was given me by a senior PX officer.

In the Danang PX an American civilian employee indulged in collusion with local Vietnamese concerning the maintenance and hiring of motor transport. He was caught. He was sent to the PX in Cam Ranh Bay, with a more responsible job than he had had in Danang.

It is no secret that the PX and the commissary are supplying just about everybody in South Vietnam (who has the money) with luxury items via the black market. An importer told me that he stopped dealing in legitimately imported refrigerators and tape recorders. Customers could get them cheaper and quicker from the PX, via the black market. Foreign-food importers are in the same fix. I myself have seen an Army truck with Filipinos and South Koreans *in uniform*, stop in front of the Continental Hotel at 6 A.M. and unload a truckful of Spam and fruit juices. The menu at the Continental Hotel advertises "American Spam." When one orders tomato juice for breakfast, the waiter brings a small can, with the U.S. commissary stamp still on it—ten cents. At four different times during my stay in Saigon, I saw this truck deliver PX and commissary edibles to the Continental Hotel. Once a large package of meat with General Westmoreland's name on it was delivered to the Continental along with the tomato juice. There is hardly a bar in Saigon which does not have liquor which comes from the U.S. supplies.

There is a black market which specializes in food and liquor from the PX and U.S. commissary. It is adjacent to the Redemptorist Church. There, openly for sale, is canned ham, bonded whiskey, soap, soup, candy, canned vegetables, etc. It is a supermarket of American goods.

In investigating PX practices, I requested an interview with a responsible PX officer. The interview was granted with a colonel on the condition that I would not use his name and that I would not quote him directly.

I was ushered into the colonel's presence and was given a small lecture on how newspapermen are always saying bad things about the PX. Why can't they write something good for a change?

I described to him the malpractices I had discovered, and what follows is his explanation.

The PX, he said, employs over 5,000 Vietnamese women, because it is the duty of the United States to train these women in merchandising practices. It is America's duty to Vietnam. After the war is over, the women will know how to be skilled clerks in the stores of Vietnam and will be able to aid the commerce of the country. This seemed crazy to me. Any store which was run like the PX would soon go bankrupt.

He said that they were using Vietnamese women as clerks and Koreans and Filipinos as merchandising executives because it was far cheaper than using Americans, and the Filipinos and Koreans have had PX experience in Seoul and Manila.[6]

I pointed out to the PX colonel that the service was bad, that perhaps $75 million a year of merchandise was stolen or diverted to the black market largely because of employment of foreigners, including clerks, executives, truckers, longshoremen, and so forth. He denied that the service was bad—which is contrary to the opinions of his customers (who have no other place to shop). He denied that there was any sizable black-market leak from his stores.

He denied that there was $65,000 worth of pilferage from the small Saigon PX. I myself had seen the Saigon PX's own estimates of pilferage. Either the colonel did not know what was happening in his own stores or he was lying.

He said that another reason for employing over 5,000

[6] In Seoul and Manila the PX's supplied the black markets so lavishly that it almost made one ashamed to be an American. However, they were not as bad as in Vietnam.

foreigners in the PX's was to give work to worthy Vietnamese of good character, which helped the war economy. I asked him if he knew how the employment racket worked. He denied there was such a racket.

The facts are, however, that each clerk employed has to get a recommendation from someone who is in the Vietnamese government. This recommendation has to be paid for—and the standard payment is approximately a month's wages.

The colonel said he had never heard of any such thing.

The colonel then got on his soapbox and told me what a wonderful thing the PX was. It was being operated so that there could be profits made to supply the Army and the Air Force with money to pay for the motion pictures shown to the troops and for other recreational activities. He also said that the PX was a place where restless Americans could spend their dollars—instead of unloading their money on the Vietnamese economy and thus causing inflation.

I asked him, "Isn't the primary mission of the PX's to give the troops a service?"

He said it was.

As I observed it, the troops come last as far as the big Saigon PX is concerned. Training Vietnamese comes first. Then comes making money for recreational service. Then comes improving the economy of Vietnam. Then comes "looking good." Last and least is the GI.

The original function of the post exchange was to provide the men (at the men's personal expense) with those few items which the government did not supply—for example, tobacco, shaving equipment, pieces of uniform in excess of what was issued, and such things as stationery, hair tonic, and so forth. But today the PX and the commissary have gone far beyond this function. The PX now stands as a gigantic bribe. It is supposed to take the sting out of being in combat and give the Americans in tough areas the "good American way of life." Bizarrely enough, it is not the small percentage of men who are actually in combat who make the most of the post exchange. It is the fat boys in the cities and headquarters, and also the thousands of civilians, such as construction workers, newspapermen, AID employees, and the staff of the Embassy.[7]

A Vietnamese businessman told me the PX gives convenience and profits to the rich Vietnamese; but in some ways the post exchange defeats the American war effort. The luxury items in the post exchange are bought by Americans, and also by the Vietnamese elite—via the black market or American friends. The garish and blatant way in which the American and Vietnamese officials exhibit these things can do nothing but widen the gap that separates the masses from the local rich and the Americans.

The wider the gap between the people and the Americans and the administration of South Vietnam, the less the people identify themselves with us and the more with the Vietcong.

The PX as it is run now makes the United States a collaborator in the worst kind of corruption. Everyone—including the Americans—knows that some Americans involved are corrupt. They know that many Vietnamese clerks are corrupt; they know the Filipino and Korean PX as-

---

[7] The people eligible to use the PX in Vietnam—either in full or limited capacity (according to the Directive from United States Military Assistance Command, Vietnam) is as follows: (1) U.S. Armed Forces personnel, (2) Retired personnel of the U.S. Armed Forces, (3) Personnel from the following countries who are serving in Vietnam: Australia, Korea, New Zealand, the Philippines, Nationalist China, and Thailand, (4) U.S. Embassy personnel, (5) U.S. Agency for International Development personnel, (6) Joint U.S. Public Affairs Office personnel, (7) United States Civil Service employees, (8) Official visitors to Vietnam, (9) United States press corps (journalists), (10) U.S. contractor personnel (that is, civilians—thousands of them—engaged in engineering work for private companies), (11) Masters, Chief Engineers, and Pursers of MSTS vessels, (12) Celebrities and entertainers, representatives of USO and other social agencies, and six educational institutions and persons in similar status providing direct services to the United States Forces. Just about everyone in Vietnam—except Vietnamese—have direct access to the PX (and commissary). The rich Vietnamese gain access through their friends among the allies and through the black market.

sistants often are in cahoots with their friends. Therefore, because of the PX and the commissary, the average Vietnamese believes the Americans to be corrupt. Almost every day there are fifteen or twenty Vietnamese National Police standing within a block or two of the small Saigon PX. They approach Americans going into the store and ask them to buy them cigarettes, soap, and other commodities. This is illegal, and everyone knows it; yet many Americans comply with the requests.

What is happening to the PX and the commissary in Vietnam is not new. The same corrupt and inefficient operations occurred in the Philippines and in Korea. It is happening in Thailand. It happened in Germany, Italy, and Greece.

12 THE PX foul-ups and the sale of millions of dollars of PX products in the black market turned out to be almost microscopic compared to what turned up later. I can best describe it by showing it in action as I witnessed it.

We were walking along the Saigon River. With me was my old friend Tran Trong Hoc. He is an old man now, but he knows the Saigon bureaucracy—of both underworld and overworld. In a sense, Tran is sort of a retired mandarin who sits back, observes everything, listens to the rumors and gossip, reads the papers, and watches the ever-present power struggle in Vietnam politics. He has children and grandchildren all over Southeast Asia. Some are employed by the South Vietnamese government, some by the American government, and some by the National Liberation Front. Several are in business. Tran Trong Hoc is a miniature Central Intelligence Agency. But this for him is a pastime, a hobby. He is not in the intelligence business, yet when I remarked on the danger implicit in his hobby, he said, "How else can an old man help his country?"

During the 1950's, Tran spent eighteen months in

Los Angeles, studying American police techniques. While there he learned the American way of life. He takes delight in using American slang as much as possible when he is with his friends. It is his small vanity.

We turned left and went north, past the German hospital ship, which is West Germany's humanitarian contribution to Vietnam. Tran told me that the hard-working German doctors and nurses unwittingly are contributing to a crooked racket. All charity patients must have a "permit" to visit the foreign ship. For this they must pay a "tax" to a police organization. But German medicine is among the best in Vietnam; and many sick Vietnamese want to be treated on the hospital ship. Actually no Vietnamese gets on board unless he is a friend or relative of an important official, or has the money to bribe his way by paying "the tax." The same racket was applied to the American hospital ship, the SS *Hope*, when it was in Saigon. The visiting foreign physicians think they are doing good by helping the "people." In reality they are either treating or enriching the Vietnamese elite. Everything in Vietnam requires a payoff, even medical charity.

Moored in the river we saw several American freighters. The nearest was a big, gray cargo vessel. Her booms were swinging back and forth, and she was discharging cargo to barges alongside.

"That is the one we will watch," said Tran. "But it will be safer if we watch from my car. After all, we are spying. We are gathering intelligence. We are spooks. We want to see who cops the American military supplies. Standing here in the street, using binoculars, is asking for . . ." He drew his forefinger across his throat. We turned and walked down Ben Chuong Duong until we reached Pasteur Street. We turned right there and went north about seven blocks until we reached the RAND Corporation Building—Number 176. That was where Tran's car was parked. It was an old and beaten-up Citroën. The front seat was covered by an imitation leopardskin. The back seats had oilcloth over them. Although old, the

Citroën started quickly, and in a few minutes we were back by the river. We were about five hundred feet from the wharf to which the barges from the American freighter were headed.

"Those barges," said Tran, pointing, "belong to a Vietnamese company owned by a couple of Vietnamese generals. You Americans pay for the use of those barges. *You Americans pay for the privilege of sending ammunition and food and war supplies to this country.*"

The barges approached the wharf. Standing on the dock were eight five-ton trucks. Once they had been U.S. Army trucks, but now they were painted a slightly different shade of brown.

The barges swung alongside and secured to the wharf. Vietnamese longshoremen began to carry the cargo off, loading it directly into the brown trucks.

"The United States pays the wages of those Vietnamese longshoremen," said Tran.

There were no American soldiers or civilian officials about, supervising or checking. I asked Tran about this.

"The South Vietnamese government has told the American government to keep its nose the hell out of something which is an internal affair."

I said angrily, "That cargo is American war materiel. The wooden crates are marked 'Department of Defense, ELECTRONICS, this side up.' They come from the United States, and are paid for by U.S. citizens . . ."

"Bill," said Tran, "the United States has no Customs rights in Vietnam. You must understand that you are only guests here. That is your country's official attitude. Even every American military man has been ordered to carry a card which lays down a code of behavior. It says that you are guests here, and that the Vietnamese are always right. Perhaps that's why there is no one here checking on these war supplies. Guests, you know, do not check up on the dishonesty of their hosts. That would be bad manners."

"But this is American equipment for American troops. . . ."

"Yes."

We continued to watch; it took about an hour to load the eight trucks with their forty tons of American cargo.

The truck drivers clearly were restless. They kept looking at their watches and talking agitatedly among themselves.

Tran said, "Ordinarily, time means very little to us. Therefore when Vietnamese drivers are nervous about a schedule, it means only one thing. They are about to go through VC territory. The VC are paid off to let a convoy come through at a specified time. If the convoy is early or late, the trucks might be blown up."

A Vietnamese Army jeep, with a small Vietnamese flag flying on the left front fender, drove up to the wharf and stopped. A stout Vietnamese, about thirty-five, dressed in khaki (but wearing no insignia), got out. He carried a new black leather briefcase, which he opened on the hood of the jeep. The truck drivers clustered about him. To each of them the fat man gave a piece of paper. He talked intensely to the drivers, looking almost like a football coach instructing his team. Finally, he nodded his head, and the drivers fanned out, moved quickly into the cabs of their big trucks, and started their motors. While doing this they were putting the pieces of paper into a plastic envelope attached to the sunshade of the truck. One driver folded his paper and tucked it into his wallet.

The fat Vietnamese in khaki nodded his head again. The first truck started off and the others fell in behind. The convoy left the river area and headed inland, moving slowly through town. We lost sight of them then, but Tran knows their route as well as their routine. Among his literally hundreds of friends and informants is one who rides regularly in this convoy route.

When the eight trucks carrying 40 tons of U.S. electronic equipment reach the Saigon-Bienhoa Highway, they are stopped by a Vietnamese guard accompanied by an American soldier. The drivers show their pieces of paper. The Vietnamese guard walks down the line, looking at each paper for a moment. He waves the convoy on. The Vietnamese guard says something to the American soldier (who, after all, neither speaks nor reads Vietnamese and is dependent on his Vietnamese opposite number), says "Okay," and returns to the side of the road, leans his rifle against a house, and finishes his half-empty bottle of Coca-Cola.

The convoy moves on to Old Route One, the highway which leads to Cambodia and to Nhom Penh. It is only fifty miles to the Cambodian border. The convoy keeps moving straight to Cambodia. Near Trang-Bang there are holes in the road where a military convoy was blown up by Vietcong mines. Despite the presence of South Vietnamese and American troops, the Vietcong control this stretch of land.

The drivers look at their watches. They steer around the holes in the road and speed up. Four times on the way the trucks are stopped by armed guards; four times they have their papers examined. Twice the armed guards are in South Vietnamese Army uniforms, and twice they are in the black pajamas of the peasants. The trucks finally are at their destination, Go Dau Ha, a village almost on the Cambodian-Vietnamese border. Go Dau Ha is fifty miles and about two hours and twenty minutes from metropolitan Saigon.

The trucks pull up at a street called Tu Xuong. There is no street sign, but that is what the dirt road is called. At the intersection of this and an even smaller road called Van Lang is a rather large wooden house with a thatched roof. The trucks stop there. Armed South Vietnamese soldiers come from the house. One of them collects the pieces of paper from the drivers. He gives each a receipt in return. One of the soldiers bellows something. The drivers get out of the trucks. They go to a table by the side of the thatched house. Two women in black pajamas bring the drivers some lunch. It comes in a large, blue bowl, and it smells like fish and garlic.

While the drivers are eating, a convoy of black-painted trucks arrives from the other direction. They have just come from Kompong (Cambodia), and they have Cambodian licenses. The Cambodian trucks stop and, immediately, a crew of laborers swarms from the rear of the thatched house. Without instructions they get to work. The cargoes of the two convoys are swapped. The American electronics gear goes to Cambodia, the cartons from Cambodia go into the Vietnamese trucks.

The laborers work fast.

It is now half an hour later. The Cambodian convoy goes back to Cambodia. The Vietnamese convoy is returning to Saigon. In the Vietnamese trucks are tons of Red Chinese merchandise. There is no attempt to disguise anything. Everything is marked clearly on the large cardboard cartons. The boxes contain toothbrushes, tooth powder, vitamins, imitation Parker fountain pens, and thermos bottles, among other things.

Now it is three hours later. The trucks go to Cholon, on the outskirts of Saigon. They are parked outside a block-square warehouse. The Chinese Communist products are carried inside. Several National Policemen stand by in their white shirts watching. One asks a driver how things are at the border. Inside the warehouse are big stacks of tires for jeeps and other U.S. military vehicles. Piled up in the rear are hundreds of bags of U.S. cement (with the USAID markings on them) and hundreds of bags of U.S. rice. The warehouse belongs to a Chinese named Hop Tan.[8]

That was what happened to the trucks with the forty tons of U.S. military supplies. It is a story with a clear meaning; it needs no further detail. But, in fact, there is further detail, and it is important.

The fat man in khaki who met the trucks at the Saigon wharf is Nguyen Kai.[9] He is from the office of

[8] His real name.
[9] His real name.

Captain Kham,[10] who is the Chief of the Province Police for Tay Ninh Province (which is on the Cambodian border). Every day Nguyen Kai arrives at the wharf *at least* once to give pieces of paper to truck drivers. The paper is an official document which says that the materials in the truck are being delivered to the South Vietnamese Intelligence Forces and are for the use of the Intelligence Forces.

Of course the materials in the trucks are *not* going to the Vietnamese Intelligence Forces. They are going up the Old Route One to Go Dau Ho, or perhaps Ta Loc, or Nan Pi—all of which are gateways to Cambodia. Once there, the contents of the trucks are turned over to Ho Ting,[11] a Nationalist Chinese from Taipei. Mr. Ho represents an international black-market cartel. *The role of the South Vietnamese Intelligence Forces in this operation is an interesting one.* The Chief of Intelligence, Thanit Tung,[12] receives a *minimum* payoff of 2 million piasters a month from Captain Kham of the Tay Ninh Province Police Force. That's about $12,500 a month for Thanit Tung personally. It is delivered in greenbacks or U.S. credits (in Thanit Tung's name) to the director of the Saigon Airport. The airport director sends it via diplomatic pouch (along with similar monies from other South Vietnamese officials) to his brother, who is the Vietnamese consul-general in Hong Kong. The consul-general passes it to Nguyen Huu Co—the ex-minister of defense—who now acts as banker in Hong Kong for the South Vietnamese generals and officials.

The entire operation is beautifully coordinated among the various South Vietnamese government agencies.

The vice-director of the port of Saigon, Chung Duc Mai,[13] and his boss know which American ships and what American cargoes will be coming to Saigon. They control the unloading. Perhaps two weeks before an American

[10] His real name.
[11] His real name.
[12] His real name.
[13] His real name.

freighter arrives in Saigon, the contents of the American vessels have been broadcast among various possible custo-.mers. There are many. The Vietcong is one, the North Vietnamese are another, and sometimes Red China, or perhaps a middleman in Hong Kong, or any nation in the world who needs the cargo and is willing to pay a high enough price. According to a Filipino source, Israel was one of the black-market customers in the summer of 1967. She desperately needed the large mortar shells which only the United States was making in considerable numbers. They cost about $400 each. The mortar shells, designated for the U.S. Army in Vietnam, were diverted via Manila. From Manila they were transported, by a different ship, to Israel.

Who pays for the billions of dollars' worth of stolen U.S. goods?

Whoever receives them. The Vietcong, or the Viet-namese, or the Red Chinese, or the Nationalist Chinese who manages the Hong Kong office, or Filipino members of the cartel.

What do they pay for the goods with?

Either American dollars, American credits, or barter.

Who handles these deals?

There are many people. After all, it is multi-billion dollar operation. But in order of profit and numbers, the following are involved:

1 South Vietnamese generals and officials.
2 South Vietnamese businessmen who are friends of the Vietnamese in official power.
3 The National Liberation Front (Vietcong).
4 American black-market operators.
5 North Vietnamese agents.
6 Nationalist Chinese businessmen, both in Vietnam and in Taiwan.
7 Korean troops, businessmen, and officials.
8 Filipino troops, businessmen, and officials.

In other words, just about everyone plunders and rapes the United States war effort in Vietnam.

13 IT IS a Wednesday in June. We are at the Saigon wharfs again. We are sitting in Tran Trong Hoc's car close to a different pier, but one not too far from where we were yesterday. Alongside the pier is a small Vietnamese steamer —one designed for coastal and river trade. Piled up near the ship on the street are what I estimate to be 1,500 tons of materiel. It includes U.S. rice, U.S. sheet metal, bags of U.S. cement, drums of U.S. oil, and what appear to be cases of ammunition. Several South Vietnamese soldiers, armed with automatic rifles, are guarding the supplies.

A Vietnamese Army jeep, with the flag on its left front fender, arrives. The same stout Mr. Nguyen Kai, in the same khaki clothes and carrying the same new black leather briefcase, gets out of the jeep. He walks about the supply dump, checking things off a list.

"Down! Down!" Tran shouts. He roughly puts his hand on my shoulder and pushes me below the level of the windshield.

"Stay down!" he says, backing his car slowly, turning it, and moving away from the pier.

We are now about a block away. Tran turns the car and parks it. We can still watch what is happening and see much through the binoculars.

"Whew," says Tran. "Nguyen was walking toward us. We couldn't take a chance. He knows both you and me. If he spotted us we'd both get our asses into jams."

"He doesn't know me," I say, getting off the floor and sitting up in the seat again.

"You are a dope," says Tran. "Everyone knows everyone in this town. My daughter-in-law is an interpreter at JUSPAO. She told me that Major Hogben was scolded by the colonel in Public Affairs because the major had lunch with you. . . ."

"Of course I had lunch with Major Hogben. What's wrong with that . . ."

"Nothing, nothing, as far as you're concerned. But in this can-of-worms town, everyone must protect himself. Especially from newspapermen. It is okay for the enemy to know what's happening—and the enemy usually does—but not the American Embassy or the American people. I tell you, Willy-boy, the word gets around. You have been discussed several times at the JUSPAO morning meetings. They want to know who your sources of information are. That's why the colonel scolded the major. Was the major giving you the poop? And if that bugger Nguyen Kai recognized you and me together, the crap would hit the fan. Nguyen Kai would send word to Thanit Tung, and in the end my daughter-in-law would be fired from JUSPAO for being a poor security risk—which she is, as is every other Vietnamese employed by the U.S. government."

Up the street, stevedores are now carrying the supplies—sheet metal, U.S. rice, U.S. cement, U.S. ammunition, U.S. oil—aboard the Vietnamese steamer. Nguyen is supervising.

"There is no use in our staying longer," says Tran. "It will take several hours to load the ship. I just wanted you to see what goes on board. That ship leaves this dock every sixth day. It goes south, then up the Mekong River to Chau Doc Province, which also is on the Cambodian border. There it off-loads; and the supplies go easily to the Vietcong—or whoever else needs and can pay for them."

"What about the U.S. Navy?" I ask. "Doesn't the U.S. Navy inspect all the shipping along the coast?"

"Of course your precious Navy stops every ship and inspects it. But that inspection isn't worth a fart in a whirlwind. The ship's papers are in perfect order. The captain of the Vietnamese ship has a document, signed by Thanit Tung, saying that the ship is carrying urgently needed supplies for the South Vietnamese intelligence units near An Phu. Not a single American on any U.S. Navy ship speaks or reads Vietnamese. All your goddam Navy can do is glance at the document with the Intelligence Force's letterhead and Thanit's signature. So, of course, your Navy permits the ship to go on. How in hell does the U.S. Navy know the ship's carrying black-market materiel stolen from the U.S. Army?"

"Does the steamer bring a cargo back?"

"Of course. It brings back the same Red Chinese products you saw in the trucks. There is a small fleet of steamers working this racket. There are three on the Mekong run alone."

I ask, "Who owns the steamship company?"

"It is chartered by the South Vietnamese Navy."

I ask, "When I was in Hong Kong I saw USAID rice for sale there. Do these steamers transport it there?"

While we are talking, Tran is driving his car through the swarms of scooters which buzz along the Saigon streets. After a while he answers me.

"Under your Public Law 480, rice and other materials are sent to Vietnam. They are supposed to be transported in Vietnamese bottoms. But South Vietnam has no big ships of its own. Therefore the United States lends ships. The arrangement is, then, that when the American ship departs an American port for Vietnam, *the Vietnamese take possession of the cargo at that moment.*

"The American ship captain, therefore, has very little to say about what happens to the cargo. It belongs to Vietnam the moment the ship leaves the U.S.A.

"There are many shiploads of American supplies going to Vietnam. Ships often are sent to Manila to stand by until anchorage or mooring space opens up in Vietnam. I am certain that is where most of the bulk stores such as rice or cement are transshipped to other ports and sold on the black market."

Tran has stopped his Citroën on the corner of Han Thuyen and Cong Ly. This is where I am to get off and walk the rest of the way to my hotel, the Caravelle. No sane Vietnamese would escort an American to his hotel, especially the Caravelle. The doorman and elevator boys are members of Colonel Ngoc's[14] Intelligence Police. Every Vietnamese who comes into the hotel with an American is identified and noted.

Before I get out of the car, I ask Tran how this hijacking and black marketing of U.S. war and aid materiel could be stopped.

He says it would be simple to reduce the stealing. "The obvious way is to get rid of the Vietnamese longshore-men and replace them with Americans. Have Americans unload their own ships and deliver the materiel in their own trucks, driven by Americans. Have Americans guard their own warehouses."

"Why can't this be done?" I ask.

"Not long ago one of your ambassadors tried to. But the Vietnamese government—it was Marshal Ky—said no, it would put too many Vietnamese out of work. The Viet-namese government refused to let you Americans unload your own ships in Saigon."

"Wouldn't it be economical," I say, "if we put Ameri-cans on as stevedores, and just paid the Vietnamese long-shoremen for doing nothing?"

"Of course," he says, as I get out of the car. "Of course. But you Americans have had neither the initiative nor the courage to do it."

A policeman is walking toward us. Tran Trong Hoc stares ahead as if he does not know me. He puts his Citroën into gear and drives away.

The next day Tran told me, "I have been reading Spengler. Now I believe the United States is in a strange downward spiral. Don't you see it? America is doing every-thing to lose the war. It makes a big show, spends billions, has thousands of its men killed, but *really down deep is trying to lose.*" He raised his eyebrows and wrinkled his forehead. This is a Vietnamese expression which means approximately, *My God, is it possible?*

[14] His real name.

Tran Trong Hoc continued, "Whenever you allow these Vietnamese big-shot crooks to enrich themselves at the expense of the common good, at the expense of the common people, do you know what you're doing? You are helping the Vietcong to win the war!

"Do you know who Sam Van Khanh[15] is?" asked Tran.

I did not know.

"Sam is a Vietcong who is a professional killer. He is a skilled saboteur, a terror maker, a marvelous propagandist for the Vietcong. He propagandizes by acts, not by talk. He works with thirty assistants here in Saigon. It was he who bombed the My Canh floating restaurant, the Metropole barracks, and the American Officers' Club, and mortared the Independence Palace during the presidential ceremonies. It is he who bragged, 'We cannot bother to blow up the old American Embassy. We'll just toss a bomb or two in. We will wait until the new one is built. Within a month after that, we will not bomb it. No, we will raid it, enter it.'[16] Do you know what the poor people of Saigon call Sam?"

"No."

"He is called 'Protector of the Poor.' That's almost the literal translation. A more accurate translation for what the people call Sam might be 'Knight in Shining Armor.' Spooky, eh? And you Americans who think you're doing good, the people have contempt for you. You Americans could learn a lot from Nguyen Van Tam, the killer, the 'Knight in Shining Armor.' You should study his techniques."

The people in Vietnam, particularly in the cities, and most particularly in present-day Saigon, generally have a

15 This is the alias by which the people know him. His real name is Nguyen Van Tam.

16 On 31 July 1967 Sam Van Khanh was captured in Saigon. Still, on 31 January 1968, the Vietcong entered and raided the new U.S. Embassy—almost at the predicted time.

low regard for police. The police are considered a group of privileged characters whose major responsibility is to keep the current administration in power; in return for this they have the privilege of shaking down the people of the precincts.

Policemen are exempt from military duty. Policemen may knock on the door—or break into a private home—and search the place without a warrant or forenotice. Any member of the household can be dragged to jail without trial, and without any given reason.

The various kinds of Vietnamese police "protect" the populace the same way that Chicago gangsters "protected" businesses from which they wanted to squeeze a profit.

In the Sixth Police Precinct of Saigon the police had been wallowing in a very lucrative racket. They "protected" the farmers who brought their eggs, vegetables, meats, and other foodstuffs from the country into the Saigon markets. What the police were "protecting" the farmers from, no one knows. The poor peasants already had paid an official tax to the South Vietnamese government; they had paid a tax to the Vietcong at their villages or along the roads; and they already had given half of their crops to the absentee owner of their land and a percentage of the crops to the person who owned the water rights to their farms.

Now, in Saigon's Sixth Precinct, the police were grabbing still another slice of the peasants' small profits by "protecting" them from hoodlums who were policemen out of uniform. If they didn't pay, they were physically abused, or their ID cards were taken.

This illegal and unjust practice had been well known to the Americans who act as advisers to the South Vietnamese police. (There are American advisers to almost every official in South Vietnam.) One of the American advisers, "an honest cop," tried to persuade the police of the Sixth District to stop their shakedowns. The Vietnamese police chief of the Sixth Precinct complained to his political boss that the American adviser was meddling.

Two days later an official from AID told the American adviser to keep quiet. "After all," said his American superior, "this is their country, not ours."

Later still, another American official scolded the American adviser. "Remember, we are guests in this country. You are here to advise police on law enforcement techniques, not to interfere with their personal behaviors."

Both the Vietnamese farmers and the Vietnamese city dwellers who consumed the foodstuffs felt that the action of the police was a social injustice. They did not grumble, at least not publicly, for fear that they would be identified as being Vietcong or anti-administration. Almost anyone who complains of the police or army is arrested as a Communist. But deep within themselves the peasants and poor people resented and chaffed over the crookedness of the police. Also, they wondered about the United States of America. They listened to the propaganda broadcasts which described how badly the unfortunate people were being treated in North Vietnam. The propaganda described the democracy and justice for which the South Vietnamese and the United States were fighting.

The South Vietnamese people of the Sixth Police District knew that the American advisers were familiar with the police malpractices, and they became silently angry when the Americans did nothing to correct the crookedness.

One day, the police station in the Sixth Precinct was blown up by Sam, the Saigon terrorist for the National Liberation Front. The next morning the NLF radio described how the Sixth Precinct police had been abusing the people and the farmers; that was why Sam had destroyed the police station. The NLF threatened that if the corrupt practices did not stop, further measures would be taken to punish the evil police.

The people in the Saigon Sixth Precinct smiled.

The Vietcong looked like heroes, like protectors of the poor, like knights in shining armor. And, once more, the people of Saigon looked at the United States and the South

Vietnamese administration with the same contempt as they once had looked at the French who had indulged in similar exploitation of the peasants and the poverty-stricken city dwellers.

V

THE

HUMILIATED

AMERICAN

'You are an old friend, and we are here at a family celebration; so I will tell you what I think is the truth.

"America cannot win in Vietnam until two deep
flaws in American character have been made good.

"What are the flaws in America's character? Well,
the first one concerns your leaders—your diplomats and
generals. These fellows have no courage of spirit. De-
generes animos timor arguit, as Vergil said. 'Fear betrays
ignoble souls.' We professors call your ambassadors and
generals 'The Groveling Americans.' They would kiss the
backside of a North Vietnamese carpetbagger like General
Ky—at noontime in front of the Parliament Building—
rather than take a chance of offending the Vietnamese or
having him be critical of America.

"It is an American diplomatic and military tradition
in Vietnam to be subservient and obsequious, if necessary, to
'get along.' We refer to it as 'Yankee Doormat Diplomacy.'

"Well, maybe I'll have the courage to tell you details after a few more glasses of wine. . . ."

PROFESSOR VO VAN KIM after a few
glasses of rice wine on the occasion
of his 70th birthday in June 1967

14   AMERICAN OFFICIALS know about the corruption of
the South Vietnamese. A high State Department official told
me that he and his colleagues are familiar with more corruption than I could ever dig up for myself. "But," he said,
"it really isn't important."

Tragically, Americans are afflicted with a paralysis
which has made it impossible for them to force the South
Vietnamese government to eliminate corruption. Our
officials are afraid of offending the Vietnamese. Because of
this helplessness, the Vietnamese treat us with scorn and
contempt. They humiliate us at every opportunity—of which
there are many. Thus American self-esteem is diminished
and "doormat diplomacy" develops. Efficiency is wrecked.

Perhaps it is shame which causes American officials
to hide the ugly facts from their countrymen.

What follows in this chapter are a few small examples of the kind of humiliations heaped upon the United
States by her ally; and some examples of how America's
humiliations have contributed to our disgraceful performance in Vietnam.

There is a large U.S. air base in South Vietnam
which, to protect one of its officers whom I will call Colonel
John Adams, USAF, I will not identify. Possibly the U.S.

Embassy or MACV[1] can track down Adams if their files are sufficiently cross-indexed, but at least I wish to make it as difficult as possible.

At this unnamed base, one hot Monday morning, the medical officers of all services met for a special conference. Two subjects were on the agenda: (1) the shortage of broad-spectrum antibiotics, and (2) a mystery disease.

It seems that an undiagnosable and serious skin infection had appeared among an increasing number of the patients of a young Air Force doctor. It had immobilized its victims, and he hoped that his seniors could give him some help. None could, but all reported similar outbreaks in their units.

As a result of the meeting, a public-health team was flown in and an exhaustive investigation undertaken. Laboratory technicians found several different types of fungi and bacteria hostile to the human skin. They found these fungi and bacteria on the men's clothing. The dermatitis finally was traced to the home laundries run by a local Vietnamese company. The clothes of U.S. military men were being washed by hand by Vietnamese women. The water they used was cold and was contaminated by human sewage, some of which carried intestinal parasites.

The military doctors and the public-health personnel ordered the Vietnamese laundrywomen to boil their water. Also they gave them a water purifier and demonstrated how to use it. The managers of the laundries said their employees understood and would comply. Nevertheless, the washerwomen continued to wash clothes in cold, contaminated water; and the troops continued having skin ailments.

One of the service officers on the base, Colonel John Adams, USAF, an ex-command pilot now on administrative duty, found a solution to the problem. Adams negotiated with a non-Vietnamese commercial firm to come to the base and operate a modern laundry. In about six weeks the

[1] Military Assistance Command, Vietnam (General William C. Westmoreland).

laundry was set up and operating. Americans on the base were pleased. The skin-ailment epidemic stopped. The troops now were getting two-day (instead of five-day) laundry service, with the clothes sterilized, bleached, and pressed.

Everyone was grateful for Colonel Adams' initiative. Everyone, that is, except the Vietnamese laundry people, the Vietnamese Army officers, and the Vietnamese whores —a combination strange to the Americans but reasonable by local custom.

The South Vietnamese military junta controls or has a finger in almost every form of business in Vietnam—either directly or indirectly. Among them is the laundry, dry-cleaning, and clothes-mending for U.S. troops. This is about a $120 million[2] a year business. Vietnamese officials get a kickback from every washerwoman, laundry operator, and tailor who serves foreign troops. This is an accepted fact of life. Thus, when Colonel Adams established a modern laundry run by outsiders, he automatically stripped the South Vietnamese leaders of their profits.

The whores got into the act by a less direct route. As soon as the modern laundry began operating, there was a sharp drop in the sale of laundry powder at the PX. The Vietnamese laundry managers had been getting their laundry powder from the PX via the troops. For every ten boxes of soap powder delivered from the PX to the Vietnamese laundry, the men received a coupon usable at some of the better whorehouses. With the incoming of the new laundry, business fell off.

A few weeks after the laundry was working, Colonel John Adams received a letter from United States Ambas-

2 This figure was supplied by Captain Lee Van Trom of the South Vietnamese quartermaster corps, who was sent to Can Tho to organize the American troops' laundry business for the "syndicate." William Corson, whose book on Vietnam will be published in August 1968, gives a slightly lower figure. But even a $20 million difference is of small significance here. Corson lived with the syndicate's activities and describes them in detail. His book is recommended for anyone who wishes to know more on the subject.

sador Ellsworth Bunker. According to Adams, the letter
said that Ambassador Bunker had received a communication from the Vietnamese corps commander in Adams'
area. This ranking South Vietnamese general had complained about the establishment of the new laundry. The
reason given for the complaint was that the new laundry
had put Vietnamese women out of work.

Therefore, said the letter from Ambassador Bunker
to Colonel Adams, if the colonel could not find other equal
sources of revenue for the Vietnamese women, he would
have to shut down the new laundry and give the laundry
contracts back to the local Vietnamese.

Colonel Adams was not happy at his orders to become an employment agent for washerwomen and a middleman for Vietnamese racketeers. He says he went into a
temper over the fact that the welfare of perhaps a hundred
Vietnamese washerwomen and perhaps two hundred Vietnamese whores was considered more important than the
health of thousands of American servicemen assigned to
combat duty on behalf of the Vietnamese. But Colonel
Adams is intelligent and practical. He realized that he had
no choice. The ex-washerwomen were employed as mes-
sengers, picking up the soiled clothes at the barracks and
taking them to the new laundry, and, later, delivering the
clean clothes. Their service was not needed; in fact they
both slowed deliveries and increased laundry prices. But it
made it possible to continue the laundry and to keep the
men healthy.

Also it made it possible for the U.S. ambassador to
"cooperate" with the Vietnamese corps commander, and it
made it possible for the Vietnamese military junta to continue enjoying the profit which came from American troops.

Finally, it made it possible for the whores near the
U.S. base to get back in business. Even though the Vietnamese laundries were not operating, the troops still had
someone to whom they could give the laundry soap from
the PX. They gave it to the ex-washerwomen, who, in
return, produced the coupons for the whorehouses.

Instead of being used for local laundry, the soap now is sold on the black market. Often it is transported to the black-market terminals in U.S. trucks.

"Everything worked out okay in the end—at least our troops didn't get dermatitis any more," said Colonel Adams. "But it does make one realize that, if we are ever to win this war, the United States must defeat the South Vietnamese government's racketeers; then we have to defeat the U.S. Embassy and MACV. After that it will be a cinch to lick the Vietcong and the North Vietnamese. Man, then it would be a cinch."

A footnote of interest is that the Vietnamese corps commander who complained about Colonel Adams to the U.S. Ambassador was a poor migrant when he fled from Hanoi to Saigon in 1954. Today he is a rich man. He is one of those involved in selling rice and other U.S. grains earmarked for use by troops and refugees.

15   ONLY A small percentage of the over half a million Americans in Vietnam are in combat. Therefore only a small percentage of them live in the field. The others, both military and civilian, are located in urban communities.

Thousands of Americans sleep in houses rented from the Vietnamese. Officially there is rent control. But rent control for American tenants is not enforced. This does not appear important. We have rent-control problems at home. But the way it happens in Vietnam illustrates the contempt the Vietnamese elite have for Americans; and it illustrates the self-humiliations, the "doormat diplomacy," the groveling which marks the behavior of the Americans in Vietnam.

I inspected some of the houses which are rented from Vietnamese for the use of American personnel. The first was listed as a "two-bedroom villa." Upon entering it, I thought I was in the wrong place. It smelled like a cesspool. I asked about the stench. It came from sewage which backs up through the toilet every time there is rain. The sewage flows all over the floor, which is rotten. The sewage remains between and under the boards. There were holes in the roof, each with a bucket underneath to catch the rain.

One of the bedrooms was 10 feet by 12 feet. The other one was 8 feet by 8 feet. The kitchen had no stove. The refrigerator was an old-fashioned icebox which was nearly unusable because it had no drain. It had to be bailed out.

The lease stated that any furniture or equipment brought in became the property of the owner of the house when the tenants moved out. The hall leading into the two bedrooms was used as a sitting room. That was it. The rent demanded for the house 16,000 piasters a month. In other words, the U.S. government was paying $200 a month for this pigpen. This is roughly three times the rent-control ceiling. The two-bedroom dump was occupied by eight American enlisted men. The landlord is a major in the South Vietnamese Army. The American officer (whose men lived in the pigpen) complained about the house where his men had to live. His American superiors told him, "Keep quiet. The major is doing us a favor. He could raise the rent more if he wants to."

Three blocks away a South Vietnamese lieutenant colonel is building an apartment house. It is his personal, private venture. The cement, hardware, and lumber have been stolen from the U.S. government. The materials, plainly marked, are in an open lot near the main street. It is near the USAID building. American officers pass there daily.

Many of the new, large apartment houses in Saigon are owned by senior Vietnamese military officers. The building material used in them—much of it—is USAID goods intended for refugees. The labels on the packages clearly show that they belong to USAID. No one bothers to disguise or hide the labels. Some of the construction labor is

done by South Vietnamese Army personnel. The U.S. government does not complain. One USAID official told me,
"At least it relieves the housing shortage. That's how I got
my apartment."

The second rented house I looked at had four miniature bedrooms. It had one room which *might* be called a
bath. It consisted of a toilet bowl and a shower. The shower
had only cold water. There was no sink. Two of the bedrooms each had a basin with cold water. The house was
designated by the Vietnamese as a "three-bathroom house."
By Vietnamese zoning law, if a house has three "bathrooms"
it can be designated as a hotel. If it is a hotel, the rent can
be raised, and the minimum is $100 per month per room.
This small, miserable shack was listed as a three-bathroom
hotel, and the U.S. government was paying $400 a month
for it. There was no wallpaper. The plaster was cracked.
There was a garbage dump within fifteen feet of the front
door. In America this shack could not possibly have gotten
by even a bribed health inspector.

In Saigon I was invited to a house which was a
pleasant three-bedroom home in a respectable residential
area. It had a garden about it, and an airy porch on two
sides. It was well furnished with tropical furniture. It was
occupied by three Embassy officials. My informant told me
that the rent was $2,000 a month.

On all these houses, the tenant pays for the electricity;
and the electricity rate is ten cents per kilowatt hour—
about three times as high as in the United States.

The rent-control law in Vietnam is a farce. The
majority of rental contracts involve the U.S. government;
therefore, the U.S. government is a party to violating the
law in a way which does harm to Americans who reside in
the overpriced rental units.

No matter where they are in Vietnam, the Americans
permit themselves to be gouged and suckered. For example,
the Vietnamese military establishment receives equipment

which is denied the American fighting forces. I asked a supply officer why this was.

"Because," he said, "on this base if we don't give the Vietnamese what they want, they complain to Westmoreland that we are insulting them or wrecking the war effort. If I get a couple of such complaints against me, I'll get transferred and get a lousy fitness report."

He put on his cap and said, "Come along. I'll show you what I mean."

He took me on a tour of the Vietnamese base and the adjacent American base. "See," he said, "the Vietnamese have plenty of fire extinguishers, lumber, jeeps, fork lifts, and cement. But on our own base we don't even have fire extinguishers. If even a small fire started, we'd go up in flames. We receive enough materials for our own base—on delivery day. But I am forced to give first crack at everything to the Vietnamese. Our boys come next—if there's anything left."

Almost everything seems to end up in the wrong hands. There are so many jeeps stolen or sold from the U.S. military that there is a shortage of transport for our troops. It is one of the excuses offered by U.S. Army advisers for the nondelivery of necessities such as rice, grain, and plague antitoxin to troops and refugees. The shortage is so acute that for some time now the American military has been renting its own stolen jeeps from black-market operators at $250 a month. The same double indignity and multiple cost applies to U.S. government trucks.

The ancient, ritualized, and traditional system of kickbacks and almost honorable bribery of the Orient was "for services rendered"; it was reasonable. But it has been perverted in a culture made up of a massive dose of American dollars. It has become a monster of venality which is devouring the national structure of South Vietnam. It is debilitating the war effort. And, of course, it causes the Vietnamese to view us as fools.

One of the Vietnamese in Danang who is most popular with Americans is the mayor. He is a lieutenant colonel in the South Vietnamese Army, and he speaks fluent English. He gives parties and flatters the American officers. He arranges "entertainment" for them. In return for this he expects no interference from Americans in the local black-market operation. No Americans interfere, even though American materials are involved.

The mayor requested that the U.S. military pave many of the streets of Danang. He requested that the whole shoreline along the river be strengthened and shored up. The U.S. military did this for him. It is this mayor who allows Vietnamese landlords to violate the laws and over-charge the military for its housing. The landlords, of course, give him a cut.

The control which the Vietnamese have over the Americans has no end. They dictate to us as if we were their slaves, yet our military and civilian officials either are unaware or incompetent or forbidden to take action. For example, 10 per cent of all of the space on Air Force transport planes operating in Vietnam is reserved for the South Vietnamese. The South Vietnamese government would not permit us to use the airfields unless we agreed to this. Many times there are no Vietnamese passengers, but still we are not permitted to fill those seats or our own planes with our own troops. Ten per cent of the seats in the plane are often empty, while American GI's wait at the terminal for transportation.

Such things as empty plane seats are petty annoy-ances compared to some of the ways in which we are being had by our hosts.

Several years ago, when there was a terrible rice shortage in Vietnam, the United States sent shiploads of rice to Saigon—on a high-priority basis. But the unloading of the ships was so slow that sometimes they would stay at anchor as long as forty days. One of them had taken in water in a storm. The rice was spoiling because of the dampness. The captain of the ship said if his cargo wasn't unloaded quickly his rice would go bad. The American government requested that the rice ship be unloaded. (The priority of cargoes that come ashore in Vietnam is the prerogative of the Vietnamese.) Even though the ships are American and the cargoes are donated by the United States, the ships' cargoes are brought ashore on Vietnamese lighters (for which America must pay a charge) and are unloaded by Vietnamese longshoremen.

The name of the chief of the Department of Supplies for Vietnam was Tran Do Cung.[3] He turned down the request from the American government to unload the rice ship—even though the country was close to famine in some areas. Instead, he gave orders that ships carrying Honda motor scooters be given first priority for unloading.

Tran Do Cung received a 5 per cent kickback on every Honda landed in Vietnam. The U.S. Embassy and the U.S. military knew about this. I asked an Army colonel why we didn't do something. He looked at me with puzzlement. "How could we do anything? It's their country, isn't it?"

It is in the realm of pure cash and finance, however, where South Vietnamese officials and entrepreneurs are at their most adept at humbling and weakening their ally, the United States.

American economists have spent much time on the spot, advising the Vietnamese on how to stay economically healthy. The American economists recommend all kinds of measures to prevent inflation, to keep the piaster stable, and to safeguard government funds. Despite all this counsel and American supervision, the government Bank of Vietnam does as it pleases. It usually disregards American advice.

A man named Nguyen Huu Honh[4] was the director of the Vietnamese government bank. At the start of his tenure as director, the Vietnamese government funds were deposited in many banks throughout the world. This

[3] His real name.
[4] His real name.

was done as a safeguard for the security of the government funds. But Nguyen Huu Honh put an end to that.
He withdrew much of the money from all over the world,
and placed it in just a few banks.

I asked the Vietnamese economist who was telling
me about this why Nguyen Huu Honh had done such a
thing. The Vietnamese economist replied, "It wasn't so silly
for him. He received a kickback, or shall I say 'favor,' from
people connected with the 'preferred' bank. It is no accident
that he is a rich man, with money in U.S. banks."

I was astonished to hear this. I thought this was one
area where the United States government was keeping close
watch on the Vietnamese. A Vietnamese economist told me
that not only are the banks involved, but that Nguyen Huu
Honh gets kickbacks from many other quarters also. He
gets "financial favors" from the company which prints the
piasters for Vietnam. It is Nguyen Huu Honh who controls
the printing contract.

The Vietnamese economist continued, "It is true that
officials in the Vietnamese government are corrupt. But they
could not be this way without considerable cooperation
from American officials. If your Department of Internal
Revenue would check up on the hidden earnings of several
thousand Americans over here during the last fifteen years,
you would be in for some surprises."

The free-market exchange rate of the piaster is about
160 piasters to 1 dollar. The many thousands of Vietnamese
who are employed by the United States are paid in piasters.
The hundreds of millions of dollars which have been paid
by the United States to Vietnam for the rent of land and
buildings and other services are paid in piasters. To get
these piasters the United States gives dollars to the Vietnamese government, which converts them to piasters
(which the United States will pay out). But the rate of
exchange which the United States government gets is arti-
ficial—about 80 piasters to the dollar instead of the free-
market rate of 160 piasters to the dollar. In short, Uncle
Sucker is paying twice as much as he should for everything.

And this is done with the full knowledge of the American government. I was told that this was done to help prevent inflation. It may help. It also breeds corruption which keeps the money in the hands of a few well-connected Vietnamese. They buy import licenses, then apply for dollar credits. They pay for these at the 80 to 1 exchange but sell the U.S. imported merchandise in a 160 to 1 exchange free market. Everything thus brought into Vietnam by the U.S. for importers means at least the doubling of the Vietnamese importers' investment.

Vietnamese officials make profit from all kinds of U.S. imports. Near Canlo, for example, there were approximately 10,000 refugees. In order to help them, the United States supplied enough cement to build foundations for refugee housing.

The Vietnamese lieutenant colonel who received the cement sold it on the black market in Hue. U.S. officials knew about this. But they were unable or unwilling to stop it or do anything about it.

Near Khe Sanh 6,000 tons of rice were sent by the United States to the Special Forces camp for resettled Vietnamese. The Vietnamese camp commander sold the rice on the black market.

The national law of South Vietnam says that the landlords may charge a maximum rent for farmland, not to exceed 25 per cent of the total crop. This law is violated from one end of the country to the other. Eighty per cent of all farmland is owned by absentee landlords; the standard land rental which is demanded and gotten is 50 per cent of the gross crop. Every American official in AID, in the U.S. Embassy, in USIS, and in the military knows this is true.

The Vietnamese landlords (a large number of whom are in the South Vietnamese government, either directly or by being related to an official) could be forced to abide by the 25 per cent land-rent rate. If this were done, the National Liberation Front would receive a great blow. The biggest plank in their political platform concerns land reform. Just one bit of reform in land rental probably would do more to win the political front of the war than any other single item. The present land law, of course, could be enforced, but the Vietnamese government is making too much graft out of it. The American advisers—including the Ambassador and the ranking general—are unable to do anything about this. Since 1961 American ambassadors have pleaded, cajoled, and threatened the South Vietnamese government regarding land reforms and corruption in general.

The South Vietnamese officials publicly agree. But nothing happens. Instead conditions get worse.

The illegal profits from violation of the land-rent law prolongs the war because it hands the Vietcong a vital argument to keep the loyalty of the peasants. Also, it damages the United States directly. When U.S. troops move into a Vietcong area, the Vietnamese landlords often come too, and, with U.S. protection, begin charging the high rents which the Vietcong had abolished. The peasants, therefore, blame the United States; and the peasants then assist the Vietcong even more than previously, and adhere more closely to them politically.

16   IN SOUTH VIETNAM there are more than 4 million refugees and displaced persons. A great number of them are refugees because their villages have been destroyed by U.S. bombs or artillery fire. The rest have been made refugees by the U.S. tactic of removing a village from the Vietcong rather than vice versa.

The United States pays compensation for the homes and property which have been destroyed. These payments are made whether the homes of the Vietnamese are destroyed on purpose or by accident. Assistance to the unfortunate villagers frequently is sent by CARE and AID.

Such money and supplies are *supposed* to go to the Vietnamese whose property has been damaged or destroyed. In questioning approximately one hundred Vietnamese in two widely separated sections of South Vietnam, I was unable to find a single instance in which a Vietnamese family had received the money. The consensus among the Vietnamese was that the money went into the pockets of Vietnamese officials.

Near Nam Dong a hamlet was almost obliterated—by mistake—by U.S. bombs. The Vietnamese peasants told me an American said that CARE was going to send supplies to rebuild the entire village. A month or so later an American from AID said the CARE materials had been delivered to the Vietnamese Army commander in Danang.

"But these CARE things never reached the village," said the peasant. "Even today, a year later, the people in the village have not received them."

He took me to a refugee family of five, and they confirmed the story. They also added that they had not received the personal-injury money.

Personal-injury money is a compensation paid by the United States if an individual is wounded or killed by accident. The money goes to the individual or to his family, and is known as *solatium* money.

"Oh, everyone knows," said a Vietnamese woman, "that the Americans give the money to the officials, but it never reaches the people.

"My brother is a clerk in the Army. He said that whenever his officers need money, they go to the Americans with a *solatium* claim which they make up. It is easy—they mention the name of a town where a big shell or bomb has dropped, and hand in a list of names of people killed or hurt. Sometimes the Americans send an interpreter to check on the accident. But the interpreter gets money from the Vietnamese officials. So he says the claim is true." She continued, "it is only the Marines who sometimes insist on personally inspecting the bodies and the damages. That is why the Army interpreters hate the Marines."

I asked them if they could give me any evidence of

cheating for *solatium* money, and they said yes; it concerned a district chief in Quang Nam Province.

I investigated the story, and got it firsthand from the
Marine officer involved.

One day the district chief, Major Hao, came into the
field command of a U.S. Marine Corps lieutenant colonel.

"Colonel," he said, "I've come to collect *solatium*
money for the five villagers who were accidentally killed the
other day over by the river."

"How were they killed, and by whom?" asked the
Marine.

The Vietnamese officer unrolled a map and put his
finger on it. "Your Marines were dropping mortars in here,
and some of them fell on the outskirts of the hamlet, killing
three men and two women. This is in my district, and I
have come to collect the money for the families."

"Three men and two women? When did it happen?"

The Vietnamese major gave the date and the time.
The Marine knew that at approximately that date and time
the Marines had been firing in that general direction at
what they thought was a guerrilla concentration.

The Marine said, "Let me see the bodies."

"They are outside in my jeep."

The Marine walked out and looked. In the back of
the jeep were five bodies, well wrapped in sacking.

The Marine said, "Major, put the bodies on the
ground and cut open the cloth."

"Oh no," said the Vietnamese major. "They're all
bloodied and mutilated by the shrapnel."

"Put them on the ground and cut the cloth open. I
want to look at them," said the Marine.

"Colonel, I assure you you don't want to look at
them. They are mangled and mutilated, with stomachs and
chests blown open, and with heads smashed. And putrefac-
tion has set in."

The Marine unloaded the bodies from the jeep. He laid them on the ground. Taking out his pocketknife, he cut the cloth off so that the bodies were out in the open.

They were the bodies of five men. There were no women. None of the bodies was mutilated and bloodied. In each of the men was one bullet hole. Obviously these individuals had been killed by rifle fire.

Without saying a word, the Marine lifted the bodies and put them back into the jeep. He took the Vietnamese major's elbow, led the major back into the vehicle, and pushed him into the front seat.

"Major," said the Marine bitterly, "if you wish to collect *solatium* money for dead Vietcong, I suggest you go and collect it from the headquarters of the National Liberation Front, not from the U.S. Marines. Now get the hell out of here."[5]

Major Hao drove away. Later in the book we will hear more about him.

17   AT JUSPAO and other government public relations centers in Vietnam, the U.S. Air Force is regularly awarded the "gold star" for efficiency. Suave, accommodating, cheerful, knowledgeable Air Force officers function in the very best Madison Avenue tradition. Lieutenant colonels and colonels deliver exciting combat pictures to the press almost before the pilot has landed his plane. Facts are distributed in well made-up press kits. Easy transportation is arranged for correspondents or other molders of public opinion. The U.S. Air Force public relations, with an endless supply of brass, is an efficient, effective, well-oiled machine.

Unfortunately the Air Force's performance as a mass transportation organization is not on the same high level as

---

[5] Pham Van Tang, a Vietnamese journalist, said this is one of the few instances he has ever heard of where a U.S. officer seriously has checked up on *solatium* requests.

public relations. Tactical airlift in Vietnam is the Air Force's responsibility—and it carries mostly GI's. Unlike its public information effort, the tactical airlift usually is a shabby, shoddy, disgraceful operation. Dogfaces and Leathernecks get worse treatment from the Air Force than the cattle occasionally flown over for the USAID program. Correspondents and officers avoid the scheduled tactical airlift flights if possible. They pull strings to get a special helicopter or go via Freedom Air Lines, a CIA-operated outfit.

Whereas there are platoons of lieutenant colonels, colonels, and generals pursuing and wooing and servicing the correspondents, I have never as yet seen an officer, of any rank, working at one of the Air Force passenger terminals. The GI's and Leathernecks who must use the tactical airlift (and it is their only means of getting around Vietnam) are treated with a "You're lucky to be getting a ride at all" attitude.

The Air Force terminal at Can Tho is a hot, dirty place where passengers usually are forced to wait for hours. There is no drinking water, and the filthy, fly-infested one-hole latrine is a place which forces the passenger to grit his teeth and decide to wait, no matter how miserable he feels.

Passengers—even if manifested—often doubt whether they'll get on their scheduled flights.

I saw an Air Force transport plane land in Can Tho half full of passengers. Some of the passengers, a few, were disembarking at Can Tho. The rest were proceeding to Saigon, which was the next stop. The plane taxied up close to the terminal. The tail gate was opened, and the flight orderly bellowed, "Them guys proceeding on to Saigon can get out and stand in the shade under the wings for a few minutes."

The passengers got out. A minute or so later a crowd from the terminal rushed out across the field and joined the passengers who were waiting in the shade under the wings. The members of the crowd that rushed over had no tickets, no passes, no supervision. No one knew who they were.

About ten minutes later the passenger supervisor, a sergeant at the terminal, announced, "All authorized passengers who are on my list to go from Can Tho to Saigon follow me to the plane."

About a dozen people, whose names were on the official flight manifest, followed the sergeant to the plane.

As they approached the plane, the flight orderly on the plane bellowed, "All them what was on the plane going to Saigon, get back into the plane."

The entire crowd—including unidentified members of the mob from Can Tho—pushed in. The seats were all filled. There was no room for the passengers with tickets— the passengers who had been properly manifested. This included GI's traveling under orders.

The flight orderly picked his nose for a minute, then said, "Jeez, there's no way to tell who should be in here or who shouldn't. Anyway there'll be another plane in two hours."

That was that. The American and Vietnamese troops who had gone to a lot of trouble to get on the manifest legally and to take transport to Saigon stood out on the field as the plane taxied off and became airborne. Slowly and angrily they went back to the dirty, hot terminal. About two dozen unauthorized persons were on their way to Saigon. Some may have been VC's for all the Air Force knew. Two of the passengers who got bumped were a Vietnamese paratrooper of the elite 38th—one of the finest units the Vietnamese have—and his wife. His wife was about to have a baby and, because of a complication, he was taking her to the hospital in Saigon.

The Air Force terminal at Saigon is just about the same. On their way to combat areas, Doggies and Leathernecks, heavy with packs and rifles, jostle and fall over each other in the crowded, small, dirty, hot, wooden building. Often there is no place to sit. When I was there, I talked with a Negro captain in the U.S. Army. He was traveling under orders, inspecting a string of communication units.

He had been waiting for three hours for a plane which had not come in yet. No one knew when it would arrive.

"Sometimes it's grim," the Negro captain said. "I waited here for seven hours yesterday, trying to get out, and I'll be lucky if I make it today."

Thousands of troops go through this Saigon terminal weekly. Most of them wait for at least several hours, often having to stand. The only eating place in the U.S. Air Force terminal is run by a Vietnamese outfit. The little restaurant is dirty, smells like garbage, and buzzes with flies.

At almost every stop on the Vietnam tactical air circuit it is the same. No decent toilet, no decent place to eat, often no drinking water, usually no place to sit except on the floor, no dependable schedule, and damned little consideration.

The U.S. Air Force's public relations boys will probably be getting out a press release soon telling how many million bodies the Southeast Asia airlift system has transported. The number, I am sure, will be accurate and impressive.

I queried an Air Force major about the lousy service. He replied angrily, "We know about the terminals, the restaurants, the toilets, and all that. But there's not a goddam thing we can do about it."

"Why not?"

"The South Vietnamese won't let us."

"We're financing everything out here, aren't we? We've suffered about 150,000 casualties, haven't we?"

"Just the same, the South Vietnamese won't let us." He stopped, blinked, and said, "We're not supposed to discuss these things with reporters."

I said, "That's absurd. Does the Vietnamese government order U.S. Air Force personnel to have filthy toilets for passengers? To allow filthy food? Do the Vietnamese prevent the U.S. Air Force from refilling the drinking water tanks at the terminals? Or make the planes consistently late?"

"In a way, yes," said the U.S. Air Force officer. "In a way they *do* control us and make us do these things. But I'm not supposed to discuss this with reporters. I suggest you see the colonel."

I didn't have time to see the colonel because I was on my way to Danang.

Danang Air Base is one of the largest and most important in South Vietnam. The United States has put several billion dollars into equipment and materiel for air operations from this field. The Tactical Air Command also operates from there, transporting personnel to other bases. The passengers get the same shabby treatment there as at the Can Tho and Saigon passenger terminals.

A U.S. Air Force officer, Colonel Sam Verplank, observed the way transients were treated, and he asked his commander for permission to try to improve matters by starting a place where food and liquid would be available. Permission was granted. Colonel Verplank looked about and found that near the passenger terminal was a storage shed about 20 by 40 feet. It was locked and it was empty. It belonged to the South Vietnamese Air Force.

Colonel Verplank decided the old storage shed was large enough to convert into a snack bar which the PX would operate and where military transients could get something to eat during their often long waits for planes.

But anything which an American wishes to do at Danang Air Base must first be cleared with the South Vietnamese Air Force. Colonel Verplank went to the South Vietnamese base commander and asked if he might have the unused storage shed to turn into a snack bar for passengers.

"Yes, you may," said the Vietnamese colonel, "provided you build *me* a house of the same proportions."

"It's a deal," said the American. "Where do you want it built?"

"Next to my residence."[6]

The Air Force officer got his construction gang together, and they built for the Vietnamese colonel a new storage house approximately 20 feet by 40 feet. When this was completed the American went over to the Vietnamese Air Force and asked for the keys to unlock the old dilapidated shed next to the U.S. Air Force passenger terminal. He was told it was already unlocked. When the American got to the storage shed, he found that it was not only unlocked, but that a Vietnamese family of five had moved into the shack. They were living in the back of it; in the front they were selling Coca-Cola, cigarettes, sandwiches, and the rest. The soft drinks and cigarettes which they were selling had been stolen from the Air Force PX.

The prices which the Vietnamese were charging were five times as high as the PX prices. A Coca-Cola cost fifty cents. The customers had to pay in U.S. money—which is illegal. If the U.S. Air Force had been enforcing the law, and insisted on it, the Vietnamese would have been arrested for dealing in stolen property and using illegal currency. The U.S. servicemen who gave them the American money would have been arrested on approximately the same charges.

Colonel Verplank went to the Vietnamese Air Force and complained about the family which had usurped the U.S. Air Force snack bar building. He was told that he had wanted a snack bar, and now he had one. Period.

The South Vietnamese Air Force commander wouldn't listen to any discussion of the matter. The Danang Air Base was in South Vietnam, and the Vietnamese would run it as they damned well pleased. The U.S. Air Force used the base "by permission" only.

A few days later several U.S. airmen working in the

[6] This is common practice throughout all of South Vietnam and Thailand. If the Americans want anything, the Vietnamese or the Thai official demands that the same thing be constructed for him— and usually it is to become his personal property.

passenger terminal got sick. It appeared to be dysentery. The Air Force medical officer traced the illness to the Vietnamese snack bar. The doctors examined the place, found it was "unacceptably filthy," condemned it, and forbade its use by American personnel. While they were examining it, the physicians noticed that a member of the Vietnamese family which ran the place was defecating into an open pot next to the table where sandwiches were being made.

The U.S. Air Force posted a notice outside the Vietnamese snack bar saying it was "off limits to American personnel."

A half hour later, two Vietnamese airmen, armed with automatic weapons, came to the U.S. Air Force terminal and tore down the "off limits" sign.

Colonel Verplank telephoned the Vietnamese Air Force commander and asked about the event.

The South Vietnamese colonel replied, "I ordered the sign destroyed. This is Vietnam, not the U.S.A. I will install anyone I wish in the building—and neither you nor any other American may put up notices saying it is off limits for Americans or anyone else. I have already discussed the matter with your commander. I suggest you see him."

Colonel Verplank wanted to make an issue of it. But the U.S. Air Force swallowed its pride and did nothing. A small notice was posted *inside* the passenger terminal saying that the Vietnamese food joint was off limits. But there was no notice near the entrance of the building, and Americans were still eating there, and still paying exorbitant prices for stolen U.S. merchandise, and were using illegal currency, and were sometimes getting sick with dysentery.

I asked some Air Force officers and some American newspapermen about this, and they told me this was the way things were run all over. They pointed out that, at the big passenger terminal in Saigon, there was a filthy snack bar exactly like the one in Danang. The South Vietnamese Air Force had refused to give the U.S. Air Force permission to improve things.

I had Vietnamese friends go into the snack bars at Danang and Saigon and ask the Vietnamese proprietors why their prices were so high. Their answers were simple and clear. "We have to give half of the money to the Vietnamese Air Force commander."

At Danang there is a cubbyhole of space inside the U.S. Air Force passenger terminal. It is here that Colonel Verplank hopes to build a tiny snack bar. "It'll be better than nothing," he said. "But I hope we can get it completed before the South Vietnamese Air Force hears about it and finds some excuse for stopping us."

18   MY OLD shipmate, Chief Photographer's Mate O'Leary, was going to take me on a tour of Saigon night life. But when O'Leary showed up at 7:30 P.M., he was in uniform and carried cameras. "I got a duty assignment this evening," he said, "but I don't have to leave for a few minutes yet."

O'Leary has been in Vietnam for two tours and knows his way around.

"Chief," I said, "I've been traveling some since I got here, and one of the things I've noticed is that the South Vietnamese seem to be making a good thing out of kicking us around. What's the story?"

"It's humiliating," he said.

"Then it's true?"

"True? You're damned right it's true. They lead us around like cattle. They tell us what to do, and, boy, when they tell us to jump, we jump. They also tell us what not to do.

"That's one big reason we're getting the hell kicked out of us. And we're so ashamed of our own groveling that everyone lies about it. All the brass—civilian and military— including my admiral—are scared of the South Vietnamese. They're scared of stepping on their toes. If by chance any of us complain about it, the brass is quick to remind us that we are guests here." Chief O'Leary added, "We're guests, all right. Paying guests."

The chief pointed at a big generator on the sidewalk. "You see that generator? It provides electricity for this building which has quarters and offices used by our armed forces. It's our building, on lease from the Vietnamese. We pay rent for it. Well, that U.S. Army generator makes the electricity for our building.

"We make the electricity because the power supplied by the Vietnamese is unreliable. We run our cables through the meter, and we have to pay South Vietnamese what the meter reads at the end of the month. We have to pay the South Vietnamese for the electricity which we generate."

"How come?"

"The Vietnamese say they'll throw the United States out of the building if we don't comply. So we comply and pay them for the electricity we generate. What's more, if we pay without a squawk and everything goes smoothly all up and down the line, some colonel or general gets a commendation for his 'unselfish devotion to duty and cooperation' when his tour is up at the end of a year."

O'Leary pointed to a U.S. Army truck. "See the license plate on that truck? Well, the U.S. government pays the Vietnamese the fee for the license plate—on the truck which we supply and send out here to fight their war with. The Vietnamese will hold up the delivery of the truck until the license fee is paid. Ask anyone you know well," O'Leary went on. "Go look for yourself. We invite the Vietnamese to kick us around. We almost have big signs tattooed on our foreheads saying, 'I am an American. Please kick me around.' Well, damn it all, I've got to go on duty now."

"I thought you had the day shift."

The chief spat in the street and said, "The Vietnamese Officers' Club is having a party. One of them is getting married. They've got plenty of photographers of their own, but they put a request in for an American photographer. And I'm the guy who got stuck."

"Do you make pictures of the parties for American officers?"

"Hell, no," said O'Leary. "That's illegal. It's supposed to be illegal for us to do it for the Vietnamese Officers' Club also. But you know how it is in Vietnam. When a Vietnamese says jump, then, baby, the Americans jump."

19   MAJOR TOM SMOOT, USAF, calls himself "an honest cop who happens to be in the Air Force." He is heavyset—almost stout—and is the "hairy type." He has a black beard and must shave twice a day to look neat (which he does). He has dark tufts of hair on the back of his hands, and black hair on the rims of his ears. He speaks slowly, walks quickly, and has a reputation among the men as a square shooter. In civilian life he was a police chief of a city of about 20,000. At Danang he was one of the provost marshals.

At the Air Base in Danang where Major Smoot was stationed, the U.S. Air Force has many out-of-doors storage depots. These are areas of land jammed with supplies and surrounded by high fences. There is only one gate through which people can enter, and it is always locked except when supplies go in or out. Inside there is a guard; in most instances he is not an American.

In the following incident, the guard was Chinese.

This particular outdoor storage depot contained thousands of cases of supplies. Over a period of two weeks it was observed that entire stacks of materials were disappearing. The thefts were mentioned to the U.S. Air Force provost marshal, Major Tom Smoot.

The next evening Major Smoot hid his men outside the depot. Shortly after midnight, a large South Vietnamese Air Force truck drove up. The Chinese guard unlocked the gate. The Vietnamese Air Force truck drove in. The Vietnamese crews loaded the truck with goods belonging to the

United States Air Force. When the trucks were full, the Vietnamese lieutenant who was in charge of the working party, handed an envelope to the Chinese guard.

When the South Vietnamese Air Force truck had moved outside the compound, Major Smoot gave a signal. Flood lights illuminated the Vietnamese truck, and U.S. Air Force policemen surrounded it. The truck and its U.S. contents were confiscated. Pictures were made of the truck and the Vietnamese who were with it. The Vietnamese were taken to jail. The Chinese guard, who had an envelope with 10,000 piasters in it, was jailed.

Within the hour, Major Smoot received a phone call from the South Vietnamese air base deputy commander demanding that his men be released immediately. Major Smoot refused.

By morning the South Vietnamese air base commander received a report of what had happened—along with pictures.

The next afternoon, the South Vietnamese Air Force commander officially wrote a protest to the U.S. Air Force commander: "You have again exceeded your authority. Your provost marshal arrested innocent men who were transporting food to Vietnamese soldiers—on duty.

"Your provost marshal does not know that he is forbidden to meddle in the affairs of my command. I could get along with your former provost marshal, who understood about these things. I trust you will take corrective action."

The South Vietnamese commander summoned the U.S. Air Force colonel, and in personal conversation made it plain that the U.S. Air Force should get rid of the provost marshal who had arrested the South Vietnamese airmen. After all, the U.S. Air Force was on the base only as a guest.[7]

The provost marshal had only two months to go before returning to the United States. This satisfied the

[7] Although the United States built and paid for everything on the base, it is Vietnamese property.

South Vietnamese commander, but he said he would put in a claim for compensation for the inconvenience and insult done to his men by being arrested on false charges.

Several miles outside Danang there is a mountain. On this mountain is perhaps $15 million worth of U.S. Air Force equipment. It is equipment that is secret in nature.

But the United States of America does not own or lease this mountain. It had to get permission from the Vietnamese to build the U.S. installation there. The mountain is "owned" by a Vietnamese Army officer named Major Minh.[8] There is nothing which the U.S. Air Force can do on that mountain without getting Major Minh's permission on a day-to-day basis. Whatever Major Minh wants, even if it is contrary to U.S. war interests, the major usually gets.

In early 1967, the Air Force was building a transmitter near the top of this mountain.

A large concrete base was laid on which to erect the tower. But as soon as the concrete foundation was completed, Major Minh called on the U.S. Air Force commander.

Minh told him that he had always wanted a summer home on the mountain. In fact, he wanted it exactly where the new concrete antenna foundation had been poured, and he had wanted a home almost precisely the size and shape of the new foundation.

The U.S. Air Force commander objected.

Major Minh did not compromise. He said he wanted that base for his summer home; unless this was arranged, he would not give permission for the Air Force to continue erecting their electronic units. The Air Force commander held consultations on this problem with his superiors, both in Danang and Saigon. It was suggested to him by American headquarters in Saigon that "for political reasons it is expedient to cooperate with Major Minh."

[8] His real name.

The U.S. Air Force not only gave the concrete base to Major Minh, but also built a home for the major. It furnished the home. As of this date the U.S. Air Force also is supplying the labor to maintain the house and the grounds.

Major Minh has decreed that all personal services for American airmen on the mountain will be done by Vietnamese. The cooks, servants, tailors, and barbers are Vietnamese. The charges for their services to the personnel of the U.S. Air Force are approximately twice as much as similar services on other bases around Danang. When queried about this, the barbers were frank. They said, "We have to give half the gross to Major Minh. That's why the prices are double."

There is nothing the U.S. Air Force will do about it. They have instructions to knuckle under. The U.S. Embassy in Saigon and the office of General Westmoreland have made it clear that whatever the Vietnamese want from the United States, the United States will give them. After all, "We are guests here."

The mountain near the U.S. Air Force installation is a beautiful spot. From the top there is a spectacular and famous view of the entire area. Everyone knows this, and some of the Catholic nuns who run an orphanage near Danang requested permission for the children to be driven to the summit (on the road which the U.S. Air Force built) to have a picnic. This permission was granted by the U.S. Air Force.

When the bus, full of children, accompanied by the nuns, arrived at the entrance of the Air Force installation, the American guard looked at the driver's papers and waved the bus in.

There were two guards at the entrance. One was an American and the other was a Vietnamese employed by Major Minh. When the busload of children arrived and was told to enter by the American guard, Major Minh's guard was about fifty feet away, relieving himself in the bushes. When he saw that the American guard had given the bus permission, he hurriedly pulled up his trousers and ran over to the road. Raising his rifle he aimed at the busload of children.

The American guard knocked the rifle out of his hands.

The next morning Major Minh called on the U.S. Air Force commander. He told him that the Vietnamese Air Force had been insulted by the American guard. In the first place, the American had given permission for a busload of children to enter the American installation without the concurrence of the Vietnamese guard. In the second place, he had assaulted the guard by knocking the rifle out of his grip.

Major Minh said that he wanted the American guard transferred immediately. If the American guard was not transferred immediately, Major Minh would order the removal of the trailers which were being used as quarters for U.S. Air Force officers.

Within two hours, the American guard was transferred from the mountain and was on his way to Saigon.

VI

THE

SUCCESSFUL
AMERICAN

"We are not Communists, even though we do not know exactly what a Communist is. But we admire and respect Ho Chi Minh. He led the struggle which threw out the foreign French. And he lives the life of a peasant. Our South Vietnamese generals in Saigon wear silk clothes and ride in big cars and send their wives to France and Japan for eye fixings so they can look like foreigners. Not Ho Chi Minh. He owns only two suits of clothes, wears sneakers, and rides to work on a bicycle. He may be a Communist. But we would like to have a leader like him around here."

A VILLAGE ELDER of Giai Xuan hamlet, interviewed near Can Tho, May 1967

20 THE PACIFICATION PROGRAM, which is a source of many U.S. humiliations, goes by many names. Sometimes it is called "The War to Win the Hearts and Minds of the People." Sometimes it is referred to as simply "The Other War." Basically, the Pacification Program has one broad mission: to gain the allegiance of the hamlets[1] (the rural population) for the South Vietnamese government (and the U.S.A.); and to deny the hamlets to the National Liberation Front.

If this one war, the pacification war, can be won, it could well result in a satisfactory settlement in South Vietnam; or at least it would be the first big and positive step toward an end to the war. If most of the hamlets became pro-government and were able and willing to reject the NLF, the NLF soon would become nonfunctional. The results would be dramatic: (1) the NLF would lose its source of recruits, (2) the NLF would lose a major source of supplies, (3) the NLF would lose its major source of intelligence. In short, there would be no indigenous NLF.

Again and again the Pacification Program has been described by the U.S.A., as it was by Ngo Dinh Diem, and by the French before that, as a winner. For years American

---

[1] A hamlet is about the same as an American village. Average population is about 1,000. In Vietnam a group of three or four hamlets is called a village.

and Vietnamese officials have been saying how effective the program is. Yet, to date, it is a failure.

The overall Pacification Program engages 315,000 persons and last year cost over half a billion dollars. The effort has been going on for fourteen years (with U.S. guidance, participation, and money), yet, according to 1967 official U.S. data, the government is certain of the loyalty of only 168 hamlets out of 12,537.

The government claims partial control of another 1,776 out of 12,537; but my experience indicates that "partial control" does not mean much. It means the peasants express loyalty during daylight hours if there happens to be U.S. or South Vietnamese troops nearby.

Official U.S. data indicates that the NLF controls more than twenty-three times as many hamlets as does the government; and during 1967 the number of NLF-controlled villages increased, *except in one small area where the U.S. Marine Corps Combined Action Platoons are operating.* This Marine program is a unique success. But it is tiny. It involves a mere 1,200 men in only seventy-eight hamlets, and it is enveloped in an almost inevitable tragedy. Possibly because of the success of the U.S. Marine Corps program, the U.S. Army, the USAID mission, and the South Vietnamese government are trying to choke the successful CAP out of existence. Details of this will be given in a later chapter.

News stories which involve failures of the Pacification Program seldom are made available by government spokesmen on a voluntary basis. The news reporter has to dig for them. The inclination in Vietnam is to make everything "look good." Reporter David Halberstam describes an incident during the regime of President Ngo Dinh Diem:

> Colonel Dong called over the district chief who was in the command post, and introduced him as a former aide and an old friend. "I think I trust this one," Dong said.

Then he turned to the chief and asked him how many villages there were in his district.

The district chief said that there were twenty-four.

"How many do you control?" the colonel asked.

"Eight," the chief replied.

Then the colonel smiled and asked, "And how many did you report that you controlled?"

The chief looked slightly sheepish and then answered, "Twenty-four."

The Americans nodded as Colonel Dong said, "Mr. Diem always got a false report. Mr. Cao liked his job, and he and Mr. Dam always reported that ninety-eight percent of the population was with Mr. Diem. And so Mr. Dam did not dare make any operations, because if he had casualties, Mr. Diem would ask him why there were any, when all the people were with him, and then Mr. Cao and Mr. Dam would lose their good jobs. Mr. Diem did not like casualties. They made him very angry, and he would transfer commanders, and they would lose their promotions and their money. So the Vietcong did not need to attack the chief towns. All they wanted was control over the rural areas, and so there was no fight and no casualties. When Mr. Diem would ask about the war, Mr. Cao and Mr. Dam would say that it was going well because of Mr. Nhu's strategic hamlet program, and that made Mr. Diem and Mr. Nhu very happy and very flattered. That was how they were winning the war. Once I could drive to My Tho or Can Tho at night without an escort, but while Mr. Diem was winning the war you could not drive without a big escort. It was a very funny way to win a war."[2]

The current deception practiced by the U.S. government is almost as bad.

On 1 December 1967, in Saigon, Robert W. Komer (then chief of the U.S. Pacification Program) announced that two-thirds of the people of South Vietnam were living in secure areas under South Vietnamese government con-

[2] David Halberstam, *The Making of a Quagmire*, pp. 301–302. Random House, New York, 1965.

trol. The basis given for this statement was data analyzed by the new computerized Hamlet Evaluation System in the U.S. Embassy in Saigon.

Ambassador Komer[3] appeared to have joined the top-level group which for at least three years has been using statistical analysis to convince (or deceive) themselves and the U.S. public that all goes well in Vietnam. Komer seemed to be attempting to persuade us that modern technology (and its computers) at long last had produced pacification—a goal which has eluded the French, Ngo Dinh Diem, and the United States for over twenty years.

What comes out of the computer, of course, is only as good as the information which goes into it; and the Vietnam Hamlet Estimates fed into the electronic gadget have been neither accurate nor honest.

The evaluation of conditions in approximately 13,000 hamlets is made by U.S. Army officers who are advisers to Vietnamese district chiefs. They send in Hamlet Evaluations monthly. I estimate that 99 per cent of the U.S. Army advisers have neither the language facility nor the knowledge of Vietnamese culture to know what is happening within their own districts. Those who have been to language school have learned only a smattering of Vietnamese; and, usually, it is the wrong dialect, because their Vietnamese language instructors mostly have been Northerners. The U.S. Army advisers often impress visitors by rattling off "Hello," "Good-bye," "How are you?" to the peasants; but that's about the extent of their language capabilities.

It is from Vietnamese interpreters that the U.S. Army advisers receive almost all their information about the hamlets. But the interpreters also are incompetent to evaluate conditions. Not only is their first loyalty to the Vietnamese district chiefs—whose job is to make things "look good" —but also a large proportion of them are Northerners who speak a different dialect from the Southern peasants. Even if the peasants understand them, they are traditionally

[3] As chief of the Pacification Program, Komer had the rank of ambassador.

suspicious of Northerners and therefore do not give honest answers. An additional irony is that the interpreters usually do not speak enough English to understand or report adequately to the Americans who employ them. I have interviewed many interpreters (and recorded the dialogues so that others could check on me); a majority of them know only from three to five hundred words of English.

Everything is against the evaluation techniques used by the Americans in Vietnam. For the Vietnamese peasant (who is being questioned) to survive, he must tell the interrogator what the interrogator wants to hear. This is the best way of being left alone by the "outsiders" who have been criss-crossing the land for the last five generations. Such behavior has become part of the Vietnamese life. It is impossible to know what is on a peasant's mind unless one can hear and understand him while he is gossiping as freely as he would with his family and neighbors. Naturally neither the U.S. Army advisers, their interpreters, nor the current Saigon government has this capability.

Recently television newsreels have shown U.S. reporters—via Vietnamese interpreters—interviewing Vietnamese peasants. I have been watching these telecasts with a Vietnamese, a Southerner. He has told me that frequently the Vietnamese interpreters did not repeat the question exactly as the American TV interviewer asked it; that the peasant being interviewed did not respond to the question put by the interpreter; and that the interpreter did not repeat accurately in English what the peasant had said. It is through similar daisy chains of misinformation—only far worse—that the U.S. pacification computer is operating.

I have seen samples of the Hamlet Evaluaton Estimates sent to headquarters by U.S. Army advisers. These estimates are fraudulent; or, to be charitable, they are distorted with errors. Under the present system they can be no other way. It is not only that the U.S. advisers and their interpreters are intellectually and culturally unable to make accurate estimates, but the taint of dishonesty has swept through the entire United States government reporting system in Vietnam. This pollution sinks down from the top. In Washington, Walt Rostow (who advises President Johnson) suggests—sometimes even insists—that his colleagues de-emphasize unfavorable facts. Occasionally when his assistants refuse to alter facts, Rostow goes into tantrums. Once he threw a water pitcher at a colonel who showed that Rostow's figures were biased. Unwillingness to face unwelcome facts has spread throughout the government, and it has of course reached Saigon and down to the Army advisers in remote South Vietnamese districts.

The administration's Vietnam public relations program for U.S. home consumption frequently has tried to make our win-the-war-in-the-hamlets efforts in Vietnam appear successful. True, similar attempts have been made by high civilian and military officials since 1945; but now the struggle is more cunning, more desperate, and more dangerous to America's welfare.

I have visited some of the so-called "secure villages" whose data were put into Komer's pacification computer. With the exception of a few rigged showcases reserved for the press and distinguished visitors, I found that the "secure" villages, in general, are not secure and that their inhabitants do not support the government. In the majority of villages, the conditions are so precarious that at night the government's Revolutionary Development workers often flee to the safety of the district headquarters or to the nearest city. Often the village chief, if he has been appointed by Ky[4] or was elected under a Ky-controlled election, also departs from the village at night. The villages appear secure only during the day if there are South Vietnamese troops nearby. When the South Vietnamese (or U.S.) troops are moved, members of the Revolutionary Development Teams disappear. My own estimate is that this is true for about 70 per cent of Vietnam.

The proof of pacification is in the sleeping. If and

[4] Despite the fact that Thieu was elected President of South Vietnam, Ky still controls "the organization." Ky is still the patronage boss.

when Ambassador Komer and his colleagues, both Vietnamese and American, could stay in villages at night and
sleep there undisturbed, then they would know that perhaps the village is nearing pacification. I predict that the
ambassador and his friends, if they tried this today, would
get precious little sleep, unless it were the long sleep which
accompanies a slit throat.

Another thing for the U.S. government officers to
chew on when they announce success in security and
pacification concerns food. The two and a half million
residents of the Saigon area now are eating rice grown in
Louisiana and South Carolina, pork which has been
brought in from Denmark, and frozen chicken and fish
which have arrived from the United States. Only a few
years ago, Vietnam exported 800,000 tons of rice. In 1968, it
may be necessary for the United States to send about
1,800,000 tons of rice to stop a famine. The shortage is due
to several factors, including the fear of the villagers—which
keeps them out of their fields much of the time—and the fact
that the Vietcong appropriates much of the crop. While our
troops were diverted from the rice areas by the battle at
Dakto, the Vietcong made off with two-thirds of the harvest
of one entire valley region. General Westmoreland did not
seem to realize that Dakto was a decisive victory for the
Vietcong.

Because of defoliation and the fire bombs of the B-
52's, and the savage and indiscriminate use of napalm and
cluster-bomb units by U.S. planes, and mass evictions, the
agricultural production of South Vietnam was reduced
about 25 per cent in 1967.

The "computer ruse" is one method offered by the
government to talk the public into a false optimism on
pacification. The other technique—which has been used in
the past—is the "numbers game." We are continually being
told how many South Vietnamese are under government
control. Often it has been given as about 12 million. This is
75 per cent of the total population.

The 12 million figure is arrived at by adding together

the approximately 4 million refugees and about 1 million Vietnamese who directly or indirectly work for the United States; the approximately million more who are in the South Vietnamese Army, the National Police, and other paramilitary organizations; and the 2.4 million inhabitants of Saigon. This subtotal amounts to 8 million people, or 50 per cent of the total population. This then is added to the 4 million living in areas where there are South Vietnamese and U.S. troops. From the grand total comes the misleading numbers conclusion that the government controls 70 per cent of the population. Obviously, it is spurious. The important factor in this estimate is "How many South Vietnamese *support* the government?" Over 4 million refugees of various sorts have been thrown out or bombed out of their homes. They do not support the people who evicted them or bombed them. They certainly do not support the Saigon government or the U.S.A. Quite the contrary. We know that, conservatively, perhaps one-third of the South Vietnamese government is infiltrated by members of the National Liberation Front, or is sympathetic to the Front. An indication of this is that 8,000 to 10,000 South Vietnamese soldiers desert every month.[5] Three-quarters of them take their weapons with them, which would seem to indicate that many of them are headed for the Vietcong ranks.

One cannot help but ask, "How then is the war continuing?" The answer is simple: The war is continuing because it is advantageous for the leaders of the Saigon government to have it continue. For example, the gold holdings and credits[6] of Vietnam (a nation in a major, total war) have increased in three years from $130 million to $450 million. This represents only the visible surplus, and

[5] Of the total manpower of the South Vietnamese military forces, about one-fourth deserts annually.

[6] Which can be exchanged for gold on demand. Soon after Britain devalued the pound, the South Vietnamese controllers of the Vietnamese-owned U.S. credits shamelessly and ruthlessly began making runs on the U.S. gold supply.

indicates tremendous under-the-table manipulations by the Vietnamese. Anyone wishing to explore the USAID facet of this should read the congressional testimony of Mr. Rutherford Poats, onetime administrator of foreign aid in Vietnam. A condensed version is in the 19 September 1967 issue of the *Congressional Record.*[7]

In addition to the visible increase in Saigon's gold reserve, approximately $18 billion, according to my Swiss and Chinese informants, has been sent to foreign banks by private Vietnamese individuals since 1956. Not so long ago, Madame Nhu, through a silent partner, purchased outright the second largest private bank in Paris. For cash.

Why kill the U.S. goose which lays so many golden eggs? Pacification is one of the golden eggs—even though it is one of the smaller ones, involving a mere half billion a year out of a total of $30 billion total U.S. expenses in Vietnam.

21 THE MAJOR work of the Pacification Program is supposed to be done by South Vietnamese Revolutionary Development Teams (RD's). A team consists of sixty Vietnamese who are said to be specialists in guerrilla fighting, civil development, and propaganda. The RD teams have five basic missions in the hamlets:

1 Establish military security.
2 Record the grievances of the people and alleviate them.
3 Learn the hopes and aspirations of the people and assist them—with technical advice, money, and materials—in developing an economic, social, and political atmosphere which makes possible the realization of these hopes and aspirations.
4 Discover and destroy any remnants of the NLF which still might be in the hamlet; and, at the same time, establish a democratic structure of local self-government.
5 Train and inspire the people to defend their own hamlets.

[7] See Appendix D.

An RD team is given six months in which to accomplish the above.

In the summer of 1967 I wanted to see a pacified village for myself. The officials at JUSPAO said there were some near the Can Tho area. Can Tho is eighty miles from Saigon, in the Mekong Delta area. There is a road, but the JUSPAO colonel advised me not to drive. "Some people drive," he said, "but it really isn't safe. One never knows when the VC will put up a road block or mine the road. Of course, at night it's impossible—even for an armed convoy. You better take the helicopter."

In Can Tho—a city of 80,000—I went to the headquarters of General William R. Desobry,[8] U.S. Army. I asked for the location of a pacified village which was under government control. A major pointed to a map and assured me that Giai Xuan was a safe village, a pacified village, completely loyal to the government—and all because of U.S. and Revolutionary Development Team efforts. The village of Giai Xuan could be reached by renting a boat and going up the river for about an hour.

With two Vietnamese interpreters, I leased a motor sampan and went to Giai Xuan, taking along my tape recorder with which to record all our conversations.[9]

At Giai Xuan I learned that there were about 1,500 people scattered in several small hamlets. A South Vietnamese Army major greeted me and said that the government personnel stationed in Giai Xuan consisted of a sixty-man RD team, about fifteen Popular Forces men (local militia), a U.S. Army captain, a U.S. Army Pfc., and the major himself.

The heavy rains had started; everything was wetness

[8] His real name.
[9] I informed the interpreters that when I returned to Cambridge, I would have the Vietnamese experts at Harvard listen to the tapes and check on the accuracy of their interpreting.

and mud. No one moved about. The RD members and the Popular Forces men sat around tables in their mess hall, gambling. The U.S. Army captain had gone to Can Tho for food supplies. The Pfc. sat on his cot in the hut occupied by him and the captain. His job was to stay near the radio transmitter in the hut and to call for help if the village was attacked.

The village was nervous because about a week earlier the South Vietnamese battalion stationed nearby had been transferred. The Vietcong already had started roaming about at night. The South Vietnamese major said he and the U.S. Army captain and the RD's had killed five VC a few nights ago. I asked to see the bodies, but was told they had been brought into Can Tho.[10]

The village chief told me that as soon as the VC had become active, one-third of the RD team immediately had deserted. Also about a fourth of the small Popular Forces platoon had "gone home."

In interviewing the villagers, I found them surprisingly sophisticated,[11] and willing to discuss their fears and aspirations. The first question I asked them (as I later asked in other villages) was, "What is it you want more than anything else?"

I had expected such answers as "We want peace more than anything else" or "All we want is to be left alone."

But that is not what they said.

What the peasants of the Mekong Delta area wanted more than anything else was "social justice." I doubted that a peasant would use such sophisticated terminology.

I asked the people, "What do you mean by social

[10] I inquired about this the next day at U.S. Army headquarters in Can Tho. I was told the bodies had been buried near the village.
[11] This may have been because I had a good interpreter. He is a cultured gentleman who is fluent in French, German, Chinese, English, and the three major Vietnamese dialects. I estimate that 95 per cent of the interpreters used by Americans do not know enough English to explain the nuances possible in Vietnamese.

justice?" Then I added, "I don't think you know what that means."

The interpreter repeated my question in Vietnamese. The people became excited, began speaking shrilly and gesticulating. One of them, acting as a spokesman, explained, "Social justice means there is equality for everyone. If I do something wrong, I should be punished. But if a big shot, say a general or a colonel in Saigon, does the same crime, he should be punished the same way I am. Social justice means that everyone is treated alike. If I work hard I should benefit from it. But if I work hard why should a government official take most of my earnings so that he can live a life of ease in Saigon without work?

"If there is an enemy to defend ourselves from, then we should go into the army and fight. But it is not right that the poor should do the fighting while the officers become rich from graft."

I asked, "What about the National Liberation Front, the Vietcong? Don't they come and steal and force you to pay taxes?"

There was some hesitation by the peasants before they answered this. They began discussing it among themselves. Finally, the spokesman said, "This is hard to answer. Yes, the NLF come and ask for supplies and money. But in a different way than the Saigon soldiers. If we are hungry and have no money and the NLF stay here, then they go hungry also and they do not take money. They live the same as we do. Also, we know many of them. They are the same as we are. Almost every family in the Delta has at least one member who is an NLF member."

I asked, "Are you Communists? Do you want Ho Chi Minh's government to take over?"

"We are not Communists. We don't really know what a Communist is. But there is one thing about the government up north. Maybe it is harsh on the people, and life there is hard. But the officials share the harshness and the hardness. It may be hard but there is social justice. Everyone is equal before the government."

I thought, *someone may have done a great propaganda job here—but whether it is true or not, the people believe it.*

"Most people believe Ho Chi Minh is a Communist," I said.

The spokesman replied, "We are not Communists, even though we do not know exactly what a Communist is. But we admire and respect Ho Chi Minh. He led the struggle which threw out the foreign French. And he lives the life of a peasant. Our South Vietnamese generals in Saigon wear silk clothes and ride in big cars and send their wives to France and Japan for eye fixings so that they can look like foreigners. Not Ho Chi Minh. He owns only two suits of clothes, wears sneakers, and rides to work on a bicycle. He may be a Communist. But we would like to have a leader like him around here."

I asked, "Do the NLF ever abuse you?"

"Sometimes if they are from far off, the ones who talk about politics. Sometimes they are cruel if we go against them or do not understand them. Two years ago they killed one of us who refused to desert from the army. They beat up an old man who said he had no rice. They beat him up when they discovered he had much rice hidden."

"Do the RD's here protect you?"

They did not respond to the expression "RD's," so I said, "Revolutionary Development cadres," and pointed to the black-suited men nearby.

The people answered immediately even though a few RD's were standing only a few yards away.

"No. Most of them are city boys. They are afraid of the dark. They do not know the area. They cannot defend us. When NLF come, the city boys often say they are going on patrol. But lots of times they go off and hide."

I asked, "Could you defend yourselves?"

Once more there was a hesitancy and the peasants discussed the question among themselves.

This time another man acted as spokesman. He said, "Yes, we could defend ourselves. Most villages could defend themselves, if the government would help us." He paused. "If the government would let us."

"How would you defend yourselves?"

"It is simple," said the young man, as the others, including the women, nodded their heads and smiled.

"There are about a hundred young men in this village. Have the government investigate them all and pick out those who pass the security check. Arm them and pay them the same as the army troops. Give our young men the same equipment and the same pay and privileges as the army and we will defend ourselves. We know how. We are local Vietnamese, you know. Our young men here know everyone hereabouts. If someone is a stranger he will be stopped. Our young men know every grass, every tree, every stream, and can patrol at night. These city boys who are the RD's cannot do that. They run away. Many of them ran away last night when some VC came. Our men will stay and fight."

"But," the spokesman continued, "defending our village is a full-time job. It is day and night. A man cannot farm and be a good soldier for his village also. Therefore our men need the same pay as the army, the same rations for their families, the same rifles.[12]

"Yes, we could defend our own villages. Remember, we are Vietnamese. We have been defending ourselves against outsiders for a thousand generations.

"But the government will not let us defend ourselves. They send down city boys and American foreign troops who sit in their tent all day by the radio. What good does it do if the Americans call for help on the radio if someone attacks us? It would be half a day before government

[12] I told this to some U.S. Army officers in Saigon. They became indignant. "Why should a man be paid for defending his home?" said one. Another Army colonel said, "Planting rice is easy. It only takes a couple of months a year. They have plenty of time to defend their homes. The fact is they're lazy bastards looking for a handout."

troops came—if they came at all. We don't want the American airplanes. When the American planes come, the NLF already have left and are in bunkers. This makes the NLF and the people close."

"Who builds the bunkers?"

"The villagers—under the NLF direction."

"Do they have bunkers here?"

No one answered. Most of the people looked at the ground.

I asked, "You said that almost every family in the Mekong Delta has at least one relative who is in the NLF? Why do young men and women go into the NLF?"

"In many cases because they are afraid they will be drafted into the ARVN [South Vietnamese Army]. Sometimes they join because they want revenge on a government official who has treated them or their family badly. Sometimes they join because of the glamor of it. The VC make their men feel important with the mission to free Vietnam from corrupt government and foreigners. And sometimes they join for excitement. It can get boring staying on the farm, especially if you do not own it and someone else gets most of the profits. Why work hard if the rich landlord in Saigon takes half the crop?"

I asked, "Do you want to get rid of the Americans?"

There was a courteous silence. The village elder finally spoke up. "We know that the Americans are trying to help us. But they are strangers here and do not know our ways. We appreciate what the Americans are trying to do. But maybe you should ask your question to the American troops. Ask them would they not be happier being home with their families?"

"What do you think the Americans are doing now?"

"The Americans have the power here. They have the guns and the ammunition and the money and the troops. Whatever they say is the law in Saigon . . . but . . ."

"But what?"

"They pick officials who flatter them. The Americans

are foreigners. I have never met an American who speaks my language."[13]

When our meeting was over I asked to see the results of the RD work.

The RD leader came over and showed me the community projects his men had constructed for the villagers. They had built a one-room school house and a one-room dispensary.

"These were the first things we did. We made a school and a dispensary."

We inspected the two small buildings, which were empty.

"When does the doctor or nurse come?" I asked.

"There is no doctor or nurse. The province chief said there are none available. Not now anyway. Maybe next year."

"How many children are in school?"

"None yet. We have no teacher."

I asked him what good the buildings did the village.

"It's good for the spirit of the village to have a school and a dispensary even if there are no doctors or teachers."

I said, "When the government reports say that so many schools and dispensaries have been established, are they like these?"

"Yes," he said, "mostly. But you must remember we are a nation at war and you can't do everything at once. And the buildings are useful. They can be used as storehouses until the teachers come."

At 4 P.M. the interpreter said that we had to stop the

13 Giai Xuan and Can Tho are in Phong Dinh Province. In Phong Dinh (400,000 population) there are only two Americans who speak Vietnamese, and they are really not fluent. They can jabber away with natives, but my interpreter told me (he has heard the two Americans speak), "They do not know the local dialect; and they have not lived in Vietnam long enough to know the nuances of the language. One can say, 'Where is the man of the house?' with four different tones. Each has a different meaning—which only a really fluent Vietnamese speaker would understand. Your two Americans would not understand it."

interview and return to Can Tho. I said I wanted to stay overnight. The interpreter said it was not safe.

"But," I said, "General Desobry's office said this is one of the safest villages in the area."

The interpreter laughed. "Look," he said. "That old man over there is the village chief. Do you know what he is doing now? He is getting ready to go to Can Tho. He is afraid to stay here overnight."

So we packed up our things and took the sampan back to Can Tho. There we were to make arrangements to stay at a U.S. government lodging for transients. The lodging is for guests and workers of the Americans who run the Pacification Program in Can Tho. My interpreter (who is a university graduate and a distinguished Vietnamese journalist) telephoned the lodging. When he hung up, his face was strained and white.

"What's the matter?"

"Goddam it," he said. "The fellow at the lodging said that I can't stay there. There are empty rooms, but there's a regulation that Vietnamese are not allowed in the American lodging house."

We spoke to an American official, who arranged for my friend to stay with me at the U.S. government lodging. But the incident indicated that there was more friction between Vietnamese and Americans than I had realized.

During the evening and the next morning we interviewed a variety of people in Can Tho. They had heard that the U.S. Army would be sending more troops to Can Tho, and the people did not like this.

"It is not the American politics or philosophy which concern us," said a Vietnamese school teacher. "It is what the Americans do to our economy. Now we can live—not well, but live—here for three thousand to four thousand piasters a month. We have a rural economy even though this is a city; the Americans come, even a small number of them, and then we local people cannot live well anymore."

Another Vietnamese said, "When the U.S. Army or Air Force comes the prices go up. It has happened in every city where the Americans have gone. Everything goes up in price: food, clothes, rent, movies, whores. But our income stays about the same, unless we work for the Americans, and here not many do. So what happens—the standard of living of the entire community goes down. All of us suffer."

"But don't the Americans protect you from the NLF?"

"No, they don't. But even if they did protect us, having Americans here is too high a price for us to pay for protection. Our problem is to eat and live; and it's hard enough as it is. The NLF is a government problem, not ours."

Another resident of Can Tho said, "After the Americans arrive and food gets expensive, then the VC come around and say, 'See, with the U.S.A. you cannot live. Work with us and we will kick the U.S.A. out.' Then we have the government and the U.S.A. tugging at us from one end and the NLF from the other. No, keep the troops away from our cities. If the Americans want to fight let them live in jungles where the NLF are."

The next day we were briefed by General Desobry. He told us everything was improving. The pacification was coming along well. "You know," he said, "the VC control only 57 per cent of the Delta now."

22   AT TWO different times, and from two different Vietnamese, I had heard about the CAP efforts of the U.S. Marines. And on both occasions, the Vietnamese (neither of them a government official) had praised the Marines as being the only ones who knew anything about pacification, and as the only units—either Vietnamese or American—who are successful at it.

Before this, I had not heard of the Marine

Combined Action Program. I thought, if it was such a success, why weren't we initiating it all over Vietnam? Why did not South Vietnamese General Nguyen Duc Thang utilize the same methods for his pacification and anti-guerrilla campaign? I went to JUSPAO and asked a U.S. Army lieutenant colonel if he had any information on it.

The colonel slowly filled his pipe, and in a delaying manner searched one pocket after another for matches.

"Bill," he said, "a lot of reporters have been asking me about the Marines' Combined Action Program. I hate to disappoint you, but that program isn't what it's cracked up to be. I'll tell you off the record—that is, don't tell anybody who told you—and if you use my name I'll deny it—that the whole program is a figment of the imagination of a Marine named Colonel William Corson.[14] I am sure Colonel Corson is a good soldier, but he's an even better PR man. He's what we call a 'character.' He's glib and he's colorful and he's got the big vocabulary of an intellectual. There's nobody this guy can't snow.

"Colonel Corson has a way with the press, and he shoots them a big line about this Combined Action Program, which he says General Walt started. We discussed it at a staff meeting just the other day, and the consensus was that the Marines' program goes against the principles of strategy and tactics which MACV is using." The colonel relighted his pipe, paused for about ten seconds, and then continued.

"Let me explain the feeling of the staff here on the Combined Action Program.

"The Communists are now in what they call the third phase of their war. This means they have formed their military into large units and are attacking in mass battles. That is the way we have to fight them. The mistake which the Marines are making—I'm speaking of this damned program of Colonel Corson's—is that they are going back to Phase One. Do you know what Phase One is?"

[14] Lieutenant Colonel William R. Corson, USMC.

I didn't say anything, so the colonel continued.
"Phase One of Communist aggression is when the
guerrillas try to get organized in the villages. They try to
form cadres or cells in each village composed of people who
live in that village. They do this usually by acts of terror. But
Phase One really means taking control or having the major
influence in the administration of the villages. That's what
the Marines are trying to do in their Combined Action Program. That's going backwards in history. We're now in Phase
Three of the war, and that's the way you've got to fight it to
win it. What this con-man Corson is doing is telling the
press and anybody else who'll listen that he has accomplished those things he dreams he would like to accomplish
—which anybody who knows anything out here recognizes
are impossible. He is a very brilliant but a very dangerous
man. What he tells you accept with a grain of salt."

The following day, the Pan American Airways public
relations man told me he had a story which might interest
me. Pan American was flying some hogs of a very special
breed from the United States to Saigon, destined for a
hamlet called Phong Bac, which was near Danang.
"This is interesting for a couple of reasons," he said.
"First, the villagers of Phong Bac have paid for the hogs
and for their transportation. It is a private, commercial
venture that has nothing to do with the government. The
AID people don't even know about it. Second, two of the
men from the hamlet have come to Saigon to accept delivery of the hogs. This is the first time in their lives these
peasants have ever been ten miles outside of Phong Bac."
The next day the interpreter introduced me to Nguyen and Lo. They were having "southern noodles" and pork
in a Vietnamese workingman's sidewalk restaurant. Nguyen
was about sixty, wrinkled and wizened, and with teeth
stained a dark brown from smoking. Lo, the younger Vietnamese, appeared to be eighteen or nineteen. Both were

small and thin, coming only to my shoulder, and weighing probably ninety pounds. They had the beautiful hands of the Vietnamese peasant; their hands, even though a bit dirty, didn't *look* dirty. They looked earthy.

At first it was difficult to talk with them. They appeared suspicious, as if perhaps I were a government man checking up on them. I had to start off with small talk—via the interpreter—in order to get a dialogue rolling; and they answered me monosyllabically.

"Where do you live?"

"Phong Bac."

"Where is Phong Bac?"

"Up north, near Danang."

"Are you married?"

"Yes."

"Have you any children?"

"No."

"You came to Saigon to get some American hogs?"

"Yes."

"Why are you getting that kind of hog?"

"Because Sergeant Smith says it is the best kind and it will be good for our village."

"Who is Sergeant Smith?"

"He is an American Marine."

"How is it that Sergeant Smith discussed hog-raising with you?"

"Colonel Corson brought him to us."

"Who is Colonel Corson?"

For the first time Nguyen and Lo smiled.

"He is the Marine officer who came to Phong Bac."

"Where is he now?"

"He is in Danang. But he lived in our village for half a year."

"Yes, he left us only a few months ago," said Lo.

"What did he do in your village?"

The two Vietnamese peasants from Phong Bac hamlet told me about their community and about the Marines who stayed there from September 1966 until the end of February 1967. Nguyen, the older man, did most of the talking, although Lo joined him by laughing over happy remembrances, nodding affirmation, and supplying facts when the older man could not recall them. The dialogue came through the interpreter. What follows is approximately the way the old man told me about Phong Bac and Colonel Corson.

We are (said Nguyen) a small hamlet about fifteen kilometers to the south of Danang. We are mostly farmers and, as far as I can remember, and my father before me, our only crop has been rice. Very few of us, perhaps one in ten, own our own land. Almost all of the land in Phong Bac is owned by rich men who live in Danang or Saigon. For the use of their land, we pay the landlord one-half of our crops (double the legal limit). We have always been a poor community, but we have gotten along satisfactorily. There has been much war in our country since I was a young man, but it has never affected us much. Our village life went on the same, year by year—even though some of our men went into the army.

But this is different. Many villages have been destroyed by bombs and by fire, and therefore there have been many refugees.

Where do the refugees go? They must live someplace. They go to other villages. Last year about 1,500 refugees came to Phong Bac. Soon after that the U.S. Marines came to Phong Bac.[15] At first we did not like the Marines. We did not like them because the Americans had bombed and burned our villages, leaving my countrymen homeless. This hurts our feeling of *dem voi ve day ma to.*[16]

[15] This was the Third Tank Battalion of the Third Marine Division.

[16] Literally this means "take the elephants back to stamp out the graveyards of the ancestors." But the way the Vietnamese accept it is "it is impossible for them to forgive anyone who participates in

We also did not like the Marines because they would go through the streets giving everyone chewing gum, cigarettes, candy, things to eat, and toys to the children. Maybe that would make them popular in the United States, but it does not make them popular in my village. We have a saying, *Banh ech di, banh quy lai.*[17] We Vietnamese are very proud, and we do not want to be beggars. One of the worst insults in our country is to call someone a beggar. We do not like being beggars, and we do not like foreign troops who try to make us look like beggars.

After giving us so many presents, the Marines at Phong Bac were surprised when they were attacked by the National Liberation Front during August. Everyone in the village knew that the Marines would be attacked but no one told them. The government soldiers (Regional Forces) were camped near the Marines. They knew about the attack also, but did not tell the Marines, and they did not help them during the fighting. The Marines were bitter; and they stopped giving us presents. They even stopped giving us medicines. For several weeks they talked only among themselves, and had very little to do with my people.[18]

---

the destroying of the land of their ancestors." This feeling is so strong that it is the source of much of the Vietnamese folk song lyrics. One of the most popular ones goes as follows:

> This house, this house is ours now.
> Our ancestors have built it with so much hardship
> We must take care of it and keep it
> For ten thousand years, along with our country.

[17] It means if someone gives you a cookie, you give him back a pudding.

[18] Later, when I interviewed Colonel Corson, I asked him about this. He said, "If my battalion was to serve the national interest of the United States in the field of pacification, I concluded that my program could not depend upon the Vietnamese military or political hierarchy for its successful implementation. We studied all other efforts at pacification—by the French, by the Vietnamese, by the Americans. Clearly, all of them had been failures. This took about two weeks of soul-searching and considerable scholarship. The decision, made in early September 1966, was for us to go it alone, relying on Marines, and to deal directly with the end object of pacification—the peasant. We decided to approach the problem from the point of view of the peasant. Everything had to be done within

Most of the people in Phong Bac were cooperating with the National Liberation Front. You seem surprised! It seemed to us that if the NLF would win, then at least the frightful conditions of this war would come to an end. Anyway, the NLF mostly are farmers like ourselves and come from the same district.

Also, we do not like the presence of the American soldiers and the ARVN which come to our villages to pacify us. Usually when they come, the old landlords return with them. They use the troops to collect back rent and to force excessive abuses on us. The only land reform any of us can remember was when the Vietminh gave us land a generation ago.

At the end of half a month we saw that the Marines were playing *Cò Tùong*.[19] It interested us very much that the Marines were playing *Cò Tùong*, and we watched them. We saw that their teacher was Colonel Corson. Until now we had seen little of him, and any talk between the Marines and the people of my village always came from young officers or the young men who are not yet officers.

A little while after that, the Marines put notices in all the hamlets in our area. These notices were that the Marines were sponsoring a *Cò Tùong* tournament to see who was the best player. The announcement said that the winner in each hamlet could come to Phong Bac on the night of the Harvest Festival and there play each other to see who was the best man of all. The prize was a wonderful radio, which cost about 10,000 piasters.

On the night of the Harvest Festival maybe 1,500 people came to Phong Bac to watch the *Cò Tùong* tournament to see who was the champion.

---

the framework of his social and economic structure; and to make the peasant conclude that a certain type of behavior—the one which we wanted—would be the one most advantageous to him."

[19] *Cò Tùong* is "elephant chess." It is the most popular game in Asia, and it is something like chess with some added complexities. Almost every Vietnamese male from the age of nine years old up plays *Cò Tùong*. It is an important thing in the life of the Vietnamese, and it is considered a yardstick of a man's intellectual stature.

I (continued Nguyen) won the tournament. My father taught me the game when I was about four years old. Perhaps that's why I am the hamlet chief, because I play *Cò Túong* well.

After I had won, and the people were still congratulating me, Colonel Corson came through the crowd and spoke to me in Vietnamese. It was not fluent Vietnamese, but I could see he had studied hard and practiced a lot. He asked me if I would give him the honor of playing *Cò Túong* with him. I did not want to because I was the champion and had already proved myself; and also I did not wish to get intimate with an American Marine. But there was no way out. I had to play.

The game lasted for an hour. It ended in a draw. But I knew that Colonel Corson could have beaten me if he had wanted to.

A few days later, about fifteen of the Marines went through the hamlets and played *Cò Túong* with my people. Naturally, everyone in the village would watch the game.

At first I was suspicious. But after several weeks I saw that the Marines enjoyed the game. They did not interfere with us in any way. They did not resume giving us free presents and making us look like beggars.

But at night they went on their patrols, and the National Liberation Front was unable to get through them.

Colonel Corson went to Hao Thin village and played with Ho Yin, who is the eldest and most respected man in our community. He is eighty-five years old, and I am sure would have beaten me at *Cò Túong* if he had played in the tournament. The colonel played with him. Ho Yin and the colonel spoke to each other in Chinese. The colonel speaks fluent Chinese. It impressed us very much that an American could speak Asian languages and know our ways so well. His knowledge did us honor. He was the first foreigner who was familiar with our ways. Often we have visitors, people from your government who pass through our village, showing off to visiting lawmakers. They say "Hello," "Good-bye,"

"How are you" in our language. But that is just smoke without a fire.

One day Colonel Corson and some of his men went to the families of the fishermen on the Song Cau Do River, and said that they would like to hire the fishermen to help them do some fishing. The pay he offered was higher than the pay which the Vietnamese who worked for the Americans in Danang received. The colonel was very clever. He knows a lot about Vietnamese. He didn't go to the fishermen's houses and ask them the question directly. No, he went there and played *Cò Tuong* with them for several afternoons before he slowly asked about hiring them and renting their boats.

No one in the hamlet knew why the colonel wanted the fishermen and their boats, so when the Marines went out in the river in five boats, many of us stood and watched.

When the boats were in the middle of the river, the Marines threw some sticks of dynamite into the water. There were big explosions, and soon many fish floated on the water. The Marines collected the fish and brought them ashore. It was more fish than the fishermen ever had caught. It was more fish than any of us had seen, except for the time the typhoon blew the river over the fields about twenty-five years ago.

The fish were taken to the marketplace and sold by the Marines at about half the usual price. The fishermen didn't mind. They already had earned more money than they could have from fishing.

Colonel Corson continued fishing this way several times a week. Everyone in Phong Bac liked it because we were getting fish at a low price, and many people who previously could not afford fish now could eat them.

One day Colonel Corson asked if he could talk with the village elders. We met with him. The meeting was held on the street so that anybody could listen, and maybe a hundred people came. The colonel said that, as the river belonged to Phong Bac, the community should get some of the profits of his fishing. But, he said, the money should be spent so that everybody in the hamlet would benefit. He said he would turn the money over to me, the hamlet chief, in the public square every day after the fishing, so that everybody in the village would know how much was in the village fund.

When we had about 25,000 piasters ($150), Colonel Corson suggested that the village form a business council to determine how to utilize the money for everyone's benefit. The people agreed and elected a council.

We did not know how to invest the money, and were afraid because most of our experiences had been with Chinese who knew more about money than we did. We asked Colonel Corson what would a hamlet in America do with so much money. The colonel brought in some of his young men who were farmers and fishermen in the United States and asked them their opinion. They told us about cooperatives in America. They told us about raising rabbits, raising bees, breeding hogs, and better ways of fishing which would require the spending of money for a new type of net, but would catch more fish. We decided to try these things. The young Marines worked with us when we requested it. They were not like the government men who talk big but do nothing but talk. These young Marines worked with their hands and knew how to. Our first project was a large hog-breeding barn.

We worked on many things together, and after several months the average money (that is, per family) in the village increased about ten times.

I knew that in time the National Liberation Front would try to drive the Marines out, mostly because of their success in helping us. They sent messages saying that the Marines were trying to trick us. I brought the messages to Colonel Corson.

Colonel Corson placed notices in about ten hamlets saying that the National Liberation Front were liars, and he called them many filthy Vietnamese names. Filthy names is tradition against one's enemies. Colonel Corson is the first foreigner who knows how to use filthy names with skill. In his notice he said he would be in the public square of Phong Bac a week from that day, and he invited the National Liberation Front to meet with him and to debate in front of the entire village as to whether or not the business program of the village was good for Phong Bac, and whether or not the Marines were liars. He said that if the National Liberation Front were afraid to come, he would even remove the Marine troops from the area as a guarantee of their safety.

I told the colonel that if he did that he would be killed, because already the National Liberation Front had a reward of 100,000 piasters for anyone who would capture him alive.

Never mind, he said. If they come, we will have an honest debate, and the man with the better argument will win it. If they don't come, then we know who is the liar. And if they kill me—that will be too bad and I won't like it. But at least you will know what it means.

The National Liberation Front did not show up for the debate. So, instead, we had a prosperity festival, and played more *Cò Tuong*. The Marines ate dinner in the village homes. This is good because in restaurants there may be class differences, but all who eat in a home are equals.

About sixty families in Phong Bac now are employed by the new businesses which our hamlet business council has started. This has had deep results for us. Many of the families have found the new business more profitable than raising rice. Some families told the landowners that they no longer wanted to plant rice and so they didn't need the land anymore. The landowners reduced the rentals from half of the crop to a quarter of the crop. Now rents in the whole district have dropped.

Our new businesses give the village a sense of independence. What we did, we did alone, without the help of the government. We do not have to pay off a district chief for licenses or for help. We feel like an independent hamlet, which is traditional in our history. Therefore we do not wish to get into trouble either with the National Liberation Front or the Marines or the South Vietnamese government. We want to be neutral. We will do anything to keep the fighting away from our village.

Once, we heard the NLF was going to attack Danang Air Base, and they were going to pass through our village on their way. They were going to stay overnight where some of our new hog farms were. We did not want our new businesses destroyed by artillery fire, so one of my men told Colonel Corson about the planned attack. We were not betraying the NLF or acting as informers. What we did was to make sure that the hamlet property was not harmed.

So you see (said Nguyen, sipping his tea), now you understand why we are in Saigon buying new kinds of hogs. Our village is prospering. The NLF is still strong near us. The Marines are still there. But the NLF does not come in to fight because the Marines now know the fields well (and here Nguyen winked), especially those near our new businesses. The Marines don't bother us. Nobody makes speeches about democracy or Ho Chi Minh or General Ky. The Marines mind their business and we mind ours. We understand each other. The Marines still play Cò Túong with us, and Sergeant Smith, who helps us with the hogs, has beaten everyone in the hamlet except myself. Next week Sergeant Smith is going to Hoa Tho to play the local champion. Sergeant Smith doesn't know it, but the man he will be playing is an NLF leader. The winner will get 160 piasters (about $1). The NLF officer is a champion. Probably he will beat Sergeant Smith.

The old man thought about something and began to laugh. He spoke rapidly in Vietnamese, and Lo began laughing also, and also the interpreter. When the laughter stopped, the interpreter told me what he had said. It was, "Since our village has become prosperous, a few of the NLF have come home. That's all we farmers want—a good and peaceful life. Give Colonel Corson enough time, and he'll have the NLF making so much money from new businesses and *Cò Túong* that they'll quit fighting, and then all the Americans will go home, and the war will be over."

Later I learned that this account of Phong Bac was an understatement. Colonel Corson has written in great detail of this episode at Phong Bac. In his forthcoming book he tells step by step of the Marines' accomplishment with the citizens of the hamlet.

23   WHAT Lieutenant Colonel William R. Corson, learned at Thong Bac hamlet became the pattern for the Marine Combined Action Program.

The CAP is, in my opinion, the only successful American project of any kind whatsoever in Vietnam. The program is surprisingly simple. It is inexpensive. The cost of maintaining the 1,200 Marines involved in the CAP is roughly one-fifth as much as is required to maintain 1,200 U.S. Army men employed on search and destroy missions or logistics support duties. Costwise it requires only about one-third as much money as is required by the South Vietnamese Rural Development program. In effectiveness there is no comparison at all. The search and destroy program, the official strategy under General Westmoreland, is a failure. The ARVN Revolutionary Development effort is a failure. The Pacification Program of AID is also an expensive failure which has made numerous millionaires among the already well-off Vietnamese but has not reached that 90 per cent of the population which matters.

The entire U.S. Marine Corps Combined Action Program consists of 15 officers and 1,200 enlisted men. They have lived and worked in seventy-eight hamlets in the five northern provinces. These Marines are influential in an area which has a population of approximately 260,000 Vietnamese. In this area during approximately a one-year period the

Vietcong were able to get only 170 recruits. This is a reliable estimate because when the Marine CAP units come to a hamlet they immediately take a census, including the fingerprinting of everyone; by taking similar censuses at regular intervals, and by knowing almost everybody within that hamlet, the Marines know when anybody has left the area. The average unexplained loss of any members of those areas is approximately 170 Vietnamese. When one considers that in the five northern provinces there are roughly 30,000 Vietcong, it can be seen that the recruitment of 170 new ones in one year is not enough to replace losses; and the denial of new recruits is a considerable blow to the Vietcong.

Besides needing recruits, the Vietcong require food. In most other rice-growing areas in South Vietnam, the Vietcong get, one way or another, three-quarters of the rice crop. In the five northern provinces, largely through the efforts of the Combined Action Program, much of this rice has been denied the Vietcong.

In many of the villages where the Combined Action Programs are in effect, Marines (as in Phong Bac hamlet) have created an environment which has made it possible for the Vietnamese peasants to become economically independent after several generations of virtual serfdom.

The only Americans in all of South Vietnam who are not disliked in some degree by the Vietnamese are the Marines employed in the Combined Action Program. The enlisted Marines of the CAP's are liked and respected by the Vietnamese peasants. There have been instances during the last year, after a Marine in one of the CAP units has been killed, when the entire village of Vietnamese peasants has gone into public mourning for sometimes as long as a year.

There are examples of the villagers being so loyal to the Marines that they will warn them of impending Vietcong attacks. In some areas where the Vietcong wish to attack the Marines, they have to make hostages of the peasants and threaten to murder them if anyone gives notice to the Marines.

These successes of the enlisted Marines of the Combined Action Programs, and the affectionate attitude of the Vietnamese toward them, contrasts with other American and Vietnamese relationships throughout Vietnam.

A Combined Action Program unit consists of fourteen enlisted Marines and one Navy hospital corpsman. These men are put into a Vietnamese hamlet *where they will live for approximately one year.* Working and living with these fifteen Americans are thirty-five Vietnamese Popular Forces troops. These are militiamen, local men who come from that hamlet or village. Their families live there. They know the area.

The most immediate duties of the Combined Action Program—a total of fifty men per unit—are military. They are to protect the village from the Vietcong, to deny Vietcong access to the village. This in itself is a tremendous responsibility; but the Combined Action Program accomplishes even more. The men dig wells, build roads, build bridges, look after the health of the community, find ways of increasing the agricultural yield, build medical dispensaries, build marketplaces,[20] hold school, protect peasants from local loan sharks. The Americans, in fact, become integrated members of the community.

These Marines must have had combat experience before they go into the villages. They are examined to make sure they are emotionally stable. They get schooling in the language of the area. They pick up the language quickly because they live with the people. The Marines who are around Danang learn the Quang Nam dialect; but those three CAP units who were in the area of Khe Sanh learned

---

[20] If the marketplace is properly made, one individual can observe who buys rice. This is one of the methods of controlling the flow of rice into the hands of the Vietcong.

Bru. The people there are not Vietnamese and speak a different language. In the school to which the Marines go before they join the CAP program (the school is held in Danang), the Marines learn local customs. Any Marine in a CAP unit can go into any Vietnamese home in the hamlet (and the majority of them are asked there for meals frequently) and conform with local customs and etiquette. They learn about local food and how to eat it; they learn what respects are extended toward the local Buddhist bonzes and to the Buddhist altars. They get a smattering of local religion. They learn the social customs relating to marriage, courtship, funerals, harvest celebrations, and so on.

The Vietcong realize that the CAP's are the most effective opponents they have in all of Vietnam. The Marine CAP's deliver the promises which the VC have made but have been unable to carry out. In essence the CAP's are more effective than the half million American troops or the 700,000 South Vietnamese and allied troops; they're more effective than the bombings or the defoliation or any other of the American instruments of combat. The proof of the value which the Vietcong place on these CAP units is the effort the VC have been making to destroy the CAP units. During January of 1968 almost every CAP unit was attacked frequently, sometimes several times a week, and seldom by less than 250-man expanded Vietcong companies. Time and time again, these small CAP units have defended themselves successfully—often because they have been warned by local villagers. Many of them have been killed, but the Marines are always replaced. There was one CAP unit that was completely wiped out after an all-night fight. But the Vietcong were unable to do it with a 250-man expanded company—they had to bring in a battalion of 750 men with automatic weapons, recoilless rifles, and mortars.

In early February of 1968 the three Marine CAP units beyond Khe Sanh had to be moved. The three hamlets involved were so attached to the Marines that they insisted on accompanying the Marines. The Marines helicoptered the three villages to safety, along with their forty-two Marines and three Navy hospital corpsmen. Already the members of those hamlets have had conferences with the Marines about planning, about building houses, about opening schools.

When I decided to inspect the CAP's, I thought that it would be wise to look at the weakest link first. So I went to La Chau hamlet, where what had seemed to be one of the most successful CAP projects had run into some trouble.

24   LA CHAU hamlet is only a few miles from Hoa-Phu village. The U.S. Marines had a particularly successful Combined Action Program there. The fourteen Marines and their Navy hospital corpsman were respected and popular. They had built a dispensary and held daily sick call for the villagers. They had built several deep wells in the center of the hamlet, thus saving the women a half-mile walk for water. They had started a school and raised the money for a teacher. During the rice harvest, they had stood guard and stopped both the VC and the government troops from taking it.

There was much affection between the villagers and the Marines. There was close cooperation between the Marines and their Vietnamese partners, the thirty-five-man Popular Forces company.

Yet late one afternoon in La Chau hamlet, Vietcong guerrillas ambushed and slaughtered ten of the fifteen Americans in the Combined Action Program unit. This was the first time that so many Marines in a CAP unit had been killed at once. Frequently they had lost one, two, or three in a night, but never such a complete wipeout.

I wanted to find out the cause, so I went to that hamlet.

The thing which made the slaughter possible was simple. That afternoon, without giving notice, a majority of the thirty-five-man South Vietnamese Popular Forces company had deserted and gone home. The South Vietnamese are men from the area where the unit is stationed. They are not volunteers. They are appointed by the district chief (an ARVN officer who has a U.S. army officer as his adviser).

On the afternoon of the slaughter of the ten Marines, a majority of the thirty-five Vietnamese Popular Forces men were out on patrol. The ten Marines who were ambushed were on their way out to relieve the Popular Forces men. But the Popular Forces men were not patrolling, they had left their posts, deserted, and had gone home. It was under these circumstances that the guerrillas infiltrated the area and ambushed the Marines.

I interviewed the Popular Forces men in La Chau hamlet.

"Why did you and the others desert the Combined Action Program unit?"

The South Vietnamese did not hesitate to answer. They had deserted because they hadn't had their food rations for six months. Their families were hungry, and they had to go back and feed them. The ration for each member of the Popular Forces soldier's family, per month, consists of three pounds of bulgar wheat, three pounds of corn meal, three pounds of rolled wheat, one and a half pounds of vegetable oil, and one and a half pounds of powdered milk. As there is an average of 4.8 members per family, the Popular Forces men each receive approximately sixty pounds of ration per month. *This ration of sixty pounds per month per man is supplied by the United States.* The food is sent out and delivered to Vietnam by the Catholic Relief Society—even though the foodstuffs come under Public Law 480. That means that most of it is surplus food.

What had happened then was that the Vietnamese militiamen did not get the food for themselves and their families for six months, thus resulting in the death of U.S. Marines.

To fully understand the gravity of this, it is necessary to understand the system by which the food is supposedly distributed.

The instruction, as issued by the United States command (USMACV), are:

> USAID ships Public Law 480 [supplies] into the Republic of Vietnam, transports them from dock to USAID warehouses in Saigon and Danang, and stores them until released by Catholic Relief Society. Catholic Relief Society releases these commodities for use in the Popular Forces, military civic action, and other programs. Upon release, responsibility of the commodities passes to agency which released them. . . .
>
> Commodities will be shipped to provincial capitals and consigned to sector advisors. . . . [NOTE: Consigned to sector advisors. *This means that the food is consigned to the U.S. Army officers who are advising their South Vietnamese counterparts.*]
>
> Commanders [U.S.] and senior advisors [U.S.] at all levels will continue to make maximum use of all available transportation in support of civic action programs. Advisors, particularly at sector level, will seek such assistance from counterparts [South Vietnamese]. . . .
>
> Sector advisors[21] will coordinate with counterparts [South Vietnamese] through their respective provincial committees to secure timely and equitable distribution of Popular Forces commodities.

According to official U.S. regulations, the task of the food for the Popular Forces troops, under the responsibility of COUSMACV (Commanding Officer U.S. Military Assistance Command, Vietnam) is clear and simple. In plain language, the procedure is as follows: The Popular Forces' food is shipped from the United States to a dock in Vietnam. From the dock (in this instance) it is transported to

---

[21] U.S. Army officers.

the AID storehouse in Danang. Even though the storehouse belongs to USAID,[22] the food still is the responsibility of the Catholic Relief Society, until the Catholic Relief Society releases it to the appropriate agency. From here the Catholic Relief Society consigns the food to the sector adviser, who is a U.S. Army officer. The sector adviser then coordinates with his Vietnamese counterpart in distributing the food to the Vietnamese Popular Forces.

No matter what the circumstances are, it is the U.S. Army advisers who are legally responsible for the distribution of the food.

I checked the amount of food which was released by the Catholic Relief Society in Danang to the U.S. Army advisers. For the six-month period December 1966 to June 1967, the CRS released an average of 632 long tons of food a month for distribution to the Popular Forces on duty with the U.S. Marines in the northern provinces. I also investigated and found out how much of those 632 long tons per month were delivered to the Vietnamese Popular Forces. *Less than 300 tons were delivered.*

I then went to other Combined Action Program units. Of the thirteen CAP units in the Danang area, only two were up to full strength in Popular Forces troops. The remainder were 45 per cent under normal complement.

In every hamlet the Popular Forces gave me the same answer. They had quit and gone home because they had not received their U.S. rations for six months.

Then they told me something even more revealing. Until six months earlier, the district chief (a South Vietnamese Army officer) had required them to buy the U.S.-donated rations from him. The amount he charged them was approximately one-third to one-half their total monthly

---

[22] The Danang USAID storehouse is operated by Vietnamese. I have never met a single person who has ever seen any Americans at the warehouse supervising the Vietnamese. I have witnesses who have seen the Vietnamese employees stealing large amounts of supplies from the warehouse they are paid to manage and guard for the U.S.

salary. When they complained about having to buy the food, the rations stopped entirely.

This is particularly shocking when one considers that it was the South Vietnamese Army officer's American adviser (a U.S. Army major) who was responsible for the distribution of these free rations.

But from December 1966 until June 1967, the troops received no rations at all.

I asked the troops if they had complained of these irregularities.

"We have complained to the village chief who has complained to the subsector chief and also to the province chief.[23] Last year when we had to pay for the rations we were told that the money was to pay for the transportation of them from America. Then, later, when we refused to pay, we were told that the rations had not arrived. We knew this was a lie, because we had seen the rations on sale in the black market, both in Danang and in the villages. One of our men from Hoa Luong went to the corps commander to complain. We do not know what happened to him. He never returned to the hamlet.

"There was nothing else for us to do but desert from the Combined Action Program and go home. We had no choice. Our families must eat. We knew more Marines would be killed. But that is the government's responsibility."

I went to the Marines and asked them if they had complained about the lack of rations for their Popular Forces associates. The Marines grimaced. What did I think the Marines would do? Of course they had complained. They had complained all the way up the line to the Vietnamese corps commander—Lieutenant General Lam—and his top U.S. Army adviser. Meanwhile the Marines had been feeding the Popular Forces men from their own rations. But there wasn't enough to feed the Vietnamese families also; and, furthermore, the prepared American

[23] The province chief is a South Vietnamese Army officer. He has a U.S. Army officer as his adviser.

food didn't suit the Vietnamese, and they did not like it. They ate it only to keep from starving.

The U.S. Marines said they had offered to take on the responsibility of distributing the rations. The Marines offered to pick up the rations directly from the Catholic Relief Society and distribute the full amount promptly, on a monthly basis, to the Popular Forces. The Catholic Relief Society thought this was a good idea because it would guarantee the Popular Forces' receiving the full contribution on time.

When this was suggested, there were objections from Colonel Hamblin and Lieutenant Colonel Dailey,[24] the U.S. Army advisers to Lieutenant General Lam. These officers also were on the advisory staff of General Walt[25] (the Third Marine Amphibious Force commander); and they told General Walt that the Marines' proposal was a bad one. They argued against the direct distribution of food by the Marines; and they said their arguments reflected the opinion of Lieutenant General Lam, the Vietnamese I-Corps commander. Their reasons were: (1) If the Marines delivered the food directly, it would indicate a mistrust of the South Vietnamese Army (to which the food now was being turned over illegally for delivery to the Popular Forces). Therefore it would be bad public relations; (2) If the Popular Forces in the I-Corps received full rations, and the Popular Forces in other areas did not, it would create jealousy.

This dispute had been going on for months, with the U.S. Army advisers to General Lam constantly taking his side against the U.S. Marines. Meanwhile, the food was not being delivered, and the Popular Forces were deserting.

What had happened to approximately 1,800 tons of Popular Forces food which had not been delivered to the troops?

[24] Real names.
[25] General Walt has been relieved by General Cushman.

This is what had happened. Instead of the food being delivered to the Vietnamese villages by the Americans, the food was illegally turned over, by the USAID and U.S. Army advisers, directly to the Vietnamese corps commander, General Lam. This is a violation of U.S. Public Law 480, which orders that the food be delivered directly to the consumer for whom it is intended. Once the Vietnamese military (General Lam and his associates) had their hands on the food, over half of it disappeared. Everyone in Danang knows where the food went. The Popular Forces men themselves said that they saw it for sale on the black market. I also saw it for sale on the black market in Danang.

When the Marines captured the Vietcong supply dump near An Hoa they found several tons of the American grain, which had been sold by the South Vietnamese corps commander. Also they found American anti-plague serum which was kept cool in an American refrigerator powered by a U.S. Army generator. There was enough serum to inoculate 5,000 people.

25 I THEN went to nearby Hoa Vang district headquarters because over half of the Popular Forces troops there also had "gone home." Through several interpreters I queried the villagers. They told the same stories—the U.S. supplies had been sold before they had reached the village. They blamed the Vietnamese army major who was the district chief. But in Hoa Vang the people had more to say about the occasion of a bubonic plague outbreak than about any other subject. What they told me was hard to believe. So I went to the Marine CAP unit stationed in Hoa Vang and asked them. They confirmed what the villagers had told me—and more.

It seems that several months earlier the hospital corpsman who was with the Marine CAP unit discovered plague in one of the nearby hamlets. Four of the people were already dead. The instructions for this kind of emergency are clear. A report is to be made immediately by the Marines to the U.S. Army adviser to the Vietnamese district chief.

The Marines put the four dead people in the back of a jeep. They drove to the district chief's compound, approximately half an hour away. The Marines went into the U.S. adviser's office at 2 P.M. and found that everyone was enjoying a "siesta." It is the custom in Vietnam for businessmen and government officials to have a three-hour rest every day after lunch. The U.S. adviser and his staff did the same thing. So, when the enlisted Marines entered on business, the people in the U.S. advisory group were irritated. They did not want their off-time disturbed.

"We have plague in our village, sir," said the Marine sergeant to the American major who was the adviser. "We have come to request the inoculation team."

"I don't believe you have any plague at all," the major said, pouring himself a glass of beer.[26]

"Sir," said the Marine sergeant, "I've got the four bodies outside in the jeep. You can see them for yourself. The glands are swollen, and the bodies are turning black. I'm on the way to the hospital now to have it confirmed."

The major muttered and walked away.

At the hospital the bodies were identified as having died from plague. The Marines stopped by the U.S. adviser's office on the way back, but the major had departed.

The next morning they again made desperate pleas at the U.S. adviser's office. The Marine sergeant said, "If my villages aren't inoculated, I may lose four thousand people in the next two weeks."

But the medical team was not sent to help the villagers.

The enlisted Marines of the CAP unit at Hoa Vang

[26] The Marines told me that the major was intoxicated.

telephoned all the military installations in the area, begging for the plague serum. They drove frantically around to various hospitals, collected the serum, and returned to the village.

The fourteen enlisted Marines and their hospital corpsman then inoculated 4,000 villagers. They did it alone. The official medical team and serum never came from the district headquarters.

After checking this story out with the Marines, I asked the villagers, "Why didn't the medical team come?"

The villagers were positive in their response. They said, "The medical team didn't come because the district chief had sold the medicine on the black market—just the way our food rations are sold."

I do not know if the plague serum was sold on the black market by the major who is the military chief of Hoa Vang district. But I do know that serum and antibiotics which are intended for the use of the South Vietnamese and the American troops are being used by the North Vietnamese and the National Liberation Front guerrillas. And the facts on the plague scandal in Hoa Vang district are: (1) The district chief and his American Army adviser did *not* send the plague inoculation team to the village; (2) The villagers know it is the responsibility of the U.S. adviser to prevent such things from happening. With the exception of the fifteen enlisted men who are in the Marine CAP unit, the villagers have no confidence in anyone in the South Vietnamese or the U.S. government.

The villagers also told me that the Vietnamese district chief had been collecting *solatium* money, and keeping it for himself.

At Hoa Vang there were only thirteen instead of thirty-five Vietnamese Popular Forces troops with the Marines. As in the other CAP units the missing troops had "gone home" because the district chief had failed to deliver the American food rations.

Twelve of the thirteen villages in the area were short of Vietnamese Popular Forces because of desertions.

Twelve of the thirteen U.S. Marine CAP units were in hazard because of the many corruptions of the South Vietnamese; and it appears that the corruption occurred with the permission of the U.S. advisers.

26   AT THE Officers' Club in Danang a USAID official and a U.S. Army lieutenant colonel were drinking martinis.

"Those goddam Marines have been heckling me to give a water pumping rig to the peasants at Hoa-Phu. . . ."

"Did you give them the pump?"

"I called Major Hao, the district chief. Good guy. Speaks good English. He said for God's sake don't give them the pump, that it'll wreck the economy of the district. I told him the Marine sergeant said if they don't get the pump the village may starve and go Commie. Major Hao says the Marines don't know from beans about Asian politics. . . ."

"The only way to keep a stable government here is let the generals make a few bucks on the side. The peasants will get along somehow. It's the power structure we have to support."

Marine Combined Action Program No. 3-2 is in Hoa-Phu village in the district of Hien Duc.

This village has about 1,600 hectares (3,600 acres) in which rice is grown. It is rich, flat land, capable of a higher yield than most areas.

The Marines who are stationed in Hoa-Phu have an extraordinarily good relationship with local Vietnamese, almost all of whom are Buddhists. The success of the Combined Action Program is so marked that the Vietcong often have tried to attack and dislodge the Marines. The attacks have been thwarted because people in the village informed the Marines when the Vietcong approached.

The local people have cooperated cordially at all
levels. During one period of four months there were heavy
rains, the road was washed out, and helicopter operations
were impractical. The Marines could not get their normal
food supplies, so the villagers fed them for four months. It
was during these four months that the Marines noticed how
terribly poor the people were—despite the rich land and
two annual rice crops—and they investigated the reason for
such poverty. The cause soon became apparent.

Most of the water for irrigating the rice comes from a
tributary of the Song Cau Do River. When the river is at
high level during the fall–winter monsoon, the water is
raised even higher by a small dam, perhaps sixty feet long,
and the water goes to the rice paddies by gravity. When the
river is low, during the dry season of summer–early fall, the
water is pumped from the river to the heights of the river-
bank and from there flows to the fields.

The owner of the dam, a small Catholic church
several miles from Hoa-Phu, received one-third of the fall
crop as payment for the use of the dam—that is, when the
river was high, during the monsoon season. The villagers
claim the dam was built by them thirteen years ago with
the money lent them by a French priest. They were to repay
the church by giving over one-third of the crop for twelve
years. The twelve years were over, but a new priest insisted
that the church owned the dam and that the payments
continue.[27]

When the river was low, the owner of the pump
received what amounted to one-third of the winter crop. It
was the pump-owner's decision how much water the villages received. A U.S. farm specialist said that if more
water were pumped, the rice crop would almost double its
yield. But the owner could not be forced. He always
insisted on being paid before he started pumping.

One-sixth of both crops went to the South Vietnam-

[27] The funds which come from the "water-rent" are used by
the church to maintain a school. But the school is located in another
village in another district populated by Catholics.

ese government in taxes. Another one-sixth (before the Marine CAP arrived) had been going to the guerrillas. Yet another one-sixth of the crop paid for transportation of the rice. This money went to the South Vietnamese Army, which controlled the transportation. Then also there were local taxes. In the end there wasn't much left for the peasants.

The Marines figured that if they could help the peasants help themselves to become prosperous, then in self-interest, the peasants would defend themselves against the Vietcong.

The Marines held a meeting with the village council. Representing the United States of America were six enlisted Marines, headed by Sergeant Carrol Soape, from CAP No. 3-2. Lieutenant Colonel Corson was present. There were no AID executives present. There were no diplomats present. The interpreting was done by Sergeant FitzPatrick, USMC, along with one of the village teen-agers who had been studying English with the Marines. As people spoke, each of the interpreters gave his version so that there would be no mistaking the meanings of the dialogue. The meeting was held in the school yard that served as the village square. The people from Hoa-Phu and several nearby hamlets—perhaps one hundred fifty peasants—stood around and listened.

Sergeant Soape proposed that the Marines give the village its own pump. If this were done, the village would not have to pay one-third of its crop to the company which owned the pump and the engine. The Marines said that they would give the pump, as well as a year's supply of gasoline, and also teach the villagers how to maintain the pump and the engine. But there was one condition to this offer. The villagers would receive the pump, provided that they would form a cooperative. A cooperative has the legal right to borrow money for agricultural purposes; and once the cooperative was formed, then, the Marines suggested, the village might borrow enough money to buy the dam and all rights from the Catholic church. Sergeant Soape had spoken to the priest. He had agreed to sell a quit-claim for the dam for approximately $5,000.

The village council decided they would like some time to discuss the matter. Another meeting was arranged a week later.

At the second meeting, there were about three hundred people listening, and it seemed that almost everybody contributed his opinion to the discussion.

The village council had reached a decision. The village would like to have the Marines' pump and would like to form a cooperative and buy the dam. Not only would this save approximately one-third of their total crop but, as a cooperative, they could arrange their own transport into Danang and thus could save another one-sixth of the crop.

There was one thing the hamlet council insisted that the village had to be sure of. Would the Marines' pump and engine work well? Before the villagers would make a commitment, they had to see the pump in operation. They could not take the chance of having no pump at all during the low water season.

The Marines thought this was reasonable and said they would produce a pump.

Then came the search for the pump. The USAID officials in Danang said they had no such equipment; and their attitude indicated they wanted nothing to do with the affair, even though it is their function to deal with such matters.[28] A couple of Marines went down to Saigon and inquired further. AID and other U.S. civic development organizations had pumps available, but the Marines were unable to get official help. The project had to be approved by AID in Danang and Saigon; and it would have required signatures from seventeen U.S. officials to release the pump.

However, after making a "midnight requisition," the Marines showed up at Hoa-Phu village with the pump.

[28] We know, as mentioned earlier, that the USAID officials had inquired about the pump of the U.S. district adviser and a Vietnamese district chief. Both of them had recommended against the pump.

Incidentally, there were no Americans tending the U.S. warehouse in Saigon. It was supervised by Japanese.

On the day of the demonstration, the men of the village carried the pump from the highway for a distance of over a mile to the small river. Approximately six hundred people followed. They walked past the old pump which was still operating, with its owner sitting next to it.

The Marines erected a platform. They lowered the pump's nozzle into the river, and started the engine. Soon water rushed and gurgled into the fields. The peasants shouted and cheered. Running over to the owner of the old pump, they shook their fists at him and screamed, "You've been sucking our blood long enough, you monster. Now we will show you what we can do for ourselves."

There was celebration in the hamlets that evening.

The Marines (a third of whom are farmers in civilian life) discovered that their new pump was not adequate. It worked at the present level, but if the river dropped three or four feet, the spout was not long enough and the engine would not be powerful enough for sustained use.

The Marines began searching for a more powerful pump and a more powerful engine. They made another "midnight requisition" trip to the AID storehouses in Saigon; but they couldn't find adequate equipment.

"We knew that the only solution," said the sergeant, "was for us to manufacture our own pump. We went to the Seabees of MCB-8. They crashed through and modified the pump and gas engine and pipes so that they functioned well even at the lowest possible river level. But soon after we installed the pump, we found that the peasants had been screwed from a new angle."

The priest who owned the dam had come around with bad news. He had received word from the Bishop's office in Danang that the dam could not be sold without the Bishop's permission.

The investigation of the church's change of mind brought out some strange facts. Major Hao, the district chief of the neighboring district, Hoa Vang, personally had

204) OUR OWN WORST ENEMY

been receiving approximately one-quarter of the revenue of the dam from the Catholic Church. The major also had received approximately one-quarter of the rent paid by the peasants to the owner of the pump.

This was why he and his U.S. Army adviser had instructed USAID not to supply a pump. Also, Major Hao is the nephew of the Bishop of Danang, and had gone to him requesting he forbid the priest to sell the dam.

While this was going on, still another factor entered the picture. An American Catholic priest who acts as a journalist for Catholic publications came to Danang and heard about how the Marines were trying to help the villagers of Hoa-Phu. He was against what the Marines were doing. He believed that if the villagers acquired ownership of the dam, the Catholic church would be losing a source of income which was being used to help Catholics in another area, while the people of Hoa-Phu were only pagans.

The priest sent a complaint back to the United States. Soon after the priest departed, the Marines received a letter from Ambassador Komer requesting that the Marines desist from helping the villagers of Hoa-Phu to get their dam. Komer requested that the Marines work through normal channels, and that they report the graft and mal-administration to South Vietnamese Army officers (the ones guilty of the graft); but keep away from the dam.

The Marines went ahead anyway. They called on the Bishop of Danang. They pointed out to him that they had been protecting both the Catholic churches and the Buddhist temples.

"Bishop," said one of the Marines, "suppose that the Vietcong suddenly decide to blow up the Catholic churches in your diocese. That would be worse than the loss of the dam, wouldn't it?"

A few days later the word came through that the church would sell the dam to the village.

But the long, strong hand of corruption continued to

push. When the villagers went to the agricultural bank to register as a cooperative group and to apply for a loan, they were frustrated. Major Hao had been there first. For a dozen reasons which no one understood, the agricultural bank could not grant the loan.

Again the Marines got busy. They went to another source of funds beyond the reach of Major Hao's influence and got the villagers a $5,000 loan.

Soon the village of Hoa-Phu had its own pump. It owned its own dam. The peasants in the area had formed a cooperative. Now they also could control their own transport to market. The half of their crops which they formerly had to pay to others now remained their own. They were accumulating capital. They were making plans for raising hogs and other agricultural products. They began thinking about buying land from the absentee landlords.

They felt secure enough to publicly insult the Hoa Vang district chief, Major Hao, as the "sucker of turtles' eggs," and to speak of his U.S. Army adviser as "Major Hao's American puppet."

The people of Hoa-Phu control their own irrigation; and they have increased their rice yield by over 50 per cent.

When the elder of Hoa-Phu village was telling me about the Marines of CAP No. 3-2, he concluded with, "The Vietcong came because of the corruption and the officials' maltreatment of the people. To stop the war it is not necessary to win the war. It is necessary to help the people be prosperous and happy. When this happens, soon there will be no more Vietcong. My people are happy. There are no more Vietcong in Hoa-Phu. They come and they go, of course, to visit relatives here, but—and it is hard to explain—what the Vietcong are fighting for, we already have it."

VII

THE

ANGUISHED
AMERICAN

"I speak Vietnamese," said the lieutenant who was a West Pointer, *"and I know what's going on around here. You have bum information."*

> U.S. ARMY ADVISER to the South Vietnamese subsector chief, in conversation with author near Danang, June 1967

27   WITHIN A short period of time I had learned about some scandals which—in my opinion—were hurting the United States, and which were driving the Vietnamese toward Communism. The Vietnamese were blaming the South Vietnamese administration and its U.S. advisers. Therefore I felt I had to interview the American officers concerned. I started out by going to the quarters of the two young Army officers who were the advisers to the subsector chief. One was a U.S. Army lieutenant, a military academy graduate, and the other one was a captain who was reluctant to discuss his background. These two officers were responsible for the hamlets in the subsector. They were supposed to be intimate with everything happening there. Why U.S. Army officers had such duties within an area which was a Marine command, I did not understand. But MACV headquarters had put them there.

Neither of these two officers had heard anything about the Vietnamese Popular Forces not getting their rations for six months. Nor did they know that the district chief extorted money from the troops for the rations before that, or that the resultant desertions from the Popular Forces had brought about the deaths of Marines and had impeded the Pacification Program.

They had not heard of the plague incident, nor of the *solatium* money affair, nor of the crookedness which was going on in Hoa-Phu concerning the shakedown of approximately half the total rice crop by the district chief, the local priest, and the man who owned the pump. They not only had never heard of these things. They denied them.

"I speak Vietnamese," said the lieutenant who was a West Pointer, "and I know what's going on around here. You have bum information."

I congratulated him on knowing Vietnamese, and asked if I could bring my interpreter in to have a discussion with him in Vietnamese.

"Well," he said, "I don't know if I'd like that. I've only had the three-month course in the language."

The Army captain, in a surly manner, indicated that *he* knew what was going on, and everything was okay. I asked him what his job was, and he said he was the intelligence officer.

"Do you speak Vietnamese?" I asked.

"No."

"Well, how do you know what's happening, then?"

"I have an interpreter."

"May I meet him, please?" I said. "I'd like to have my interpreter speak with him to see how much English he knows."

"He's not here now."

"Where is he?"

"He's inspecting the hamlets, getting information."

"I'm willing to go down to wherever he is," I said. "In which hamlet is he?"

"I don't know."

"May I interview him later?"

"No. Tonight he'll be busy making up my daily report."

I next went up one echelon to the district chief. The U.S. advisers' buildings were in the same compound. When I went there it was 2:15 P.M. The U.S. advisers and their men were sitting around drinking beer. I asked for the U.S. Army major who was the district chief's adviser. He wasn't in, but was expected shortly.

I began a discussion with a U.S. Army captain who said that he was the staff expert responsible for the administration of the Popular Forces. I told him about the Popular Forces deserting because they hadn't had their rations for six months. The captain became angry, began pounding the table, and said this was a lie. I told him if he wanted to come along with me I would take him to the villages and show him.

"You should know that that isn't true," the captain said. "Those villagers are always bitching and lying, they get plenty to eat."

"Where do they get the rations?"

"The Marines feed them."

"But what about their families? What about the sixty pounds of grain per month—which they've not been getting?"

The Army captain said, "Look, those Popular Forces men make enough money to feed their families and then have some left over."

"How much money do they make?"

With arrogance, the Army captain said, "Between four thousand and seventy-five hundred piasters a month."

"How do you know that?" I asked.

"How do I know it? From the handbook. It states in black and white how much pay they get."

"Would you show it to me?"

"You bet I will," he said. He went into the hall and brought back a book and began paging through it. After about ten minutes he said he couldn't find the information.

I said, "You're mistaken. The Popular Forces make sixteen hundred piasters a month. That's ten dollars a month."

I looked at him and asked, "Do you know how much a kilogram of rice costs? Do you know how much one melon costs?"

He didn't answer.

I said, "Sixteen hundred piasters a month is nothing. It's not enough to feed their families for a week."

"I'm sure they make somewhere between four thousand and seventy-five hundred piasters a month," he said.[1]

I asked him about the water rates and the land lease rates in Hoa-Phu, and he hadn't heard about that either.

The captain didn't even know that the Vietnamese Popular Forces troops were supposed to get sixty pounds of grain per month—the very thing for which he was responsible. He did not know that in seventy-eight villages half of the Vietnamese troops had "gone home," thus endangering the lives of 1,200 U.S. Marines.

By now the major had arrived—the American who was the adviser to the district chief. He asked me what I wanted and how I was making out. I was angry now. I told him that I wasn't getting the information I needed and that his staff seemed to be having several hours of recreation—drinking beer—in what to me was the middle of the working day in the middle of a war.

The major—who smelled and acted as if he had had several beers himself—became indignant. He shouted, "The district chief and his staff have a three-hour siesta. It lasts from lunch until three in the afternoon. Are you saying that we shouldn't have the same three hours off, goddam it? We're here in Vietnam, and we're supposed to observe the Vietnamese customs, whether the U.S. press likes it or not."

I decided it was useless to stick around there any longer. Instead, I thought, I'll go right to the top.

It took me three days to arrange the appointment, but I finally got to see a U.S. Army colonel, one of the senior advisers to Lieutenant General Lam, the Vietnamese I-Corps commander. After all, it was General Lam who gave the orders and instructions to the province chiefs, the district chiefs, and the subsector chiefs.

---

[1] Popular Forces members made 1,622 piasters a month at that time. Now it has been raised to 2,400 piasters a month. Many of the Popular Forces members do not know this, and the district chiefs pocket the difference. Also, the roster of Popular Forces men which is maintained at the district headquarters where I went had almost twice as many names on it as there were men on duty. Again, someone was pocketing the difference.

28 MY INTERVIEWS with the U.S. Army colonel who was the senior adviser at the Vietnamese I-Corps commander's headquarters were among my most painful experiences of the recent Vietnam trip. It served as the catalytic agent which suddenly put American activities in Vietnam into perspective for me. I now clearly saw how the United States is its own worst enemy; and how we Americans are directly responsible for our being beaten, humiliated, and made fools of.

I was driven to the headquarters of the Vietnamese I-Corps commander by a public information officer. As we neared the entrance, the young officer said, "Oh, good. General Lam is in."

"Why is that good?"

"When the general is in his headquarters, then the front gate is open. But when General Lam is absent he has the front gate locked. Then all Americans have to enter the back gate with the servants."

The American adviser to General Lam was a U.S. Army colonel. The public information officer said he had been there a long time; in fact he had been the adviser to General Lam's predecessor.

I asked, "What are the colonel's duties?"

"To advise General Lam."

"On what?"

"On anything—supposedly—to do with the war."

"Does the colonel have any other American advisers helping him?"

"Hell, yes. There are three floors of them."

"Are they very busy?"

"If being messenger boys for the Vietnamese commander and if kissing the Vietnamese commander's royal red *tuchas* means being busy—then they're billy-be-damned busy. . . ."

The public information officer saluted a tall, impressive-looking man with silver eagles on his collar, and said, "Colonel, this is Mister Lederer who's come to see you."

The colonel waved to a chair and asked me what I wanted. I had only an hour with him, so I got down to the dirt immediately. I told him that the Vietnamese Popular Forces troops in nearby areas had not received their American rations for over six months; and as a result of this they had deserted, thus hazarding the U.S. Marines' CAP program and endangering the lives of the Marines. I told him that the rations had been stolen by General Lam's command and that much of it had been sold on the black market.

At first the American Army colonel denied that any of this was true. I offered to take him around and, using his own interpreter, let him learn for himself. He could count the number of Popular Forces troops who were still with the Marines. He could see for himself that they were down to less than half strength. He could interview the Popular Forces men who "had gone home" and hear for himself that they had not received rations for over six months, and before that had had to pay the district chief for them.

I told him that if he wished I would interrogate his American Army officers for him—and would demonstrate that they were ignorant of what was happening within their districts.

The colonel doubted what I said, but even if it were true, he said, the distribution of the grain was not the responsibility of the American advisers.

I read to him the MACV directive, straight from Westmoreland's headquarters. It said that the delivery of the grain was the responsibility of the American advisers.

The colonel replied that the grain often could not be distributed because of shortage of transport vehicles.

I pointed out that the MACV directives ordered U.S. advisers to call upon the South Vietnamese Army for transport help if needed. I reminded the colonel that almost every South Vietnamese Army officer in that corps had an

American jeep which he was using for his own personal pleasure. If the colonel doubted this, all he had to do was drive through the residential districts where the South Vietnamese officers (and their families) lived. There were hundreds of vehicles available if the U.S. adviser could get the Vietnamese to divert them from their personal use to helping the war effort.

I then asked what had happened to the three and a half million pounds of missing grain which the Popular Forces troops never received. Before he answered I told him I had receipts which showed the grain had been delivered to General Lam's staff; and I had pictures of the grain being sold on the black market; and I had proof that Major Hao, the district chief, was a crook.

The colonel, who was getting angry, told me I was mistaken about Major Hao. Major Hao was a fine man. He was a dedicated man. He was a devout man, in fact he was studying for the priesthood. Major Hao spent so much time inspecting his district and helping his people that he seldom was home with his family. Major Hao was such a fine officer he was being recommended for an American commendation.

This shook me.

I gave the colonel a run-down of what was happening in Major Hao's district—the malfunctioning which had the tacit approval of Major Hao's U.S. Army advisers. I told of the failure to send the plague team to the villagers. I described Major Hao's efforts to keep his people in poverty by stopping them from owning their own dam for irrigation, by stopping them from owning their own pump, by stopping them from forming a cooperative. I gave evidence of the fraudulent way Major Hao had tried to collect *solatium* money.

I demonstrated how almost everything which Major Hao did was accomplishing the following: (1) enriching the major and the Saigon adminstration, (2) causing the death of U.S. Marines in the CAP units, and (3) defeating the U.S. war effort by treating the peasants so badly that they would be sympathetic to the Vietcong.

I then reminded the colonel that, by directive from General Westmoreland's headquarters, he, the colonel, and the U.S. advisers under him, were directly responsible for the things I had just told him about.

The colonel perspired. His angry behavior stopped. In a low, tired voice, he said, "Let's be civilized. Don't put the finger on me."

My scheduled hour was over. The colonel said he wished we could discuss the matter more, but he already was late for a meeting with General Cushman.

The next morning a major came to the press camp, where I was staying, and said, "What in the hell did you do to the colonel yesterday? I was with him at the club last night. He bent on a beauty. He said you have put him in a double bind. If he tries to persuade General Lam and his staff to be more honest, then General Lam will write to General Westmoreland, and the colonel will get kicked out of his job. And if you write newspaper articles about what's happening here, it might start an investigation. The colonel said that everyone is doing as good a job as is possible under the circumstances.

"What he's really bleeding over is that right now he's up for selection for general. His father was a general, and he wants desperately to make general also. The surest way for him to not get promoted is by trying to reform the Vietnamese corruption. That would kill the colonel's career."

I asked the major if the colonel knew the extent of the graft, the mismanagement of the war effort, the criminal way the South Vietnamese administrators and U.S. advisers were behaving.

The major said, "Hell, the colonel is just about the most experienced U.S. adviser in Vietnam. Of course he knows what's happening. But what can he do? If he interferes with the Vietnamese, man, he's had it. He, like all other advisers for the past twelve years, has been ordered to 'get along with the Vietnamese.' If the poor son of a bitch does what is his duty to do, the ARVN command will complain to MACV, and he'll never make general. He'll be punished by the U.S. Army for doing his duty."

I whistled.

The major said, "The colonel isn't unique. There are thousands of Army guys who are advisers to Vietnamese. The Army advisers have to play ball with these crooks—or their career is ruined. Man, don't you see what's happening? These poor Army bastards have been ordered 'to get along.' It's United States policy. U.S. policy supports corruption and wrecks the integrity of the advisers. If the advisers had real integrity, all of them would expose the Vietnamese— even if they got court-martialed or kicked out. But I'll tell you, feller, there aren't many profiles in courage out here.

"And," continued the major, "there's not a goddam thing you or any other newspaperman can do. No one can do anything about it but Westmoreland, Ambassador Bunker, and President Johnson—the guys who give the orders. And them, they don't know what the score is— everyone's been feeding them a line of crap—and I doubt whether they have the guts. So what happens? We've lost the war."

The next day the colonel sent me a message saying that we had not explored the subject enough because we had not had enough time. Would I like to meet with him and members of his staff?

I was eager to meet with him and his staff, and the appointment was made for the following morning.

29 WHEN I arrived at the corps headquarters for the second time, the front gate was locked because General Lam was absent, and I had to go through the back entrance, as did all other Americans.

The colonel had gone off someplace, and a lieutenant colonel met me. I was to meet with members of the colonel's staff. We assembled in an air-conditioned conference room. Over to the side was a microphone, and I wondered if everything would be taped.

There were four staff members, two lieutenant colonels, two majors. One was an Australian. Each was the staff's top expert in some phase of the advising business. Also present were two public health officials.

The staff had been well briefed by the colonel, and they went over the comments I'd made to him a few days earlier. I told them I had returned to Vietnam to gather material for a scholarly book on "the pathology of U.S. foreign relations."[2] What troubled me, I explained, was that the big, powerful United States was being kicked around by highly motivated and comparatively ill-armed peasants. Almost everything I had looked at—except for the CAP's—appeared to be a failure. I wanted to find out what the United States was doing wrong.

"Have you found out?" one of the staff members asked.

I told him I had come to a few conclusions. One of them was that the U.S. Army advisers to the Vietnamese were in an awkward spot. These U.S. Army advisers, if they are alert and observant, should know that their Vietnamese counterparts are involved in corruptions and neglect of duty, and that these malpractices are among the major reasons for the United States losing the war so far.

The U.S. Army advisers often know about these things, I said, but they do little or nothing—usually nothing —to force the Vietnamese to correct their criminal habits. The reason the U.S. Army officers do nothing, I said, is because the advisers are looking out after their own safety and security, and don't give a damn about the United States. The U.S. advisers are afraid to take action.

[2] The author is still working on this; completion date is about June 1969.

All the Vietnamese officer has to do, I said, repeating what I now had heard often, is to write a letter to General Westmoreland or to the U.S. Embassy saying that his U.S. adviser is causing trouble. He is impeding the war effort. He does not understand the Vietnamese and apparently does not like them. Therefore, it is requested by the Vietnamese government that the U.S. Army officer be relieved and that somebody else who is brighter and more understanding be put in his place.

The chances are that the U.S. Army adviser will be relieved and sent somewhere else if he is honest and is thinking of America's welfare. The chances are that he will receive a bad fitness report, and that his career will be hurt. The word and opinion of the Vietnamese officer will be taken over those of an American officer. Officers are ordered to get along with the Vietnamese at any price.

The senior staff member present exploded with anger. He stood up and shook his fist. He shouted with indignation. He informed me that Army officers were men of honor, and I was insulting the U.S. Army.

The Australian officer spoke up, "Colonel, Mister Lederer is right. There have been plenty of officers who have been sacked for trying to do an honest job with the Vietnamese."

The American told the Australian, who was his junior in the staff, to shut up.

After that, the meeting lasted about two hours more. We proceeded to discuss the U.S. war effort more as a "clogged-up U.S. system" than as a bunch of American blunders for which specific people could be blamed or perhaps court-martialed.

I repeated all the corruptions I had described to the colonel. Only now I cited names, laid out papers which proved I had done my research carefully and honestly. The relationship between the staff members and me became more friendly. No one denied my accusations.

The two public health officers told of their work in many plague areas—and how many people they had helped. But no comment was made about the time the U.S. adviser failed to send the health team to Hoa Vang—and how the Marine riflemen had to inoculate 4,000 Vietnamese.

When I departed, the senior member asked me when I would be returning to Vietnam. I told him probably in September of 1967—to cover the elections.

He smiled, thrust out his hand, and said, "When you come back in September 1967, I promise you that all of the Popular Forces troops in this corps will be getting their full ration of grain every month."

I did not return to Vietnam in September to cover the elections, as I had intended. But I receive frequent reports from Vietnam. My correspondents have written that the Popular Forces troops still are not getting all their rations, except in a few places. Corruption is getting worse. The Vietnamese generals are laughing at the "tough demands" of the Americans. The American military in Saigon has reached such a state of frustration that they are eager to do "anything" which will get them out of their unpleasant situation, and have been sending urgent and private cables to their friends in the Pentagon.

I have since learned that the Joint Chiefs of Staff, MACV, and the South Vietnamese bureaucracy still are trying to snuff out the highly successful Combined Action Program of the U.S. Marines. The JCS, MACV, and the South Vietnamese were unable to kill the program by cutting supplies, by refusing the transfer of necessary men, and by "allowing" the Popular Forces troops to desert because of corruption. They now are planning another assault on the Combined Action Program. General Westmoreland's headquarters has proposed taking the CAP's away from the U.S. Marines and placing them under the Army officers who are the U.S. advisers to the South Vietnamese.

And when it was recommended that the CAP's get an official commendation, General Westmoreland's headquarters tried to block it.

VIII

THE

ROAD OUT

———

"Our enemy pretends that we seek victory through United States peace movements. But we know that we must count mainly upon ourselves and no one else. The war will be decided in Vietnam and nowhere else."

PHAM VAN DONG,
Premier of North Vietnam

30 WE MUST find a road out.

The North Vietnamese and the National Liberation Front apparently have concluded that they can and must maintain the strategic initiative. That they have been successful is proved by their offensives at Dakto and Khe Sanh, and by their extensive Tet assaults. Their well-coordinated activities have drawn American and South Vietnamese troops from pacification efforts in the countryside. American projects and campaigns have been thrown off balance. The United States has had to go on the defensive.

We have failed to condition our troops for Vietnam's requirements. Not only pound-for-pound and man-for-man, but absolutely, the Vietcong and the North Vietnamese outclass us. Their motivation, their political skill, their military techniques, their combat integrity, their physical stamina have proved superior to ours. We lean heavily on our technology—which we do not know how to use in the Vietnamese terrain. Today, after four years of failure, our generals only call for *more*, not *different*. We can only hope that *more* will not lead to nuclear weapons in the end. The war has to be fought mostly by foot soldiers who have both guerrilla and political skills. It has to be fought in jungles and swamps and mountains and rural hamlets. For us to win we must accomplish what the Vietcong have done— only better. We have not done this.

Many of the 20,000 Americans killed in action have died unnecessarily. When they are killed by the enemy using American equipment, they have died unnecessarily. When they die because the enemy is given our operation plans, they have died unnecessarily. Many of the 150,000 American casualities have been wounded unnecessarily. Almost 2,000 airmen and $2½ billion worth of planes have been lost because of policies made in ignorance of history and Asian conditions. The infiltration of supplies and men from North Vietnam has increased ten times since the bombings started. Therefore we can say that the death of many pilots and the loss of many planes has been tragically futile.

This is not to say that fighting and dying have not been required in Vietnam. They have. But the way in which we have conducted the Vietnam conflict has hurt us terribly. And it has hurt those we came to protect. To a large degree we are responsible for the 4 million Vietnamese who are homeless refugees, and the several million who have been killed or wounded. It is hard to accept the full extent of what we have accomplished without seeing it in person—the burned-out countryside, the unplanted fields, the bombed villages, the millions of refugees living in slums and camps and cemeteries and fields. All this has brought no victory and, in fact, no progress.

We cannot lay all the blame on the Department of Defense, the Department of State, the military, and the AID missions. We all share the blame—all of us, including the American contractors in Vietnam who have cheated on their budgets; all of us, including the national network TV team which bribed the village idiot to pretend he was dead, and, then, after squirting catsup over him, photographed him in color as an example of Vietcong atrocities.

It may be because the North Vietnamese and the National Liberation Front have used our failures as a basis for assessment that they have taken an "all or nothing" public posture. Their actions and public statements add up approximately to this: "Defeat us, or we will defeat you.

There is no room for diplomatic accommodations or compromises. We do not trust you. You betrayed us in 1945; you betrayed us again in 1955 and 1956 after the Geneva Agreement; and you thwarted us with your intrusion in 1961. Three times we have earned victory and three times you have cheated us out of it. For us it must be all or nothing. Furthermore, this is our tradition."

Pham Van Dong, the Premier of North Vietnam, confirms this. He said, "Our enemy pretends that we seek victory through United States peace movements. But we know that we must count mainly upon ourselves and no one else. The war will be decided in Vietnam and nowhere else"[1]

A leader of the National Liberation Front said substantially the same thing to Professor Everett Mendelsohn of Harvard University in an interview held in Phnom Penh in January 1968. He said the National Liberation Front and the North Vietnamese would defeat the United States militarily and were not relying on any debilitating social unrest in the United States.

The concept of "all or nothing" is not generally held in the United States. It is the opinion of the American people, from President Johnson through the full social and political spectrum, that what the United States seeks is a cessation of hostilities on terms acceptable to both sides. We are not striving for a total and unconditional military victory —with all its macabre and frightful aftermaths. Only a few extreme military hawks would disagree.

But the National Liberation Front and the North Vietnamese keep shouting their reasons for their "all or nothing" behavior. They strongly feel that no satisfying terms for negotiations have been offered by the United States, or that the United States is incapable of offering satisfying terms upon which the Vietnamese can rely.

In the past, the one major term insisted upon by both the North and the NLF is that the National Liberation Front participate in any and all negotiations that might

[1] As quoted in *The New York Times*, March 2, 1968, in an article by Professors David Mozingo and John W. Lewis of Cornell University.

possibly occur. This *sine qua non* is repugnant to the South Vietnamese government which the United States supports. Therefore, negotiations at this time appear utterly impossible unless the United States persuades the South Vietnamese government to change its mind and concur. Our past pattern has been to permit the South Vietnamese to tell us what to do. We seem unable to provide a climate for negotiations; and we have been unable to win the military victories necessary for bargaining leverage.

United States leadership, therefore, finds itself in a dilemma. Problems at home are piling up on top of international complexities. A new and powerful political force has recently erupted. The domestic social cost of the Vietnam war is begining to become intolerable to many people. Protest movements and manifestos are flaring up with more and more frequency and magnitude. Even though these protests get the newspaper headlines, they are insignificant in comparison to still another national turbulence—a turbulence which as yet is not noisy, but which we know goes deep into the nation.

There is an unpleasant feeling, a discomfort, a restlessness among a majority of U.S. citizens. It comes from a growing conviction that the Vietnam war is bereaving the United States of far more than lives, money, international prestige, and creditability. People from Maine to Arizona, from Washington State to Florida, feel that the war is gnawing at our self-esteem, our self-confidence, and our innate sense of morality. People are becoming afraid that we are losing our capacity to continue the domestic progress which we proudly believe has been the soul of America for two centuries.

People are disturbed by the realization that the longer the war continues, the heavier the losses to all participants and the less likely the possibility of a satisfactory solution of any kind for anyone.

It is an eerie situation.

For many there is the vision of a not-too-distant economic calamity, a social calamity, a political calamity.

For some there is the specter of an approaching national demise. The United States, for the first time in its history, has become the most powerful and wealthiest nation in the world, and for the first time doubts its future.

We Americans hope these fears, these negative attitudes, are based on temporary confusion, perhaps temporary ignorance, on temporary—even though expensive—mistakes. We try to clear our heads, striving for solutions. Our great vitality and wealth, our inherent political strengths and decencies are limitless. But how to harness them and terminate the current and unwanted discord?

It is not like Americans only to criticize and fail to offer some kind of solution. But even though we are unhappy with conditions, few of us are specialists on Southeast Asia. Few of us are specialists in domestic economic or legislative matters. Fewer of us are specialists in foreign affairs. But all of us have the capacity to make commitments and become involved in our nation's problems.

If many of us actively discuss the subjects which trouble us, if many of us scratch and dig for ideas and solutions, then we can hope to move off dead center. Even if our individual solutions are not perfect, still, the continued efforts and expressed ideas of several million Americans cannot help but have a cumulative result. The effect—and there is no doubt about this—will nourish and vitalize the nation. Such is the strength of a democracy. It is only apathy, disinterest, and fear which can destroy us.

It is everybody's responsibility to participate.

31   THERE ARE two categories of national problems which can benefit from the collective thinking of Americans. First, there is the immediate crisis of the Vietnam war. Second, we have the troubles which may come in the future.

As a starter, there follow some suggestions concerning the first category, our current urgent problems in Viet-

228) OUR OWN WORST ENEMY

nam. There is, of course, an endless list of possibilities which might improve our situation, but I have limited myself to Vietnam actions which I feel could be accomplished in a hurry, and which would require little if any legislation.

1. We must develop an effective working relationship with the South Vietnamese government. First we must extricate ourselves from the stranglehold of a Saigon government whose goals are inimical to ours. We must cease to be an apologetic guest and become at least a partner, with a partner's rights guaranteed and enforced. It is intolerable that we are dictated to on our own bases. Our installations in South Vietnam must be on a basis which will allow us to administer our diplomatic and military affairs effectively, without bureaucratic clearance from Saigon or its representatives. This will be difficult to achieve since the Thieu-Ky government is well aware of our involvement; any threat to pull out would be empty, and they know it. Nevertheless, we can develop a working relationship if we simply have the courage to insist.

2. Eliminate the "adviser" system. We do not have now, and cannot produce soon, American advisers qualified in knowledge or language to counsel the thousands of Vietnamese officials who are administering the country (and robbing it). The system breeds its own destruction. It is so set up that the few advisers who are both qualified and brave enough to report accurately and completely can be removed at the whim of those on whom they report. Unwittingly our advisers have become a vast "cover" for corruption and inefficiency.

3. Enforce the provisions of U.S. Public Law 480, which requires that we ourselves deliver aid materiel to the designated recipients. Under this provision, rice, cement, money, and all the rest would be delivered to the refugees, to the villagers, to the Popular Forces, and other designated recipients by Americans, instead of being turned over to South Vietnamese officials. Rejected draftees whose physical

standards are below combat requirements could be of enormous help in this work—while easing the draft problem at home.

4. Obtain dock areas where we can unload our own ships, warehouses where we can guard our own supplies. In other words, eliminate the corruption which sends an estimated 60 per cent of our billions of dollars' worth of materiel to either the enemy or the international and local black markets. Again, below-combat-standard draftees could be used, thus eliminating the thousands of non-Americans now involved.

5. From the American academic and business worlds, obtain the services of as many specialists on Vietnam as the nation has. Place them in key spots in Vietnam as intelligence gatherers, policy advisers, and interpreters of the life and language of the people of Vietnam.

6. Be realistic about the political nature of the war. If we do so, we will place far greater emphasis on the Combined Action Program of the Marines—our one successful effort. It should be spread to every corner of rural Vietnam.

7. Recognize, at the same time, that the National Liberation Front is a going and, until now at least, a growing concern and that no meaningful negotiations can take place without it. It will be necessary to persuade the present Saigon regime to accept this fact. Strong measures may be necessary because the Thieu-Ky government has no stake in peace. On the contrary, peace would mean the loss of both power and profit to its officials.

8. Be realistic about the nature of the conflict in Vietnam. In a people's war (as contrasted to a national or governmental war), politics are more powerful than tonnages of bombs. Guerrilla warfare is highly specialized, and it is of maximum effectiveness against an army which relies on technology rather than on knowledge of the people and their reasons for fighting.

9. Finally, if we decide that we truly want negotiations, then stop bombing north of the DMZ and turn the

problem over to the Secretary General of the United Nations as he has requested. He has assured us that if we would do so, negotiations would start at once. If he is right, we will have succeeded that far. If he is wrong, we will at least, in the eyes of the world, have put the burden of proof on the shoulders of Hanoi. In a war between a giant and a pygmy only the giant can make the first move toward peace.

Those, then, are some of the short-range specifics which might help make a bad job better and disaster less certain. But what about the future? What sort of actions can we take to make us less susceptible to a repetition of folly and failure?

There *are* some ideas for long-range solutions.

The United States must develop human talents capable of coping with international patterns yet to come. We must have an organization with such flexibility and speed of decision that today's problems never again are attacked with yesterday's solutions. Some suggestions for this follow.

1. A new and widely expanded program for the training and motivation of specialists with knowledge of foreign countries. The time is long past when we can afford a Foreign Service populated by men who worked their way around the world with the final goal as Paris, London, or Rome.

2. A new method of formulating foreign policy must be developed. At present our government, through its Department of State, does not originate and plan its policies. Instead it responds, on a day-to-day basis, to the actions of other nations. We must move on long-range policy lines which cause other nations to respond in a way that we desire—ways which are beneficial to us and, we hope, to them.

3. One of the first requirements for formulating long-range policy is the creation of an effective method of collecting and assessing intelligence. At present, particularly in

Asia, Africa, and South America, our intelligence "community" has been consistently in error.

4. The Congress must be actively brought into the formulation of policy, and therefore must be informed. At present the busy Congress is either unable to assimilate the vast amount of helter-skelter information with which it is inundated, or the Congress does not receive pertinent information from the executive branch of the government without asking for it. A system—however radical—for getting information to the Congress must be created.

5. A method for training non-specialists who are sent overseas. These are the military and civil service persons sent to other nations for short tours of a year or two. They need not become linguistic experts, but they should be familiar with the history, culture, religion, aspirations, needs, and foreign policies of the nations to which they are going. The history, culture, aspirations, and so forth must be those of the majority of the inhabitants, not only of the ruling class.

6. Citizens of other countries—from every level of society, not just the English-speaking elite—should be brought to the United States by the thousands and educated in the skills their countries need and which we can provide. Teaching these foreigners English, so that they can attend our schools, will bring added dividends. Among them is the fact that they will learn to know America and understand us as we are, instead of having their image of us painted by hostile propagandists.

Can all this be done? Why not? It is practical and possible that a commission granted sufficient authority could, within a few months, draw up necessary legislation and methodology to accomplish the above. And more. The ideas are not difficult. It is only change which is difficult and which requires uncommon courage.

But there is no comfortable, easy answer. In Vietnam we have gotten ourselves into a position where—even if we

completely devastated North Vietnam, killed every Vietcong, or negotiated the war to completion—victory is still
remote, perhaps impossible.

Moreover, a victory in the classic, military sense of
the word, might well be a disaster to us. Total victory means
total responsibility. The mind boggles at the thought of
bearing total responsibility for Vietnam into a distant future.

The significant, long-range question on which our
survival hangs is not, "Shall we abruptly pull out of Vietnam
or shall we, instead, try to gain military victory by using our
most deadly weapons?"

The significant question and decision is: Have we, the
citizens of the United States, the character, the vitality, to
improve our national competence? Have we, as a nation,
the capacity, the integrity, to learn how to survive inter-
nationally (and, at the same time, domestically) in a strange,
swift, new world which is a potpourri of technology, nationalism, affluence, poverty, superabundance, and starvation?

Or is the United States like the dinosaur, which once
was the mightiest beast on earth but which became extinct
because it could not adapt to a changing environment?

We must think about this. We cannot carp and flail
and start looking for someone on whom to place the blame
for America's shameful and unnecessary failures. The people
who have botched things up are your neighbors, your
friends, your relatives, your countrymen. They are ourselves.

APPENDICES

Contents

APPENDIX A

Biographies

Vo Van Kim, a native of Long Xuyen, was Professor of Vietnamese History at the University of Hue. Today, at 70, he works as a translator for an American construction company in Saigon. He works eight hours a day and earns 17,000 piasters a month—about $150. This is about one-fourth the amount an attractive bar girl makes. Professor Vo is fluent in French, English, Vietnamese (three major dialects), Chinese, German, and Russian. His American employees do not know that this gray-haired man with the cauliflower ears (he was champion flyweight boxer of the French Union Forces) and thick eyeglasses is one of the world's great authorities on Vietnamese history. They do not know he has refused the position of Minister of Education to Ngo Dinh Diem and later refused ambassadorial status under Ky.

"I did not agree with their policies. Therefore it was impossible for me to work for them. But the government lets me alone as long as I stay entirely out of politics. My job with the Americans is easy; and I make enough money to live on. I am not happy because my nation is badly governed. But my own life is well ordered, and I have my health and family. At night I work on my history."

Professor Vo is writing the History of Vietnam from 1940 to the Present. At 20 he was a student in Paris. He was an eyewitness to Ho Chi Minh's attempt to get Vietnamese independence at Versailles in 1919. He spent the World War II years in Saigon, Long Xuyen, and Hue.

Huu Te Ton was born in Haiphong in 1905. Her father was employed by the Customs Service and was moved to Saigon when Huu Te Ton was eight years old. In 1922 she went to France. At first she majored in Asian history, and then switched to medicine. In 1932 she was graduated from medical school. From 1934 until 1943 she practiced medicine in Saigon. The French police arrested her for aiding the freedom movement. She escaped to

Nhom Penh. After the war she returned to France. She came back to Vietnam in 1955; in 1959 she once more went to France, where she is today.

NGO DUC LIEU comes from near Hue. He is 49. He has a Master's degree in Philosophy which he earned at the University of Lyons. When Ngo Dinh Diem first came into power, he became an assistant to the Port Director of Saigon.

"None of us Vietnamese ever had heard of Ngo Dinh Diem before 1954—he was a product of American publicity. But we were told he was both anti-French and anti-Communist, which pleased us. Also he was chaste and moral in the Buddhist tradition. We accepted him sort of on probation—and I went to work for his administration. I soon learned the Customs was crooked. Also Madame Nhu wanted me to be payoff man to the Vietcong. She bribed them so they wouldn't molest her saw mill in the Highlands. When I protested I was arrested on the charge of being a Communist. I escaped and went to the NLF —who welcomed me."

Ngo Duc Lieu now owns a drugstore in Saigon.

"Mostly I deal in black market antibiotics—which come from U.S. Army stores. Of course my best customers are the NLF."

APPENDIX B

Documents

Declaration of The French Government on the Status of Indochina

Issued on March 23, 1945. Text translated from Notes Documentaires et Etudes, *No. 115, Serie Coloniale XV. Ministère de l'Information, Paris.*

The government of the Republic has always considered that Indochina was called upon to occupy a special place in the organization of the French community and to enjoy in it a freedom adequate to the degree of its evolution and capacities. The promise of it was made in the declaration of December 8, 1943. A little later the general principles enunciated at Brazzaville concretized the will of the Government.

Today Indochina is fighting; troops, French and Indochinese together, the elite and the peoples of Indochina, unaffected by the maneuvers of the enemy, are showing prodigious courage and are offering resistance in behalf of the cause which is the cause of the whole French community. Thus Indochina is acquiring new rights to the role it is called upon to play.

Confirmed by events in its earlier intentions, the Government considers it its duty now to define the status Indochina shall have when it is liberated from the invader.

The Indochinese Federation will comprise, together with France and the other sections of the community, a "French Union" whose foreign interests will be represented by France. Indochina will enjoy, within this Union, its own freedom.

The inhabitants of the Indochinese Federation will be Indochinese citizens and citizens of the French Union. In this capacity, without discrimination of race, religion, or origin, and with equality of merit, they will have access to all Federal posts and employment in Indochina and in the Union.

The conditions under which the Indochinese Federation will participate in the federal organisms of the French Union, as well as the status of the citizen of the French Union, will be fixed by the Constituent Assembly.

Indochina will have a federal government of its own presided over by the Governor General and composed of ministers responsible to him who shall be chosen from among the Indochinese as well as among the French living in Indochina. Under the Governor General, a Council of State will be charged with the preparation of federal laws and regulations. An Assembly elected according to the mode of suffrage most appropriate to each of the countries of the Federation and in which French interests shall be represented, will vote on taxes of every description as well as on the Federal budget, and will deliberate on proposed laws. Treaties of commerce and friendship concerning the Indochinese Federation shall be submitted to its examination.

Freedom of thought and belief, freedom of the press, freedom of association, freedom of assembly and, in a general way, democratic liberties, shall provide the basis of Indochinese laws.

The five countries composing the Indochinese Federation and differing among themselves in race and civilization and traditions, will preserve their own special character within the Federation.

The Governor General will, in the interests of each, be the arbiter over all. Local governments will be perfected or reformed; positions and employment in each of these countries will be specially opened to its own citizens.

With the aid of the mother country and within the general system of defense of the French Union, the Indochinese Federation will create its land, sea, and air forces, in which Indochinese shall have access to all grades and equality of qualification with personnel coming from the mother country or other parts of the French Union.

Social and cultural progress will be pursued and accelerated in the same direction as political and administrative progress.

The French Union will take all necessary measures to make elementary education compulsory and effective and to develop secondary and higher education. The study of local language and thought will be closely associated with French culture.

By putting into effect an independent and efficacious inspection of work and by trade union development, the well-being, social education, and emancipation of the Indochinese workers will be constantly sought.

The Indochinese Federation will enjoy, within the framework of the French Union, an economic autonomy which will enable it to attain its full agricultural development and to realize in particular the industrialization which will enable Indochina to handle its demographic situation. Thanks to this autonomy and beyond all discriminatory regulation, Indochina will develop its commercial relations with all other countries and especially with China, with whom Indochina, like the French Union as a whole, expects to have close and friendly relations.

The status of Indochina, such as has just been examined, will be established after consultation with the qualified organs of liberated Indochina.

Thus the Indochinese Federation, in the peace system of the French Union, will enjoy the freedom and organization necessary to the development of all its resources. It will be able to fulfill in the Pacific the role which belongs to it and to make felt in the whole of the French Union the quality of its elite.

Abdication of Bao Dai, Emperor of Annam

Carefully trained and educated in France from his earliest youth, Bao Dai assumed the position of Emperor of Annam in 1932, subject to the rule of the French Resident. He served the French as a puppet king and retained that position during the Japanese occupation. On August 25, 1945, he abdicated his throne with this remarkable declaration and in accordance with his wishes, the Government of the Republic of Viet Nam appointed him a counsellor of state in the new regime as plain M. Nguyen vinh Thuym. Text is translated from La République, *Issue No. 1, Hanoi, October 1, 1945.*

The happiness of the people of Viet Nam!
The Independence of Viet Nam!

To achieve these ends, we have declared ourself ready for any sacrifice and we desire that our sacrifice be useful to the people.

Considering that the unity of all our compatriots is at this time our country's need, we recalled to our people on August 22: "In this decisive hour of our national history, union means life and division means death."

In view of the powerful democratic spirit growing in the north of our kingdom, we feared that conflict between north and south would be inevitable if we were to wait for a National Congress to decide us, and we know that this conflict, if it occurred, would plunge our people into suffering and would play the game of the invaders.

We cannot but have a certain feeling of melancholy upon thinking of our glorious ancestors who fought without respite for 400 years to aggrandize our country from Thuan-hoa to Hatien.

We cannot but feel a certain regret over the thought of the twenty years of our reign during which it was impossible for us to render any appreciable service to our country.

Despite this, and strong in our convictions, we have decided to abdicate and we transfer power to the democratic Republican Government.

Upon leaving our throne, we have only three wishes to express:

1. We request that the new Government take care of the dynastic temples and royal tombs.

2. We request the new Government to deal fraternally with all the parties and groups which have fought for the independence of our country even though they have not closely followed the popular movement; to do this in order to give them the opportunity to participate in the reconstruction of the country and to demonstrate that the new regime is built upon the absolute union of the entire population.

3. We invite all parties and groups, all classes of society, as well as the royal family, to solidarize in unreserved support of the democratic Government with a view to consolidating the national independence.

As for us, during twenty years' reign, we have known much bitterness. Henceforth, we shall be happy to be a free citizen in an independent country. We shall allow no one to abuse our name or the name of the royal family in order to sow dissent among our compatriots.

Long live the independence of Viet Nam!

Long live our Democratic Republic!

Signed: BAO DAI

Hue, August 25, 1945.

Declaration of Independence of the Republic of Viet Nam

Issued at Hanoi, September 2, 1945, following establishment of the new republican regime. Text is translated from La République, *Issue No. 1, Hanoi, October 1, 1945.*

"All men are created equal. . . . They are endowed by their Creator with certain inalienable rights. Among these are life, liberty, and the pursuit of happiness."

These immortal words are from the Declaration of Independence of the United States of America in 1776. Taken in a broader sense, these phrases mean: "All peoples on earth are born equal; all peoples have the right to live, to be free, to be happy."

The Declaration of the Rights of the Man and Citizen of the French Revolution of 1791 also proclaimed: "Men are born and remain free and with equal rights."

These are undeniable truths.

Nevertheless for more than eighty years the French imperialists, abusing their "liberty, equality, and fraternity," have violated the land of our ancestors and oppressed our countrymen. Their acts are contrary to the ideals of humanity and justice.

In the political domain, they have deprived us of all our liberties.

They have imposed upon us inhuman laws. They have established three different political regimes in the North, the Center, and the South of Viet Nam in order to destroy our historic and ethnic national unity.

They have built more prisons than schools. They have acted without mercy toward our patriots. They have drenched our revolutions in rivers of blood.

They have subjugated public opinion and practiced obscurantism on the broadest scale. They have imposed upon us the use of opium and alcohol to weaken our race.

In the economic domain, they have exploited us without respite, reduced our people to the blackest misery and pitilessly looted our country.

They have despoiled our ricelands, our mines, our forests, our raw materials. They have retained the privilege of issuing banknotes and a monopoly of foreign trade.

They have invented hundreds of unjustified taxes, condemning our countrymen, especially the peasants and small merchants, to extreme poverty.

They have prevented our capital from fructifying; they have exploited our workers in the most barbarous fashion.

In the autumn of 1940 when the Japanese Fascists, with a view to fighting the Allies, invaded Indochina to organize new war bases, the French imperialists, on their knees, surrendered our country.

Since then, under the double Japanese and French yokes, our people have literally bled. The result has been terrifying. From Quangtri to the North, two million of our countrymen died of famine in the first months of this year.

On March 9, 1945, the Japanese disarmed the French troops. Once again, the French either fled or unconditionally surrendered. Thus they have been totally incapable of "protecting" us; on the contrary, in the space of five years they have twice sold our country to the Japanese.

Before March 9, the League of Viet-Minh several times invited the French to join it in struggle against the Japanese. Instead of responding to this appeal, the French struck all the harder at the partisans of the Viet-Minh. They went as far as to murder a large number of the political prisoners at Yen Bay and Caobang during their rout.

Despite all this, our countrymen have continued to maintain a tolerant and human attitude toward the French. After the events of March 9, the League of Viet-Minh helped many Frenchmen to cross the frontier, saved others from Japanese prisons, and besides protected the lives and property of all Frenchmen.

In fact, since the autumn of 1940, our country has ceased to be a French colony and became a Japanese possession.

After the surrender of the Japanese, our entire people rose to regain their sovereignty and founded the democratic Republic of Viet Nam.

The truth is that we seized our independence from the hands of the Japanese and not from the hands of the French.

The French fleeing, the Japanese surrendering, Emperor Bao Dai abdicating, our people broke all the chains which have weighed upon us for nearly a hundred years and made our Viet Nam an independent country. Our people at the same time overthrew the monarchical régime established for tens of centuries and founded the Republic.

For these reasons we, members of the Provisional Government, representing the entire population of Viet Nam, declare that we shall henceforth have no relations with imperialist France, that we cancel all treaties which France has signed on the subject of Viet Nam, that we abolish all the privileges which the French have arrogated to themselves on our territory.

All the people of Viet Nam, inspired by the same will, are determined to fight to the end against any attempt at aggression by the French imperialists.

We are convinced that the Allies who have recognized the principles of equality of peoples at the Conferences of Teheran and San Francisco cannot but recognize the independence of Viet Nam.

A people which has obstinately opposed French domination for more than eighty years, a people who during these last years ranged themselves definitely on the side of the Allies to fight against Fascism, this people has the right to be free. This people must be independent.

For these reasons, we, members of the Provisional Government of the Democratic Republic of Viet Nam, solemnly proclaim to the entire world:

Viet Nam has the right to be free and independent and is, in fact, free and independent. All the people of Viet Nam are determined to mobilize all their spiritual and material strength, to sacrifice their lives and property, to safeguard their right to liberty and independence.

Hanoi, September 2, 1945

Signed: Ho Chi Minh, *President.*

Tran Huy Lieu, Vo Nguyen Giap, Chu Van Tan, Duong Duc Hien, Nguyen Van To, Nguyen Manh Ha, Cu Huy Can, Pham Ngoh Thach, Nguyen Van Xuan, Vu Trong Khanh, Pham Van Dong, Dao Trong Kim, Vu Din Hoc, Le Van Hien.

Agreement between France and Viet Nam

Signed at Hanoi March 6, 1946. Text translated from the Bulletin Hebdomadaire, *No. 67, Paris, March 18, 1946, Ministère de la France d'Outremer.*

1. The French Government recognizes the Republic of Viet-Nam as a Free State having its Government, its Parliament, its army, and its finances, and forming part of the Indochinese Federation and the French Union.

With regard to the unification of the three Ky (Nam-ky, or Cochin China, Trung-ky, or Annam, Bac-Ky, or Tonkin), the French Government undertakes to follow the decisions of the people consulted by referendum.

2. The Government of Viet Nam declares itself ready to receive the French army in friendly fashion when, in accord with international agreements, it relieves the Chinese troops. An annex attached to the present preliminary convention will fix the terms under which the operation of relief will take place.

3. The stipulations formulated above shall enter into effect immediately upon exchange of signatures. Each of the contracting parties shall take necessary steps to end hostilities, to maintain troops in their respective positions, and to create an atmosphere favorable for the immediate opening of friendly and frank negotiations. These negotiations shall deal particularly with the diplomatic relations between Viet Nam and foreign states, the future status of Indochina, and economic and cultural

interests. Hanoi, Saigon, and Paris may be indicated as the locales of the negotiations.

Done at Hanoi, March 6, 1946.*

Signed: Sainteny,
Ho Chi-Minh,
Vu Huong Khanh.

* There was an appendix to this agreement which guaranteed the departure of French troops within five years.

Declaration of the Viet Nam Government on the Franco-Viet Nam Conflict

Issued at Hanoi, January 6, 1947. Text, slightly abridged, is translated from a release of the Viet Nam News Service in Bangkok, dated January 25, 1947.

1. The Viet Nam Struggle for Independence

At a time when the democratic powers have just emerged from a long war against fascism, Viet Nam, victim of French colonial aggression, must still defend itself with arms. It is no longer necessary to emphasize the misdeeds and crimes of that particular form of colonialism, upon its constant and deliberate attempt to poison an entire people with alcohol and opium, its policy of exploitation, pressure, and obscurantism imposed upon Viet Nam by a handful of colonialists and from which the French people themselves have derived no real benefit. Suffice it to recall that since the French conquest more than three-quarters of a century ago, the people of Viet Nam have never ceased striving to regain their independence. The long list of uprisings and revolts, although harshly quelled, have marked this painful period without interruption and have demonstrated the invincible strength of our national spirit.

2. The Viet Nam Democratic Republic

During the recent world war, French colonialists, who considered nothing but their own selfish interests, betrayed the Allied cause. Not only did they yield Indochina to the Japanese but after allowing them to enter Tonkin˙ (June, 1940) they further cooperated with them by signing a pact with them for the "common defense of Indochina." Viet Nam, on the contrary, very quickly ranged itself on the side of the democratic nations and actively participated in the struggle against Japanese fascism.

With a *coup de force* on March 9, 1945, the Japanese Army entirely eliminated French administration throughout the territory of Indochina but Viet Nam resistance, far from giving up, continued with increased intensity. On August 18, 1945, Japan having capitulated to the Allies, the Viet Nam resistance came out of the wilds and installed themselves in Hanoi, the capital, where they seized the sovereign power. The government of Ho Chi Minh was unanimously acclaimed and recognized throughout the country, in Bac Bo (Tonkin), Trung Bo (Annam), Nam Bo (Cochinchina). On September 2, 1945, amidst unprecedented popular enthusiasm, the Democratic Republic of Viet Nam was solemnly proclaimed.

Thus after eighty years of struggle . . . the Viet Nam Republic was born and the independence of its people regained.

3. Franco–Viet Nam Agreements

As a result of the landing of French troops in Nam Bo (Cochinchina) to undertake the reconquest of this country by force of arms, war broke out in that part of Viet Nam on September 23, 1945. Viet Nam resisted this rash attempt to reinstall the old French colonialism. The war was about to extend to Bac Bo (Tonkin) in 1946 when French troops were getting ready to enter there to relieve the Chinese troops and the Viet Nam Government was determined to oppose this entry in this part of its territory. However, to avoid further bloodshed and convention of March 6, 1946, with representatives of the French with a sincere desire for peace and willingness to collaborate with the French, President Ho Chi Minh signed the preliminary Government. By the terms of this preliminary convention:

(1) Viet Nam was recognized as a Free State, with its own government, parliament, army, and finances, forming part of the Indochinese Federation and the French Union.

(2) A referendum would be held in Cochinchina to allow its people to decide their own political status (i.e., whether to join Viet Nam or remain autonomous).

(3) Hostilities would cease on all fronts and troops on both sides would remain in their respective positions. The relief of the Chinese troops would be effected by 15,000 French and 10,000 Viet Nam troops respectively.[*]

(4) Negotiations would be opened immediately, bearing principally upon the diplomatic relations of Viet Nam with foreign nations, the future status of the Indochinese Federation and the question of French economic and cultural interests in Viet Nam.

[*] From an annex to the March 6 agreement.

As a result, a Franco-Viet Nam conference took place at Fontainebleau in June and July 1946, but it failed because of the excessively wide divergencies between the points of view of the two delegations and especially because of the maneuvers of the colonialists, viz:

(a) The setting up on June 1, 1946—the very day following the departure of President Ho Chi Minh and the Viet Nam delegation enroute to France—of the autonomous state of Cochinchina with a puppet government nominated by the French authorities.

(b) The meeting at Dalat of the so-called Federal Conference on August 1, sponsored by the same authorities and which, when it convened, comprised hand-picked delegates not only from Cambodia and Laos, but also from Cochinchina, Southern Annam, and the Highlands.

Despite all this, President Ho Chi Minh, to avoid a complete rupture between the two countries, signed with the French Government on September 14, 1946, a modus vivendi (1) providing for a mixed commission to settle urgent questions provisionally; (2) ordering cessation of hostilities on both sides in Nam Bo (Cochinchina); (3) guaranteeing the population of this region the enjoyment of democratic liberties.

Thus the way was paved for the next Franco-Viet Nam conference, scheduled for January, 1947.

4. *Sabotage of Agreements by French Representatives in Viet Nam*

The March 6 convention and the modus vivendi of September 14 were systematically sabotaged by the colonialists. Documents signed by the highest representatives of France in Viet Nam and the innumerable violations by these representatives of their signed agreements indisputably prove their fixed design to re-establish purely and simply the old French domination over this country. By their policy of "fait accompli" they tried to make the agreements null and void. By their policy of force they hoped to terrorize the population, annihilate all vestiges of resistance and prove to Viet Nam the necessity for submission.

The violations of these agreements and the maneuvers aimed at disrupting Viet Nam's unity and undermining the sovereignty of the Free State (are shown by) the following facts:

(1) Continuation of hostilities in Nam Bo (Cochinchina) and in the south of Trung Bo (Annam).

(2) Atrocities and terrorism perpetrated under the name of "mopping up operations" and "maintaining law and order," such as bombardments, burning of villages, massacring the civil population, mass arrests, arbitrary execution of patriots.

(3) Creation of the autonomous State of Cochinchina with a puppet government named by the French authorities.

(4) Occupation of the Highlands of Trung Bo (Annam).

(5) The attempt to re-establish under the name of Indochinese Federation the old regime under the Governor General, a kind of super-state aimed at stifling the Free State of Viet Nam.

(6) The arbitrary setting up of the organization of Federal Commissioners for Finance, Justice, Political Affairs, Economic Affairs.

(7) Institution of the so-called Federal Customs, Federal Sûreté, Federal Ports, and the totally unjustified control of imports and exports at Haiphong.

In the garrison areas where the French "relief" troops were or believed themselves to be sufficiently strong, they provoked almost daily incidents calculated to furnish a pretext for the employment of force, either to terrorize the population or to occupy a locality. They instituted a system of provocations, assassinations, and aggressions pursued by their own military forces in the streets of Hanoi over a period of more than three weeks in November and December, 1946, both against the civilian population and the Viet Nam police. In the incidents of December 17 and 18, 1946, at Hanoi, several quarters of the city were subjected to cannon fire and ransacked. Numerous Viet Nam civilians, the majority women and children, had their throats cut. Further, the French attacked and occupied the port of Haiphong following the incidents of November 20, 1946, after blockading the same port. No clearer proof of French premeditation can be furnished than their cold, systematic and calculated attack on Haiphong and the successively more exacting ultimatums of the local French command.

From the end of November, 1946, the incidents and provocations multiplied and took an exceptionally grave turn, seriously jeopardizing public order in Hanoi itself despite the urgent and constant appeals and protests of the Viet Nam Government for restoring a calm situation. The local French authorities evidently wanted an armed conflict so as to present the Blum Government with a *fait accompli*. To the efforts by

Viet Nam at conciliation, they replied with fresh provocations, viz: the aforementioned incidents in Hanoi on December 17 and 18, 1946; the occupation of the Secretariat buildings of two Viet Nam ministries in the same city; the unacceptable ultimatums of December 18 and 19, 1946, demanding the destruction of Vietnamese defense works, disarmament of Viet Nam military forces, and the handing over of the police services to the French command during the night of December 19, 1946, when the latter had already completed all its preparations.

5. Viet Nam Appeals to the World

The era of colonial conquest and domination is over. Viet Nam is firmly resolved to persevere to the very end in her struggle for her most sacred rights, viz., the territorial integrity of her country and her political independence. . . . The Viet Nam Government in signing the agreement of March 6, 1946, offered France a policy of open door and cooperation. Yet the representatives of France in Indochina have sought to render this policy abortive in the hope of re-establishing over Viet Nam the old regime of domination which was for them a veritable monopoly of exploitation. . . .*

* These documents were gathered by Harold R. Isaacs. A complete selection is in the book he edited: *New Cycle in Asia*, Macmillan, New York, 1947.

APPENDIX C

The Geneva Agreement

The Geneva Agreement, which was signed on 20 and 21 July 1954 by the representatives of France, Great Britain, the Soviet Union, the People's Republic of China, the three Associated States, and the Vietminh Government, was worded as follows:

"(1) The conference takes note of the agreements ending hostilities in Cambodia, Laos, and Vietnam, and organizing international control and supervision of the execution of the provisions of these agreements.

(2) The conference expressed satisfaction at the ending of hostilities in Cambodia, Laos, and Vietnam. It expresses its conviction that the execution of the provisions set out in the present declaration and in the agreements on the cessation of hostilities will permit Cambodia, Laos, and Vietnam henceforth to play their part, in full independence and sovereignty, in the peaceful community of nations.

(3) The conference takes note of the declarations made by the Governments of Cambodia and Laos (see below) of their intention to adopt measures permitting all citizens to take their place in the national community, in particular by participating in the next general elections, which, in conformity with the Constitution of each of these countries, shall take place in 1955 by secret ballot and in conditions of respect for fundamental freedoms.

(4) The conference takes note of the clauses in the agreement on the cessation of hostilities in Vietnam prohibiting the introduction into Vietnam of foreign troops and military personnel, as well as of all kinds of arms and munitions. It also takes note of the declarations made by the Governments of Cambodia and Laos of their resolution not to request foreign aid, whether in war material, personnel, or instructors, except for the purpose of the effective defence of their territory and, in the case of Laos, to the extent defined by the agreements on the cessation of hostilities in Laos.

(5) The conference takes note of the clauses in the agreement on the cessation of hostilities in Vietnam to the effect that no military base at the disposition of a foreign State may be established in the regrouping zones of the two parties, the latter

249

having the obligation to see that the zones allotted to them shall not constitute part of any military alliance and shall not be utilized for the resumption of hostilities or in the service of an aggressive policy. The conference also takes note of the declarations of the Governments of Cambodia and Laos to the effect that they will not join in any agreement with other States if this agreement includes the obligation to participate in a military alliance not in conformity with the principles of the U.N. Charter or, in the case of Laos, with the principles of the agreement on the cessation of hostilities in Laos, or, so long as their security is not threatened, the obligation to establish bases on Cambodian or Laotian territory for the military forces of foreign Powers.

(6) The conference recognizes that the essential purpose of the agreement relating to Vietnam is to settle military questions with a view to ending hostilities, and that the military demarcation line should not in any way be interpreted as constituting a political or territorial boundary. It expresses its conviction that the execution of the provisions set out in the present declaration and in the agreement on the cessation of hostilities creates the necessary basis for the achievement in the near future of a political settlement in Vietnam.

(7) The conference declares that, so far as Vietnam is concerned, the settlement of political problems, effected on the basis of respect for the principles of independence, unity, and territorial integrity, shall permit the Vietnamese people to enjoy the fundamental freedoms, guaranteed by democratic institutions, established as a result of free general elections by secret ballot. To ensure that sufficient progress in the restoration of peace has been made, and that all the necessary conditions obtain for free expression of the national will, general elections shall be held in July, 1956, under the supervision of an International Commission composed of representatives of the member States of the International Supervisory Commission, referred to in the agreements on the cessation of hostilities. Consultations will be held on this subject between the competent representative authorities of the two zones from July, 1955, onwards.

(8) The provisions of the agreements on the cessation of hostilities intended to ensure the protection of individuals and of property must be most strictly applied and must, in particular, allow everyone in Vietnam to decide freely in which zone he wishes to live.

(9) The competent representative authorities of the northern and southern zones of Vietnam, as well as the authorities of Laos and Cambodia, must not permit any individual or collective reprisals against persons who have collaborated in any

way with one of the parties during the war, or against members of such a person's family.

(10) The conference takes note of the declaration of the French Government to the effect that it is ready to withdraw its troops from Cambodia, Laos, and Vietnam at the request of the Governments concerned and within a period which shall be fixed by agreement between the parties, except in the cases where, by agreement between the two parties, a certain number of French troops shall remain at specified points and for a specified time.

(11) The conference takes note of the declaration of the French Government to the effect that, for the settlement of all problems connected with the re-establishment and consolidation of peace in Cambodia, Laos, and Vietnam, it will proceed from the principle of respect for the independence, sovereignty, unity, and territorial integrity of Cambodia, Laos, and Vietnam.

(12) In their relations with Cambodia, Laos, and Vietnam, each member of the Geneva Conference undertakes to respect the sovereignty, independence, unity, and territorial integrity of the above-mentioned States, and to refrain from any interference in their internal affairs.

(13) The members of the Conference agree to consult one another on any questions which may be referred to them by the International Supervisory Commission in order to study such measures as may prove necessary to ensure that the agreements on the cessation of hostilities in Cambodia, Laos, and Vietnam are respected."

French, Cambodian and Laotian Declarations

The following declarations were issued by the French, Cambodian and Laotian Governments:

France. "The Government of the French Republic declares that it is ready to withdraw its troops from Cambodia, Laos, and Vietnam at the request of the Governments concerned and within a period which shall be fixed by agreement between the parties, except in the cases where, by agreement between the two parties, a certain number of French troops shall remain at specified points and for a specified time."

The second paragraph of the French declaration was that referred to in paragraph (11) of the eight-nation declaration—see above.

Cambodia. "With the aim of assuring harmony and unanimity among the people of the Kingdom, the Royal Government of Cambodia declares itself willing to take all necessary measures to integrate all citizens, without any discrimination, in the national community, and to guarantee them the enjoyment of all rights and liberties provided for in the Constitution of the Kingdom. It also confirms that all Cambodian citizens will be able to participate freely, both as voters and candidates, in general elections to be held by secret ballot.

The Royal Government of Cambodia is resolved never to take part in an aggressive policy and never to permit the territory of Cambodia to be utilized in the service of such a policy. It will not join in any agreement with other States if this agreement carries for Cambodia the obligation to enter into a military alliance not in conformity with the principles of the U.N. Charter or with the principles of the agreement on the cessation of hostilities, or, as long as its security is not threatened, the obligation to establish bases on Cambodian territory for the military forces of foreign powers.

The Royal Government is resolved to settle its international disputes by peaceful means, in such a manner as not to endanger peace, international security, and justice.

During the period which will elapse between the date of the cessation of hostilities in Vietnam and that of the final settlement of political problems in Cambodia, the Royal Government will not solicit foreign aid in war material, personnel, or instructors, except for the purpose of the effective defence of its territory."

Laos. A declaration similar to the Cambodian was issued by the Royal Government of Laos, which undertook not to request foreign aid "except to the extent defined by the agreement on the cessation of hostilities."

It also stated that the Laotian Government would "promulgate measures with a view to setting-up, during the period between the cessation of hostilities and the holding of general elections, a special delegation attached to the administration of the provinces of Phong-Saly and Sam-Neua for the benefit of those Laotian nationals who did not participate in the fighting on the side of the Royal forces." (The two provinces were those which had been designated as "regrouping areas" for the Laotian rebel forces who had fought with the Vietminh.)

Unilateral U.S. Declaration

The following unilateral declaration by the U.S. Government was issued by Mr. Bedell Smith (Under Secretary of State):

"The Government of the United States, being resolved to devote its efforts to the strengthening of peace in accordance with the principles and purposes of the United Nations;

Takes note of the agreements concluded at Geneva on July 20 and 21, 1954, between (*a*) the Franco-Laotian Command and the Command of the People's Army of Vietnam [i.e. the Vietminh military authorities]; (b) the Royal Cambodian Command and the People's Army of Vietnam; (c) the Franco-Vietnamese Command and the Command of the People's Army of Vietnam; and of paragraphs (1) to (12) inclusive of the declaration presented to the Geneva Conference on July 21, 1954;

Declares with regard to the aforesaid agreements and paragraphs that:

(1) It will refrain from the threat or the use of force to disturb them, in accordance with Article 2 (4) of the U.N. Charter dealing with the obligation of members to refrain in their international relations from the threat or use of force; and

(2) It would view any renewal of aggression in violation of the aforesaid agreements with grave concern and as seriously threatening international peace and security.

In connexion with the statement in the declaration concerning free elections in Vietnam, my Government wishes to make clear its position, which it has expressed in a declaration made in Washington on June 29, 1954 [by President Eisenhower and Sir Winston Churchill] as follows: "In the case of nations now divided against their will, we shall continue to seek to achieve unity through free elections, supervised by the U.N., to ensure that they are conducted fairly.'

With respect to the statement made by the representative of the State of Vietnam [see section "Reactions in Indo-China" below], the United States reiterates its traditional position that peoples are entitled to determine their own future and that it will not join in an arrangement which would hinder this. Nothing in this declaration is intended to, or does, indicate any departure from this traditional position.

We share the hope that the agreements will permit Cambodia, Laos and Vietnam to play their part, in full independence and sovereignty, in the peaceful community of nations, and will enable the peoples of that area to determine their own future."

Main Provisions of Cease-fire Agreements

(Never officially published, they are given here as reported in the U.S., French, and British press.)

Partition of Vietnam. The State of Vietnam would be partitioned into two approximately equal areas by a demarcation line near the 17th Parallel, the northern part (including the ports of Hanoi and Haiphong) passing under the control of the Vietminh Government and the southern part remaining under the control of the Vietnamese Government.

Regrouping Areas. French Union forces north of the demarcation line (e.g. those in the Red River Delta), and Vietminh forces south of that line, would be concentrated in regrouping areas and would be withdrawn from North and South Vietnam respectively within 300 days.

Vietnam Elections. Elections would be held simultaneously in both parts of Vietnam by July 20, 1956, with the aim of establishing a unified Government. They would be organized after consultation between the Vietminh and Vietnamese Governments, and carried out under the supervision of an International Supervisory Commission consisting of India, Canada and Poland.

Supervision of Armistice. International armistice commissions (one for each of the Associated States), consisting of representatives of India, Canada and Poland, would supervise the implementation of the cease-fire agreements and ensure, *inter alia*, that there were no military reinforcements by either side during the armistice. The more detailed work of supervising the withdrawals to regrouping areas would be left in the main to mixed commissions of representatives of both sides. The Indian member would be chairman of each of the three commissions.

Cambodia. The independence and political integrity of Cambodia would be recognized by the Vietminh Government, and all Vietminh forces would be withdrawn from the country.

Laos. The independence and political integrity of Laos would similarly be recognized by the Vietminh, who would withdraw all its forces from the country. The Laotian "dissidents" (i.e. the supporters of the pro-Vietminh *Pathet Lao* movement) would for the time being be concentrated in the north-eastern provinces of Phong-Saly and Sam-Neua and would remain under their own control, though under the supervision of a Laotian Government delegation. These areas would subsequently be reintegrated with the Kingdom of Laos after elections to be held in 1955.

Foreign Bases. No foreign bases would be established in any of the Associated States. This would not apply, however, to the existing French bases at Savannakhet and Xieng Houang, in Laos, nor to the French Expeditionary Force, which would continue to remain in South Vietnam.

Other Provisions. War prisoners and civilian internees on both sides would be liberated within 30 days; political reprisals would be prohibited, both against individuals and their families; and exchanges of prisoners-of-war and civilians wishing to move from the Communist to the non-Communist side, and *vice versa*, would be carried out without impediment.

APPENDIX D

Congressional Record, 90th Congress, 1st Session,
Vol. 113, no. 147. Washington, Tuesday, Sept. 19,
1967, concerning aid program mismanagement.

VIETNAM

Mr. Riegle. Mr. Speaker, I ask the attention of all
those who are in the Chamber at this time to the remarks that I
will be offering in the next few minutes. The subject upon which
I am about to speak is Vietnam. My remarks concern the fact
that I think significant new information on the Vietnam problem,
the Vietnam war, is now available and needs to be aired. These
new facts are objective; they are the truth. I think they stand on
their own, irrespective of who may stand here in the well and
present them.

The facts I refer to come from testimony offered on the
question of Vietnam before the Foreign Operations Subcommittee of the Committee on Appropriations. This testimony was
taken in May of this year and was released, publicly, this last
week. The committee hearings I feel contain some very important disclosures, so significant and important that I have
taken this time today on the House floor to present this information in detail to my colleagues.

By way of background, let me say that I serve on the
Foreign Operations Subcommittee of the Committee on Appropriations and in May of this year Mr. Poats, who previously was
the Administrator of our U.S. economic program in South
Vietnam for 3 years, appeared before our subcommittee to
discuss that program for the coming fiscal year.

Mr. Speaker, when I learned that Mr. Poats was to
testify before our subcommittee, I made an effort to gather all of
the information heretofore assembled on the subject of our
economic program in South Vietnam, to analyze this information, to cross-reference it, and to develop specific testimony
which would try to establish once and for all—for the record—
whether the alleged mismanagement of the AID program in
Vietnam was fact or fiction.

Some 18 different sources were used in preparation for cross-examination. These 18 sources are now cited on page 986 of the committee print. They range from the Moss report with which many of us are familiar, to five heretofore classified and secret reports which have been declassified are now available in the public record, as they ought to be.

By arrangement with my subcommittee chairman, the gentleman from Louisiana [MR. PASSMAN], I was granted the opportunity to cross-examine Mr. Poats on the basis of this information for some 3½ hours. I wish to extend here and now my deep appreciation and feeling for the conscientious approach of my subcommittee chairman and for the great privilege he afforded me as a freshman Member of this body to conduct an examination on so serious a subject. This testimony is contained in the book labeled "Foreign Assistance and Related Agencies Appropriation 1968, Hearings Before a Subcommittee of the Committee on Appropriations, House of Representatives, 90th Congress, First Session, Subcommittee on Foreign Operations and Related Agencies," part II, "Economic Assistance."

Mr. Speaker, the critical testimony to which I wish to refer in the minutes just ahead extends from page 986 to 1069 of the hearings.

In discussing this testimony, I am going too talk primarily about the economic program in Vietnam and will not refer in any detailed way, to our military effort in Vietnam.

Now, let us think for just a moment about what it means to have objective testimony on this subject from Mr. Poats who as I say for the past 3 years has been the No. 1 man overseeing our economic program, the so-called "other war" in Vietnam. He is the ranking administrative spokesman on this issue, who because of his work and in recognition of his ability to understand the situation, was just promoted by the President of the United States to the No. 2 spot in the Agency for International Development and is now Deputy Director of AID.

Mr. Speaker, when Mr. Poats appeared before our subcommittee he not only was the top man in this area of the conduct of the "other war" in Vietnam but he was fresh from the field, fresh from 3 years of direct experience in this area. His prior background was as a newsman and his views as documented in the testimony are as candid and objective as one might expect from a man of that background.

Mr. Speaker, I further feel it is important that we note that after offering his testimony, some 90 pages thereof, Mr. Poats had an opportunity in later weeks to sit down and confirm and discuss every single statement he made in the record. He had the opportunity to decide whether he really meant what he said under cross-examination. There was an opportunity for him to further elaborate upon and to revise the wording of any statement which he had made, but which he thought might be misconstrued. He had the opportunity to "classify it" and take it off the record or to work out compromise language. In many instances compromise language was worked out. But, upon reflection, he decided to leave most of his original statements in the record. I think that is significant.

What does his testimony establish? When I began my questioning in this area, I was concerned about documenting the alleged inability of our aid program in Vietnam to work, and I might say that the testimony very quickly began to establish the fact that our aid program is an administrative nightmare. There is ample documentation of mismanagement. To prove this and test out this premise, was like shooting fish in a barrel. This is what we found in the subcommittee. However, as the questioning went on, other imminently more important conclusions began to come to light, conclusions that I feel are profound, and add a brandnew perspective to the Vietnam situation.

The two main conclusions that developed from this testimony are these—and these are not my conclusions—these are the conclusions of Mr. Poats, the top man in this whole area of conducting the economic program in Vietnam.

First. That the South Vietnamese lack the commitment in this war—that we need to win the war—it just does not exist.

Second. If our economic program in South Vietnam is ever going to succeed, it is only going to succeed because we completely Americanize it from beginning to end.

What does this mean? It means there is not the indigenous wherewithal in South Vietnam to get this job done—the job of meeting shared objectives necessary to win the "other war."

Now you say, can this be so? I mean—is this an admission that we can believe? That it is now a matter of public record? The answer is—very frankly—yes. And these are not my statements. This is not my subjective opinion—these are Mr. Poats' objective statements. And the ranking administration spokesman in this area acknowledges very candidly that the South Vietnamese commitment to the war effort is so inadequate that the annual U.S. $200 million commodity import program in Vietnam is actually a political ransom paid to powerful South Vietnamese commercial interests to insure political stability in South Vietnam and to insure continued support of the war by these South Vietnamese commercial interests, and two, that only by totally Americanizing the U.S. economic program in South

Vietnam would the AID program be able to achieve its goals of significantly improving the quality of life of the South Vietnamese—a policy incidentally that will make South Vietnam permanently dependent upon U.S. subsidy.

Let me just give you some direct quotes from the record of this committee print which was made available to the press on Friday of last week.

This is on page 1022, and I am speaking to Mr. Poats and I say the following:

MR. RIEGLE. You are saying in essence then, if this war were conducted in a way that required greater economic sacrifices by certain elements in Vietnam, the political instability is such that the country might fly apart; is that right?

Mr. Poats answered: Exactly.

I responded: That, to me, is a most discouraging thing.

Then Mr. Poats said: Fear of violent political repercussions or even personal physical attack has sometimes prevented forceful Vietnamese government action in collecting taxes. A minister once described these personal threats in a conversation with me.

I then said: What that says, in other words, is that with our Commodity Import Program we are really paying a price for political stability. That is what it says.

And Mr. Poats responded: That is what it is.

Mr. Speaker, it is a ransom, it is a ransom that we must pay to prop up a house of cards in Vietnam. And I said at that point in the testimony: I object to that.

The gentleman from Louisiana [MR. PASSMAN], our subcommittee chairman, then said: I am frustrated, discouraged, and disappointed after hearing this testimony this morning, so much so that I am frightened. We have an unmanageable mess.

Then from page 1023 of the testimony I quote:

MR. RIEGLE. We are continuing the CIP program at a very substantial level. I assume we do that only because we cannot force on the people of South Vietnam a higher degree of sacrifice than they are willing to make at this point.

MR. POATS. We cannot force the kind of tax collections that is required to reduce the requirement for this substitute device.

MR. RIEGLE. That is right. So, the people with the wherewithal in South Vietnam are unwilling to pay for any more of this war than they are now paying for, and we have to supply the balance.

MR. POATS. They have increased the tax payments, of course. The nouveau riche, the fellows profiteering from the

258

American military presence, running the bars, cabarets, and so on, are not being taxed adequately.

On page 1025 of the testimony:

MR. RIEGLE. We are talking about motivation now, and we are talking about what motivates these commercial leaders in the non-combat areas. Are we not saying, essentially, that they do not really have the level of commitment that they need to have to get this job done?

MR. POATS. Right.

Mr. Speaker, it is clear that they do not have a level of commitment necessary to get the job done.

And on page 1060, again I was speaking to Mr. Poats:

MR. RIEGLE. It seems to me that we have just established in this colloquy that if we were to withdraw our AID program, that the government would likely collapse over there, and for all intents and purposes the war would be over. Namely, short of a tremendous initial or additional military effort, we would not be able to continue to maintain any sort of operation in this country. Is that so?

MR. POATS. That is what I have said in effect, yes.

What does that mean? It means there is not enough South Vietnamese commitment to this effort. It seems to me that if we want to continue to have the support of the all-powerful commercial interests in Vietnam to the war, and their commitment to the stability of the Government, we have got to be willing to pay ransom, and where does that come from? It comes from the pockets of the American citizens, and that is not all of the ransom, because just last week we lost 247 American boys in Vietnam from every part of this country, and yet we now learn that we do not have a sufficient commitment from the South Vietnamese to even begin to win the economic war. What a sorry state of affairs.

On the Americanization of the war, of the economic war, on page 1043 in this testimony I received the following answers —and bear in mind that these answers do not come from some flunky in the State Department offering some observations and assessments, this is the administration's top man in this area, the President's appointee who is making these points.

On page 1043 I said to Mr. Poats: Coming back to the point of management and the fact that we established this as more or less a shared job, that we cannot do it by ourselves and repeatedly we have expected South Vietnam to sort of bridge with us in doing the job, and we found for many reasons they were not able to deliver on their side, do you think it will be possible for us to really sustain a much-expended effort over there until this basic problem is resolved?

Mr. Poats answered: I think it will be necessary to use Americans increasingly in operational jobs as distinguished from advisory jobs.

I then said: In other words, if it will become a greater program it will have to be a bigger American program?

His response was: Yes, American and other foreign.

On page 992 of the testimony Mr. Poats said at this point: We are to an increasing degree, putting in Americans and other foreigners to do these jobs for the Vietnamese.

On page 993 I said to Mr. Poats: Is there a way we can combat that and try to save those dollars which are lost in terms of this inability of hooking up with the South Vietnamese in some areas?

Mr. Poats' response was: We are combating it by introducing more foreigners into the system at all possible levels.

For example, we have put enormous numbers of people into warehousing and commodity management in the past year. We have put over 1200 foreign medical personnel, including nurses and technicians, into the medical system.

He continued: We have put people into the provinces in considerable numbers. At first we had only one aide, a provincial representative. Now we may have as many as a score of foreigners working on civilian affairs in some provinces.

On page 1001 Mr. Poats said again: We are still increasing the American participation in what are normally the host government responsibilities.

So I ask you, Are we building self-sufficiency out there? I asked that question of the top man in this area who just returned from 3 years in this field. His very candid admission is, Of course we are not. Words to the contrary are a facade.

I state one other quotation at this time. This comes on page 1001 under the heading of "Lack of Vietnam Self-Sufficiency." And I say at this point:

The thing that concerns me the most is this: If we cannot establish some sort of balance between self-sufficiency, on the one hand, a growing self-sufficiency, versus a growing dependency, then we will never get out of this situation. We will be mired down there forever.

It seems to me that all the evidence that piles up on the military side and on the nonmilitary side shows that the Vietnamese, rather than becoming more self-sufficient, more independent and better able to manage these problems, that systematically in area after area we are constantly having to act in their behalf and plug the holes in the dike militarily and nonmilitarily.

I then asked Mr. Poats: Is that a fair conclusion in your judgment?

He said: That is certainly a danger, and in some instances a fair conclusion. It is a dilemma arising in part from the fact that we set standards of performance and integrity which are not native to Vietnam, and particularly not achievable by that country with its own manpower and leadership and management in this chaotic situation today.

I then said: It seems to me that the conclusion we are reaching is that to ever really get on top of this thing from a management point of view, we virtually have to be in every step of the program from beginning to final implementation.

As you say, we have unused supplies sitting out in village hospitals, and construction equipment ready to build schools that is gathering rust. Does this not mean that there is an absence there and probably we are going to have to fill it finally?

MR. POATS. Yes.

That is the story. What has gone into Vietnam so far? Some $100 billion thus far. We will invest this year a quarter of our national budget, some $30 billion. Over 13,000 American men have been killed. There have been some 90,000 American casualties. Why have we invested all this military effort? There are over one-half million American troops over there now, nine divisions. Why? We have done this, as I have listened to the arguments of the administration, to create a military shield, a temporary military shield, so that South Vietnam can have a chance to develop its own self-sufficiency, that it can have a chance to develop its economic capability and its independence.

But what does the record show as admitted by the top man in this field? That basically the South Vietnamese are not becoming more self-sufficient. Rather, the reverse is true. They are becoming more and more dependent. The South Vietnamese economy is growing fat on a U.S.-financed war economy, the people in the noncombat area actually need a ransom in order to continue their commitment to this war that our boys are fighting in their behalf.

So as things stand presently, the other war is not being won, and with these conditions it cannot be won.

What then does this mean for our military shield? Have we seen the end of it? Of course we have not. We know there has been a request for more troops. We do not know how many more troops will be asked beynod the 45,000 recently asked for. But we know this, that as long as South Vietnam is unable or unwilling to develop itself and stand on its own two feet, that we are going to have to continue to act in their behalf and do for them what they will not do for themselves.

That means that from a military point of view we are at the mercy of the enemy, because they control the initiative. If they decide to keep the pressure on, and if we decide to continue to meet their pressure, we are going to have to keep our men there indefinitely. It will be the enemy who determines how many men we have there, by the amount of pressure they put on us. I think that is a poor way to maintain a foreign policy.

What has to happen in the light of these new facts and these disclosures? First, let us face these facts. Let us be willing to reappraise our foreign policy. The stakes are too high to perpetuate a policy based on myth or wishful thinking. Frankly, the policy today is not working. We all know that. There is not anybody in the country who would dispute that.

We need to encourage public discussion. This new, confirmed information has got to be incorporated in the dialog, because I think it makes a difference in assessing the problem. I think the South Vietnamese have to care enough, and this has to mean enough to them that they are willing to put everything they have got on the line. I do not think we ought to put everything we have got on the line if they are not willing to do the same.

And, unfortunately, we do not get that much good information. We talk about managed news. It is almost impossible to get factual information on Vietnam. Here is 90 pages worth. It is 90 pages, not from the third ranking or the 10th ranking or the 15th ranking man in this area, but it is from the top man. He admits we are losing the other war.

These are facts that have meaning to me. And when we finished this testimony, I made five specific recommendations, and they have all been accepted by the subcommittee and are presently being implemented by the administration.

One is for an annual presentation of the entire Vietnam AID program to the Congress for an evaluation of its effectiveness. If we are not getting the job done, let us pin this down. Let us not have to wring out the truth like we did in this testimony.

Second, we have got to have a complete GAO audit of the field program. There had not been an audit of this, and I am happy to say it is now underway in Vietnam. We will now find out where these commodities are going. Mr. Poats admitted that many of our AID drugs had gone to the Vietcong and had been found in their caches that have been uncovered. How unfortunate.

Third, a 5-year plan to show how we are phasing out our economic program and transferring this responsibility to the

Vietnamese. We have to develop this plan, or we will not begin this necessary transfer.

Fourth, a recommendation that our subcommittee go to Vietnam and study these AID procedures in the field and recommend changes on the basis of what they find. This has been agreed to.

Fifth, a study of the ability to buy American commodities for use in Vietnam within the limits of economic sense. We found that AID is now buying from other suppliers around the world, and that we have not been able to rely on the quality of these purchases. We have been cheated time and time again.

I am going to submit for the RECORD the rest of the significant quotes—in my judgment, significant quotes—in this testimony, to have it in the CONGRESSIONAL RECORD. I urge every Member to read and study this testimony and draw his or her own personal conclusions based on this new information.

It seems to me there is something else that comes out of this, and that is that we need a new policy in Vietnam. I think it has to be an "either/or" policy with respect to the South Vietnamese power structure and their inadequate commitment, because America's military involvement in Vietnam has been justified on the basis that it is only an interim action designed to provide a temporary protective shield while South Vietnam works to achieve economic and military and social and political self-sufficiency.

It is now clear that South Vietnam has become dependent upon the United States for its economic support and internal development, and that on that basis the U.S. military forces will be required indefinitely to support the present policy and economic structure in Vietnam. This is unsatisfactory.

I talked to Gen. Lew Walt just last week, who is back from Vietnam, from the Corps I area. I asked him: How long are we going to have military actions out there to win control of this situation?

He said: Twelve to fifteen years.

This testimoney shows that the only possible hope in Vietnam now is to secure an immediate all-out commitment from the South Vietnamese. They must knuckle down and clear the decks and undertake urgent reforms needed to build national self-sufficiency.

I believe that without these changes the United States is left with two choices.

One of these is to either indefinitely send U.S. troops to defend a South Vietnam which is growing fat on a U.S.-financed war economy in Vietnam, a Vietnam that would be unable to hold any victory won by American forces and whose weakness would require a permanent U.S. occupation force.

Or, No. 2, to negotiate the best possible arrangements and to begin to withdraw our troops.

There is now clear evidence that the South Vietnamese are not pulling their share of the load in the war there. They are pulling less and less of their share of the load each day. I believe it is time we asked the South Vietnamese to make total, all-out, across-the-board commitment. If they should refuse, then I believe we must begin a systematic military withdrawal.

The stakes are too high. This is their war. They have to fight it.

Yes, we can help, but only if they are willing to help themselves, and at the present time they are not getting their share of the job done, and they evidence no interest in wanting to get it done.

Am I saying so? I am quoting Mr. Poats who has said so.

We cannot permit this to continue.

There are many specific reforms needed in South Vietnam today, and urgently needed. They ought to be implemented tomorrow morning.

What are they?

Higher taxes.

The profiteering is unconscionable in the noncombat areas. The South Vietnamese are gearing up to a prosperous standard of living in the noncombat areas that cannot be sustained and cannot be justified.

I say that it is time the South Vietnamese got just as tough as the North Vietnamese. If the North Vietnamese can implement these sorts of policies, disciplining their national resources, why cannot the South Vietnamese?

We need rationing in South Vietnam. We need price controls. We need to restrict our commodity import program to absolute necessities and to quit sending in luxury items.

We have got to require that they clamp down on the black market. I know of no publicity of a black market in North Vietnam.

There are reforms needed in the Government of South Vietnam. If South Vietnam is going to get its share of the job done, it needs new people and new purpose in its Government.

More of the U.S. aid being pumped in there has to find its way out to the villages. The testimony would make you sick, in terms of where our aid assistance goes. Does it get to the little fellow in the village, where the struggle for commitment is going on out in the villages of Vietnam? No, it does not, only a tiny trickle finds it way there.

South Vietnam has to be willing to go on a total war footing. Either this war is worth it or it is not. It has to be worth it to the South Vietnamese first.

So I am going to place in the RECORD today seven sections, which are quotes from this committee testimony.

The first is entitled "Insufficient South Vietnamese Commitment to War Effort."

The second is entitled "Americanization of 'Other War.'"

The third is entitled "Policy of Growing Americanization of the War; Overruling of Recommendations of Field Administrators."

The fourth is entitled "Mismanagement of Drugs Abuses; Overconsumption of Wide Spectrum Antibiotics in Vietnam."

Section 5 is entitled "Impact of Aid Program on Average Vietnamese Citizen."

Section 6 is entitled "Mismanagement of Aid Program in Vietnam."

Section 7, finally, is the "Recommendations" and their rationale and intent.

These seven sections are presented in detail at the end of these remarks.

Mr. Speaker, it nets out to be the fact that we have to look the truth in the eye. I would not presume to stand in the well of this House as a single Member of Congress, whether I had been here for 2 weeks or for 50 years, and say to you I think I have access to the total truth about Vietnam, or on any other issue for that matter. I do not pretend to have it today. Rather I call your attention to the truth as it is offered to us by the top man in the administration who understands and has lived with the "other war," the economic war in South Vietnam, the man who said very candidly on the public record that we are losing that war.

The SPEAKER pro tempore (MRS. MINK). The time of the gentleman has expired.

(MR. RIEGLE asked and was given permission to proceed for 2 additional minutes.)

MR. RIEGLE. We are not building South Vietnamese self-sufficiency today, I am sorry to say. The war cannot be justified on that basis. As I have said earlier, if there is no change in the South Vietnamese commitment, we ought to start bringing our boys home. If there are strategic reasons that are so overriding and fundamental that we have to hold this piece of real estate regardless of the cost, let the administration say so and make the argument on the basis of that truth and not on the basis of the present myth. Let us recall that we are spending $30 billion a year, 25 percent of our national budget, 500,000 troops there today, with over 13,000 killed and 90,000 casualties. And this war is just beginning. These are the facts. We look here at home and we see that we do not have enough nursing homes, we do not have enough classrooms and we cannot begin our job-training programs. We have sprawling slums that pockmark every city in the country. The list is endless of things which we have to do here which we cannot do at home partly because we are investing $30 billion a year in Vietnam. If there is a strategic overriding reason, let us hear it. If the President is willing to come here and make the argument that it is worth holding Vietnam whatever it costs, whether it is $40 billion, $50 billion, or $60 billion, and whatever the troop commitment may be, then let us recognize that fact and justify it on that basis. Certainly the South Vietnamese are not concerned enough to make an equivalent commitment. I happen to think that the justification does not exist. But my mind is open. If that case can be made, then the administration should make it. Certainly let us not continue to proceed on the basis of a faulty rationale when the facts stand out as clear as light that there is just not the wherewithal in South Vietnam and the commitment to this struggle necessary to bring this thing to a conclusion. Let us either reconcile ourselves to being there forever or let us decide that it is time we take a new look at this commitment, and develop a new policy based on reality.

Mr. Speaker, I am now inserting the seven sections of testimony referred to earlier:

The first is entitled "Insufficient South Vietnamese Commitment—to War Effort":

[P. 1021 and 1022]

MR. POATS. In Korea during the Korean war, prices increased 2,400 percent in 3 years, 7½ times in 1 year. That is real runaway inflation. In Vietnam it is a high but manageable level of inflation.

MR. RIEGLE. If that happened in Korea, if the rate of inflation were that dramatic, we still managed to hang on in Korea and they were able to withstand inflation many times greater than this. What is to say this country could not do the same thing? It seems to me what is happening is that this country, by controlling its inflation more effectively than Korea did, is getting rich at the same time that it is waging war. I am not suggesting that the whole country is getting rich because I am sure that the poor villager out in the hamlet is on the receiving end of all which is unfortunate and unhappy in the country. It appears to me that somebody is profiting greatly in Vietnam. Is this a fair statement?

MR. POATS. Yes. Let me answer the first part of your statement first, though.

In Korea you had a simple, clear external aggression, a unified South Korea fighting a unified action against that aggression. It was a short war, 3 years.

These people in Vietnam have been involved in war off and on now since 1946. There is not nearly the unity in South Vietnam that we had in Korea.

MR. RIEGLE. I am just talking about the inflation problem.

MR. POATS. I know. I am saying the political and social fabric that we are supporting in Vietnam is not nearly so cohesive and strong or resilient as in Korea.

MR. RIEGLE. You are saying, in essence, then, if this war were conducted in a way that required greater economic sacrifice by certain elements in Vietnam, the political instability is such the country might fly apart, is that right?

MR. POATS. Exactly.

MR. RIEGLE. That, to me, is a most discouraging thing.

MR. POATS. Fear of violent political repercussions or even personal physical attack has sometimes prevented forceful Vietnamese Government action in collecting taxes. A minister once described these personal threats in a conversation with me.

MR. RIEGLE. What that says, in other words, is that with our CIP program we are really paying a price for political stability. That is what it says.

MR. POATS. That is what it is.

MR. RIEGLE. I object to that, and I am surprised somebody else does not, too.

LACK OF NATIONAL PRIDE

MR. PASSMAN. I am frustrated, discouraged and disappointed after hearing this testimony this morning, so much so that I am frightened. We have an unmanageable mess. I do not think it is getting any better even though I think you people are trying. Unless you can get the South Vietnamese themselves to recognize that they have something to save for themselves and for their children, I do not believe we will ever get on top of it.

Undoubtedly we have failed in our program out there to generate any patriotism or pride that would make them want to defend their country. I did not think it was possible for us to get ourselves involved in this type of mess.

[P. 1023]

MR. RIEGLE. We are continuing the CIP program at a very substantial level. I assume we do that only because we cannot force on the people of South Vietnam a higher degree of sacrifice than they are willing to make at this point.

MR. POATS. We cannot force the kind of tax collections that is required to reduce the requirement for this substitute device.

MR. RIEGLE. That is right. So, the people with the wherewithal in South Vietnam are unwilling to pay for any more of this war than they are now paying for, and we have to supply the balance.

MR. POATS. They have increased the tax payments, of course. The nouveau riche, the fellows profiting from the American military presence, running the bars, cabarets, and so on, are not being taxed adequately. . . .

MR. RIEGLE. Suppose we were to announce—we are not going to, but I am wondering what you think the practical impact would be if we said: "Look fellows, the free lunch is over. We are going to stop this inflation control program. We are going to stop the CIP program other than for just those very few essential items like certain key drugs and things that are absolutely vital. The rest is gone. All discretionary items are going to be stopped. You will have to live with your inflation."

What would happen? Would these fellows then get their demonstrators in the streets and we would have a political crisis? Is this your expectation?

[P. 1024]

MR. POATS. There would be much more radical price rises and acute shortages and widespread criticism, not only of the Vietnamese Government, but of the U.S. Government, I suspect. I do not think that they could physically, technically, adequately increase their tax collection to deal with the problem.

MR. RIEGLE. What does that mean, though? You are saying that the people with the wherewithal in South Vietnam are just not willing to pay the price of this war. Is that not what you are saying? Up to a point they will pay it, and beyond that point, if the price is higher, we must pay it?

INADEQUATE TAX COLLECTON PROCEDURES

MR. POATS. It is partly that and partly the inadequate Government machinery for tax collection.

MR. RIEGLE. If the Government's survival depends upon its ability to organize and go out and collect taxes, it would be my intuitive feeling that they would make it a priority assignment and they would go out and get organized and collect them. I think they could solve that part of the problem in a crisis.

The other part, whether the people consent to pay when

the Government taxman knocks at the door, is really the relevant part of the question.

MR. POATS. * * * One of my views has been that they should radically increase the tax staff relative to other elements in the civil government, sending people from the military services in this function. . . .

[P. 1025]

MR. RIEGLE. It strikes me along the lines of the chairman's recent comment that maybe their level of commitment to this struggle, the struggle we are investing some 275 American lives a week in, is not the same as ours. Maybe these South Vietnamese commercial interests really do not give a damn.

LACK OF NATIONAL SUPPORT FOR WAR

MR. POATS. I cited some evidence to the contrary a moment ago. I think none of us is satisfied with the degree of national mobilization for war in Vietnam. I think it is improving. I think it has improved to the degree that you have stable government. We had a period of a succession of coups from November 1963 until June 1965, when government virtually disintegrated, and with that, of course, goes a breakdown of morale and willingness to contribute on the part of the whole public.

MR. RIEGLE. That is right. Have we not established that one of the key reasons we do not have that same breakdown in government happening today is the fact that we have decided to pump in hundreds of millions of dollars of CIP ransom, or whatever you want to call it, to essentially keep certain commercial interests happy enough that they will not get their sympathizers out in the streets and bring down the Government?

MR. POATS. I think that is slightly harsh, maybe more than slightly harsh.

MR. RIEGLE. It may be more than slightly harsh, but it is essentially true, is it not?

MR. POATS. There is certainly a substantial element of truth in it, the Government of Vietnam has not been able to mobilize national support in the way of sacrifices by individuals, financial sacrifices, on the order desirable.

MR. PASSMAN. Or necessary. . . .

MR. RIEGLE. We are talking about motivation now, and we are talking about what motivates these commercial leaders in the noncombat areas. Are we not saying, essentially, that they do not really have the level of commitment that they need to have to get this job done?

MR. POATS. Right.

[P. 1058 and 1059]

MR. RIEGLE. What measures do we have? What specific evidence do we have that our nonmilitary program has in fact speeded up the military solution? On what basis do we have any reason to believe that we have achieved ° ° °.

MR. POATS. There would not be military action by the Vietnamese military forces today had it not been for our provision of commercial imports.

MR. RIEGLE. You are saying they would have thrown in the towel altogether?

MR. POATS. The inflation, disruption, loss of morale would have been such as to have destroyed the Vietnamese military effort and would have changed the whole nature of our prospects there.

Secondly, I think we would have had much more severe——

EFFECT OF COMMODITY IMPORT PROGRAM
ON CONTINUITY OF GOVERNMENT

MR. RIEGLE. What is there inherent in our flooding commodities into this country which has stiffened the willingness of the Vietnamese soldier to go out and fight for his country?

MR. POATS. Because he knows that his salary is worth something. He knows that the people back home, his relatives and friends, are able to eat and afford to buy goods, and you do not have the political agitators seeking a different kind of solution from the one we are seeking, capitalizing upon the distress of runaway inflation and acute shortages of critical goods which otherwise would have occurred.

The Ambassador has repeatedly stated that this is the fact, that without this program the Vietnamese couldn't have carried on.

MR. RIEGLE. If I come back around the other way, then, if we were just to subtract the American capability from the picture, you are telling me that these people would be overrun tomorrow?

MR. POATS. No.

MR. RIEGLE. Not overrun necessarily because of the lack of strength of the military effort but they would decide the fight was not worth it?

MR. BUNDY. May I comment? I want to take it broadly.

MR. RIEGLE. Let me hear Mr. Poats' comment first.

MR. POATS. Yes, it is my view and the view of the Ambassador repeatedly stated that the social and economic distress which would have been caused by these acute shortages would have reflected against our interests and our own troops as well as the total war effort.

After all, this inflation is largely fueled by American military piaster spending in Vietnam.

MR. RIEGLE. What you are saying is that if suddenly we were to subtract the American propping up of this effort, that really the will of the South Vietnamese to defend their country from the aggression would just disappear and this country would be lost tomorrow?

MR. POATS. Not tomorrow, but it certainly would be weakened so severely as to greatly reduce our prospects of success.

MR. RIEGLE. What that really says is that there is not enough today which is indigenous to Vietnam in the eyes of the Vietnamese to really be worth a struggle.

MR. POATS. I think they feel they are in a joint effort with us.

MR. RIEGLE. We just said if we do not make it a joint effort, if we substract our participation, then they will throw in the towel. Is that what we have just said?

MR. POATS. I didn't say throw in the towel. I said this would so undermine the capacity of the Government to maintain stability and to get the support and commitment of people and to keep the Army fighting that it would greatly reduce our prospects of success in the whole war effort.

[P. 1060]

MR. RIEGLE. It seems to me that we have just established in this colloquy that if we were to withdraw our AID program that the Government would likely collapse over there and for all intents and purposes the war would be over. Namely, short of a tremendous initial or additional military effort we would not be able to continue to maintain any sort of operation in this country. Is that so?

MR. POATS. That is what I have said in effect, yes.

The second is entitled "Americanization of 'Other War'":

[P. 902]

MR. POATS. Many of the decisions (regarding AID management decisions) are made on the basis of a country team judgment by the whole U.S. establishment there and by the whole U.S. establishment concerned with Vietnam in Washington. They do not always give top consideration to management questions.

Usually the leading considerations are political, psychological support of the military effort, and stabilization.

The other problem is manpower, as I mentioned.

We could, of course, and we are to an increasing degree, putting in Americans and other foreigners to do these jobs for the Vietnamese, and we are doing that in areas where we think we can do it without a net political liability. However, we cannot do it in many of these areas I have been discussing. It would not be politically effective in the pacification program to substitute Americans and simply demonstrate that Americans are effective, efficient, generous, and so on. That will not accomplish the political purpose.

MR. RIEGLE. I tend to agree with you. When you institute a program, in hopes that the South Vietnamese will implement it as you expect they will, and then they do not, do you find this creates political and psychological disadvantages, perhaps a stage or two later, which is worse than if we had left the situation alone?

CHANGES IN VIETNAMESE GOVERNMENT PERSONNEL

MR. POATS. Yes; it can. Sometimes it creates conflict between us and the Vietnamese Government over a failure on one part to live up to one side of the bargain. One of the great problems has been that there has been such a tremendous turnover in the Vietnamese Government at all levels.

There have been times when literally only a half dozen Vietnamese officials have been available to deal with the economic problems we have been confronted with, on stabilization, industrial development, and so on, or on other financial policy aspects of the civil programs.

These people sometimes leave on short notice and there is no replacement for a period of weeks or months. A new man comes in and has to get his feet on the ground.

MR. RIEGLE. How can you build a contingency into the AID program to anticipate this? We are at a point where the pressure on dollars is so great for domestic programs and for military requirements in Vietnam that it seems we are at a point where we cannot really afford the luxury of that kind of slippage.

Is there a way we can combat that and try to save those dollars which are lost in terms of this inability of hooking up with the South Vietnamese in some areas?

MR. POATS. We are combating it (South Vietnamese inability to do their share) by introducing more foreigners into the system at all possible levels.

For example, we have put enormous numbers of people into warehousing and commodity management in the past year. We have put over 1,200 foreign medical personnel, including nurses and technicians, into the medical system.

We have put people into the Provinces in considerable numbers. At first we had only one AID Provincial representative. Now we may have as many as a score of foreigners working on civil affairs in some Provinces. These people are getting out and working down at the district level. They are watching the commodities and helping the Vietnamese manage programs. . . .

[P. 1043]

Mr. Riegle. Coming back to the point of management and the fact we established this is more or less a shared job, that we cannot do it by ourselves and repeatedly we have expected South Vietnam to sort of bridge with us in doing the job, and we found for many reasons they were not able to deliver on their side, do you think it will be possible for us to really sustain a much expanded effort over there until this basic problem is resolved?

Mr. Poats. I think it will be necessary to use Americans increasingly in operational jobs as distinguished from advisory jobs.

Mr. Riegle. In other words, if it will become a greater program it will have to be a bigger American program?

Mr. Poats. Yes, American and other foreign.

[P. 1000]

Mr. Riegle. Is there evidence to indicate that there have been seriously inadequate controls in regard to commodity imports?

Mr. Poats. Yes; I think our controls in late 1965 and the first half of 1966 were inadequate. The controls that we had in effect then were the conventional standard AID worldwide systems. They were not adequate for the special problems of a radical buildup in this program in Vietnam at that time, and particularly inadequate given the wide disparity between the realistic exchange rate, which is not the same as the black market rate, and the official rate at that time. This promoted and induced abuses.

There was also inadequate Vietnamese Government staff to carry its part of the responsibility.

[P. 1000 to 1001]

Mr. Riegle. Based on the conclusion that you just stated a moment ago we apparently were not able to tool up fast enough on the management side. In other words, the size of the program, the incremental increase in the program, was so substantial that even though, we took these staffing steps they were short of the mark. We still were not able to get on top of it.

Mr. Poats. That is right.

Mr. Riegle. Have we caught up yet? Are we on top of it today?

Mr. Poats. Largely on top of it today. We are still making changes in the procedures. We are still increasing the

American participation in what are normally the host government responsibilities.

MR. RIEGLE. This is the thing that really worries me, and I also see the same thing happening on the military side. I see it now in the pacification area. We have expected the South Vietnamese to step up to share this responsibility. For whatever the reason, they have not been able to do it. Systematically, in area after area, we have had to move in.

At first, on the military side, we were the advisers, and the Vietnamese were doing the fighting. Now it is almost the reverse, we do most of the fighting, and they do the advising, in a sense.

The same thing seems to be happening in the nonmilitary area as well.

MR. PASSMAN. That is a good statement.

MR. RIEGLE. The thing that concerns me. the most is this: If we cannot establish some sort of balance between self-sufficiency on the one hand, and growing self-sufficiency, versus a growing dependency, then we will never get out of this situation. We will be mired down there forever.

[P. 1002]

It seems to me all the evidence that piles up on the military side and on the nonmilitary side shows that the Vietnamese, rather than becoming more self-sufficient and more independent and better able to manage these problems, that systematically in area after area we are constantly having to act in their behalf in plugging holes in the dike, militarily and nonmilitarily.

Is that a fair conclusion in your judgment?

MR. POATS. That is certainly a danger and in some instances a fair conclusion. It is a dilemma arising in part, from the fact that we set standards of performance and integrity which are not native to Vietnam, and particularly not achievable by that country with its own manpower and leadership and management in this chaotic situation today.· . . .

MR. RIEGLE. It seems to me that the conclusion we are reaching is that to ever really get on top of this thing from a management point of view, we virtually have to be in every step of the program from beginning to final implementation.

As you say, we have unused supplies sitting out in village hospitals, and construction equipment ready to build schools that is gathering rust. Does this not mean that there is an absence there and probably we are going to have to fill it finally?

MR. POATS. Yes.

The third is entitled "Policy of Growing Americanization of the War; Over-Ruling of Recommendations of Field Administrators":

[Pp. 1003–1004]

OVERRULING OF RECOMMENDATIONS OF FIELD ADMINISTRATORS

MR. POATS. We have before us right now a request from the U.S. Civil Operations Office for a very large increase in its foreign staff to do a better job at the province and district level. We will try to provide these people—civilians, as much as possible, using AID recruiting devices and to the extent we cannot the military will provide them.

AID VOICE IN VIETNAMESE POLICY

MR. RIEGLE. At some point is it likely, or does AID have the responsibility, or the authority for that matter, to throw the red flag up and say to the policymakers, whether they be in the State Department or whether they be somewhere else in the executive branch, that perhaps we are crossing a line in terms of Americanizing this entire operation in Vietnam and we can never come back, we will get so far down that road that any chance of South Vietnamese self-sufficiency developing out there is going to die. It is going to be smothered, smothered by our totally moving in.

MR. POATS. It is difficult to answer this without appearing to be putting the onus on various other people.

MR. RIEGLE. Do not worry about that. I think the onus should be placed where it belongs.

MR. POATS. It is a combined judgment. Most of these questions have come up one at a time, ad hoc, and they are decided that way largely. There have been times in which AID has declared a resistance to a particular proposal. The general disposition has been to say, "How can you possibly argue that to withhold——?

MR. RIEGLE. General disposition by whom?

MR. POATS. Of the U.S. Government, the administration.

MR. RIEGLE. What part of the administration are we speaking about? The State Department?

MR. POATS. The basic Vietnam matters have been decided over the years by a Vietnam interagency group composed of representatives of the various agencies involved. Defense, State, AID, USIA, CIA, and the White House staff. Some of these things come to National Security Council attention. Some go to the President personally. Many are decided in the field and come in as a joint message or message from the country team with the Ambassador and the question is whether to oppose them.

MR. RIEGLE. Were there ever occasions when you were in charge of the AID program in Vietnam where you felt that we were moving into an area, taking this incremental step of Americanization of this whole process, where you threw up the red flag?

MR. POATS. Yes.

MR. RIEGLE. I would be interested in knowing when. If it is confidential we will take it off the record later.

MR. POATS. It is confidential, ——.

MR. RIEGLE. Before we get into the cases, I am interested more now in terms of the line of command. In other words, when you had this feeling, to whom did you communicate this feeling?

MR. POATS. Either to colleagues on the Vietnam Interagency Committee at a meeting or in a memorandum to the AID Administrator.

MR. RIEGLE. Did you send memorandums of this kind from time to time?

MR. POATS. Yes.

[P. 1005]

Obviously, I raised the red flag on some things from an AID point of view, from my view of the politics of the situation as well. When I raise questions of a political nature, obviously, I am not the final authority; or from a military point of view.

MR. RIEGLE. Let us come back to some of these times where you threw the red flag because you were concerned as the AID Administrator for this region with your ability to take on projects and do them effectively at that time.

I would like, Mr. Chairman, if it is appropriate for me to ask it, to see some of those memos that were sent not so much from the point of view of probing those specific situations, but I think we have to begin to pin down this process that is taking place, the overall decisionmaking process, where an AID Administrator in the field who has the basic responsibility for seeing the program work, when he is concerned that something new is not going to work, I want to know how and why it is that these recommendations are overridden. I want to know who overrides them.

[P. 1006]

All right. I want to make it clear I am not asking for this for the printed record. I am asking for it for the confidential use of the committee.

I want to say, too, in fairness to Mr. Poats, that I think it is very much in the interest of the American people for us to know about letters of this kind where the red flag was thrown. If possible, put them in the record.

MR. PASSMAN. I want to say that we should not be deprived of this information; we hope it will be forthcoming.

(NOTE.—None of the requested information was provided.)

The fourth is entitled "Mismanagement of Drugs Abuses; Overconsumption of Wide Spectrum Antibiotics in Vietnam." There are the drugs that end up with the Vietcong, which our American taxpayers pay for and send over there. It is unbelievable, but true. The section follows:

OVERCONSUMPTION OF WIDE SPECTRUM
ANTIBIOTICS IN VIETNAM

MR. RIEGLE. In this report it was concluded that the amount of wide spectrum antibiotics was apparently out of all size in relationship to the need. It showed kilo consumption (per thousand unit consumption) of 25,000-plus in South Vietnam, whereas in Taiwan the consumption was 3,500, and in the Philippines 2,000. Yet the populations of Taiwan and the Philippines are as large as Vietnam or larger and presumably their need is not substantially different.

This report also concluded that this amount of wide spectrum antibiotics could be misused and lead to illnesses, deaths, and things of this kind.

The pharmaceutical report also makes the observation that while there did not seem to be an apparent need in South Vietnam for this volume of antibiotics that they noted that the Vietcong do have a very grave requirement for wide spectrum antibiotics. The inference is that perhaps some of these drugs go over to the Vietcong.

Then we note the price paid for these antibiotics. If you take them by category, and I will refer to the exhibit I have just submitted for the record, the first one is tetracycline, where it cost us $245 per thousand units here whereas the cost of that same wide spectrum antibiotic in Europe would be $59.

[P. 1008]

MR. RIEGLE. Let us take the case of these antibiotics. What is happening to all these wide-spectrum antibiotics that are being consumed and sold?

MR. POATS. The reason the consumption is so large is that the Vietnamese Government is not enforcing its regulations requiring doctors' prescriptions for the use of these antibiotics. It has not been enforcing them.

MR. RIEGLE. Any citizen can buy antibiotics?

Mr. Poats. That is right.

Mr. Riegle. In unlimited quantities?

Mr. Poats. No, they are limited. The drugstores do limit them to individuals. But he can come in tomorrow and buy another bottle, and so on.

Mr. Riegle. That is not really an effective limitation?

Mr. Poats. No.

[Pp. 1009 to 1010]

Mr. Riegle. I want to summarize my thinking on this and then I want to yield back to the chairman. What this says is that we have not been able to sufficiently manage our flow of antibiotics in the country to stop the flow of, in your words, substantial quantities of these drugs to the other side where they have been warehoused and presumably used. What this gets down to is that the Vietcong, presumably Vietcong and North Vietnam regulars that have been shot up or hurt, have had access to these drugs in order to get well and come back out and mow our fellows down.

Mr. Poats. That is true of military supplies as well as pharmaceuticals.

Mr. Riegle. That is true, but military supplies are very different. When you are out on the field of battle if a man gets shot and drops his gun and somebody else picks it up, that is one thing. Hospital supplies as a general rule are different. But our hospitals as a general rule are not overrun and sacked so that it is very different. It is far more reasonable to assume that a certain amount of guns would get away from us than large quantities of drugs. We can control the drugs.

Mr. Poats. We have lot numbers on these drugs and we can trace whether they were commercial imports, project commodities, or military supplies. We have a breakdown which I will supply you.

Mr. Passman. Would the gentleman yield for a brief statement?

Mr. Riegle. Surely.

REDUCTION IN SUPPLY OF ANTIBIOTICS

Mr. Passman. It would appear to me that you have a perfect way to control this problem. Let us take the Philippines versus South Vietnam.

For one antibiotic I note the per capita consumption in Vietnam was about 12 times that of the Philippines. Why would you not ascertain from the other countries in that area what the civilian consumption of these particular drugs per capita would be? Then double that amount for safety, but do not ship in 12 times what is being used on a per capita basis in a nearby similar country.

It is just a question, it would appear to me, of not having any idea of the need. You did not study the statistics and you just shipped in the drugs. I think you will find, repeating if I may, that the shipments or consumption is 12 times that of the Philippines. It simply means to me that you provide this drug without having any guidelines whatsoever as to the requirements.

MR. RIEGLE. If you yield yield?

MR. PASSMAN. I yield back.

MR. RIEGLE. The population of the Philippines is roughly twice that of South Vietnam.

MR. PASSMAN. Then consumption in Vietnam would be about 24 times that of the Philippines. There is no justification for that type of waste. You could have very easily ascertained from the Philippines or Taiwan what the normal per capita consumption of this particular biotic would be. If you wanted to, for a safety measure double that amount for South Vietnam but not 24 times the amount.

MR. POATS. May I comment on these points? We sent out an expert in this field last summer to do just this kind of study from which these figures are drawn. From that study we concluded that we should cease financing these wide spectrum antibiotics and we should get controls established by the Vietnamese Government as to the quantities they would finance and get controls as to the sales through the retailers. This is being done. I cannot tell you that these controls at the retail level are adequate yet as to the quantities and whether that increases the Vietcong access to them.

MR. RIEGLE. You say that we have been able to more or less gage the caches of these drugs that have gone over the other side and been squirreled away that we uncovered. What percent of those captured drugs do you say can be identified by code numbers? What percentage of these drugs have been AID drugs as opposed to military drugs?

MR. POATS. I have a recent paper summarizing this whole question of the findings of the caches and percentages from each source of the types of pharmaceuticals.

MR. RIEGLE. What is the rough percentage of the AID contribution?

MR. POATS. My memory is it was as high as 30 percent in the caches found in the fall of 1966.

[P. 1012 to 1013]

MR. RIEGLE. Would you supply for the record the aggregate amount of wide spectrum antibiotics that have gone into Vietnam since 1960, the amount by year?

I want to see the buildup. This is what I worry about. I say to myself, how in the name of reason could we start to pump in large quantities of these pharmaceuticals without a commodity analyst on board to decide whether it is sound to do this? It seems to me we have the cart before the horse.

MR. POATS. We did not have any special analyst to review licenses.

MR. RIEGLE. Why?

MR. POATS. We do not have it in any country.

MR. RIEGLE. Why not?

MR. POATS. We do not because we operate on a system of agreements with a government in which it undertakes responsibilities and we do not attempt to move in and do the job of that government for it in this field. We changed this normal approach in Vietnam, beginning early in 1966.

MR. RIEGLE. There was no commodity program in recent years anywhere near the size of this one, was there, in 1965?

MR. POATS. It doubled from 1965 to 1966. It has been further increased. More than doubled. Here are some figures. For 1964, fiscal year, $9,037,000 of medical pharmaceutical products. In fiscal 1965, $13,216,000.

MR. RIEGLE. What that means is that we sent in over $13 million of pharmaceutical supplies when we did not have a qualified pharmaceutical commodity adviser or somebody who had the specific training and background to really assess whether that $13 million was appropriate or not for the job, or anything of the kind.

MR. POATS. That is right.

Section 5 is entitled "Impact of Aid Program on Average Vietnamese Citizen." This shows that the little fellow in Vietnam is being left out of this program. The section follows:

[P. 988]

PER CAPITA GAINS IN VIETNAM

MR. RIEGLE. If we take the figures for our expenditures at this time, take the aggregate aid assistance in all forms which have gone into this area, let us say for the past 20 years, it comes to a staggering sum.

Do we have any measurement as to exactly what this has done on a per capita basis for the little fellow in Vietnam, the peasant?

MR. POATS. The gage that was useful prior to the intensification of the war showed there was a steady increase in the per capita income of the country during the period from 1957 to 1960 when there was a fair amount of stability. In that period the per capita GNP was growing at a rate of about 5 percent. In that period there was a very substantial improvement in social services, education, and so on.

MR. RIEGLE. What I would like for the record would be the best expression that we have of what the per capita gains have done in Vietnam, let us say over the last 6 years.

MR. POATS. All right.

MR. RIEGLE. I would like to try to get those expressed in categories that really have meaning; in other words, not just in terms of increase in average earnings and average income but also what has happened to the median income, what has happened in the area of social services, such as schools, and what has happened in terms of the literacy rate.

MR. POATS. We cannot give you good data on recent income because there has been no adequate national income calculation during the war. It is impossible to make under the circumstances.

There was an attempt as late as 1962 to derive accurate figures for 1961. There has been no such attempt since then.

The staff engaged in that was dissipated. There were very few of them at the time and they are no longer in that unit of the Government.

(NOTE.—In response to the above request, AID provided only sketchy income information—indicates no measurement exists of alleged benefits to the Vietnamese people of continued AID assistance.)

[P. 1055]

Inflated Standard of Living in Urban Areas Versus Rural Privation—Failure of AID to Reach/ Improve Life of Villager.

MR. RIEGLE. One of the very striking parts of this—and this is a worry we all have, perhaps more acute with me than with others—is this:

This becomes doubly important when you look at the very vast difference between the kind of life the villager faces in Vietnam versus the style of living which is afforded now in Saigon. We see people in Saigon doing very well and living high off the hog. We see almost a minimal amount of our aid filtering its way out to the villager. This makes it doubly discouraging.

Does it to you?

MR. BUNDY. Yes, it does, but you have to reckon that something like this happens in wartime. I saw it happen to a degree in England during the war.

Section 6 is entitled "Mismanagement of Aid Program in Vietnam." In one instance here I ask:

How do we get rid of these excess supplies when that situation develops? I know there is a real bind on warehouse space. When we find that is true, what do we do, sell these excess supplies?

Mr. Poats answered: No. We build more warehouses. We built an enormous number of warehouses in the Saigon area.

The section follows:

(NOTE.—Numerous examples in the committee testimony document serious mismanagement of the Vietnam AID program—only three examples are illustrated below.)

[P. 1008]

DISPOSITION OF EXCESS SUPPLIES

MR. RIEGLE. How do we get rid of these excess supplies when that situation develops? I know there is a real bind on warehouse space. When we find that is true, what do we do, sell these excess supplies?

MR. POATS. No. We build more warehouses. We built an enormous number of warehouses in the Saigon area and have taken over some from the commercial community.

[P. 1027]

AUDITS OF CIP

MR. RIEGLE. Is that another way of saying there have been no GAO audits per se, of the commodity programs, apart from the system, in other words, of commodities per se?

MR. POATS. Not for quite a few years.

MR. RIEGLE. Do you think such an audit would be useful? In other words, would you feel better about the management of this program if GAO were to come in and do an independent audit, on a selective basis, of commodities?

MR. POATS. Yes, I think it would be useful.

MR. RIEGLE. I do, too.

MR. PASSMAN. I do too.

[P. 989]

OVERSATURATION OF AID

MR. RIEGLE. The next question is this; How much aid can a country like Vietnam absorb at one time: How much can we flush through their system and have it finally then work its way out into the hamlets where we really increase the quality of the life out there rather than setting people up in the city? Some people have suggested we have gone too far and it has almost reached the point of overkill in terms of pumping money in there. What would be your comment?

[P. 990]

MR. POATS. We are in several areas past the saturation point in terms of effective Vietnamese management . . .

[P. 991]

MR. RIEGLE. You said there were several areas of the AID program where essentially we were below the saturation point. What would be these areas?

MR. POATS. I think we have been attempting in many villages to provide supplies for construction where the local authorities did not have the management tools or skills or did not have, locally available, construction contractors qualified to properly do the particular job—where we have depended largely on the self-help principle which is a very sound one politically but is not necessarily the best way to build a structure.

We have provided feed for the pig corn program which was turned over to a series of individuals at various levels of government to supervise, and where many of these people were subsequently withdrawn from that service and taken off into the Army, or they quit and went to work to make more money.

We had trained teachers and medical health workers, to work in villages and district clinics. Those people have left these jobs to take higher paying jobs, or they have been drafted. We have continued to put in supplies into these clinics with sometimes inadequate management.

[P. 989]

I think that has happened from time to time in particular fields. For example, currently we are certainly putting more resources into Vietnam to operate medical assistance than the Vietnamese society, economy, and government can support. Consequently we have brought in foreigners to do it. This could not be sustained after the war and will have to be reduced.

We have put in more resources for various aspects of agricultural development at times than the Government institutions, the co-ops, credit organizations, and the Government extension workers could properly handle. . . .

[P. 992]

MR. RIEGLE. What percentage of our AID program really reflects activity which is taking place in an area faster than the ability of that sector to absorb that sort of help, things which would fall into this category of activity? Is it 20 percent? What would you guess would be the figure at the present time?

MR. POATS. It would be only a guess, Mr. Riegle. I would say it perhaps has been as high as 20 percent in pure management and economic terms, but I would not say it has been that high in terms of the political objectives of the United States in Vietnam.

Section 7, finally, is the "Recommendations" and their rationale and intent:

[p. 1066 to 1069]

BASIC RECOMMENDATIONS FOR MANAGEMENT
OF VIETNAM PROGRAM

MR. RIEGLE. Mr. Chairman, I am going to make some basic recommendations at this point that have grown out of my study of this information. I think they have been substantiated by what has gone in the record and I am going to ask you if you agree these things would be sound.

ANNUAL REVIEWS OF AID VIETNAM PROGRAM

First of all, I think it would be wise to have an annual program review of the entire AID Vietnam program. I think that program review ought to be made to the Congress. I do not mean made to the Congress in terms of a joint session but there should be a presentation made which would include the following things. I think it ought to be in quantitative terms and include all the various formal program categories you now do business in; such as economic stability, revolutionary development, and so forth, and break out the year's target objectives.

I think the cost of meeting that objective ought to be spelled out and at the end of the year we ought to have a review of the results. What are the tangible achievements and the cost to get them against the target or against what you expect to do?

I think we have to pin that down. I think we ought to go into that. Do you think this is a reasonable request?

MR. POATS. Yes; I think it is being done, to the degree the Congress is interested, in our appearances before the committees, and particularly the Subcommittee on the Far East of the House Foreign Affairs Committee. It has done this on more than an annual basis. The question of quantifying the target in a program such as revolutionary development we can quantify the RD program target for a year and show what was accomplished. I think this is perfectly reasonable, provided all concerned recognize the inevitable fluidity in the situation.

GAO AUDIT OF CIP PROGRAM

MR. RIEGLE. The second recommendation I would make is that I think we need a complete GAO audit of the CIP program, not from the point of view of the system but from the point of view of the specific commodities involved. I think a while ago you agreed this would be a useful thing to have.

MR. POATS. Yes, sir.

MR. PASSMAN. Let me say for the record, and, I hope the gentleman will agree that AID is a mess but all other spigots of aid are as bad or in a worse mess. Would you recommend this be all inclusive?

MR. RIEGLE. I would certainly be agreeable. I feel very strongly, based on what we have heard today, and Mr. Poats agrees, this sort of an audit would be useful. The fact that we agree on that now makes certain that it will take place?

MR. PASSMAN. Yes; I think it should be broader than just AID.

MR. POATS. GAO is a congressional agency.

MR. RIEGLE. How do we go about formally requesting it?

MR. PASSMAN. It will be very easy. We will go through the full committee chairman and request it.

MR. RIEGLE. Fine.

FIVE-YEAR LONG-RANGE PLAN

Thirdly, it also occurs to me it would be well for us to have a long-range plan. I mean a 5-year plan which, under the best assessment that we can make today, shows the planned transition of the AID-related activities and nonmilitary activities, the phaseout of these or the transfer of responsibility for these to the South Vietnamese as we go along. Is it possible to make this sort of projection?

MR. POATS. It is possible to make it and we have attempted it and this will be further refined by the Lillienthal study. Any such projection has to be based upon arbitrary assumptions about termination of the war, the way in which it is terminated, ——, the size of the continuing security problem, if one exists, and so on.

There are so many variables in it we have not thought it very helpful except in a broad sense of planning how we will go about sharing this burden in the post-war period.

MR. RIEGLE. I think we have to start pulling that sort of a plan together. We will never start making this transition otherwise. We may have to make some of this transition while the war continues.

MR. POATS. We are.

MR. RIEGLE. Let us make an effort to try to lay out a 5-year plan on that basis. Can you do that?

MR. POATS. We can. But you appreciate, Mr. Riegle, from some of your earlier questions, the data available in Vietnam to provide a base for such a plan, economic data, is inadequate.

MR. RIEGLE. That is right.

MR. POATS. I am simply saying that the projections we

produce and in quantitative terms are not going to be worth much by the time we get there. They will certainly give us some guidance on procedures and approaches to provide a transition, to bring other governments and other AID agencies into the act, related to the Asian Development Bank and other groups.

COMMITTEE TRIP TO VIETNAM

MR. RIEGLE. Mr. Chairman, it also occurs to me it would be well for members of this subcommittee to try to get out there this year and take a look at this. I for one would try to do that.

MR. PASSMAN. May I say to the gentleman I have been somewhat disheartened during the last 3 years. The attitude seemed to be this is what we want; this is what we are going to get, the committee notwithstanding. They must have thought they had a majority of the committee with them or they would not have taken that attitude. I now feel that we have some new friends on this committee. I am going to renew my effort to try to equal or surpass my effort in prior years just to point out what a mess we are really in. A lot of what you brought out today, I have had to associate myself with for 15 years but I have renewed hope now that we can find some open air and I think with the help of this committee, with the help of the GAO and with the approval of the chairman and all others interested, that we may be able to help AID get on top of this program. We will go there and I hope that we can spend whatever time is necessary in Saigon or in Vietnam.

MR. RIEGLE. I feel very strongly and personally the need to get some firsthand information. I would like to say to you today, and for the record, that I hope that I can go. I want to go. It seems to me, Mr. Chairman, that there is no more important official business for us than to try to get to the bottom of this thing.

MR. PASSMAN. I think that you are absolutely correct. I will cooperate and I am sure that the entire committee will.

PROCUREMENT FROM AMERICAN AND FOREIGN SOURCES

MR. RIEGLE. My final recommendation is one that the chairman made earlier. I think we ought to make a total study of the ability to buy American in all of the commodity product categories within the limits of economic sense. I do not know that we ought to go to the extremes we went to in the drug program. I think in virtually any other area, such as galvanized steel and so forth, when we possibly can we ought to deal with American suppliers if for no other reason than to insure that we are getting our money's worth and not short counts and inferior products.

MR. POATS. AID-financed procurement of iron and steel mill products are U.S.—only now with the exception of galvanized sheet, but in practice it is working out to be U.S. only.

MR. RIEGLE. I understand that there are other products in the CIP program in which we are still getting from foreign sources.

MR. POATS. That is right.

MR. RIEGLE. May we have a review of those to see which ones we can bring home?

MR. POATS. We are doing that right now, Mr. Riegle. In fact, a part of the process of reducing our commercial import program and shifting that burden to the Vietnam National Bank is exactly this—to eliminate from our program those things which are bought offshore.

MR. RIEGLE. Fine. That concludes my testimony.

I just want to say for the record, Mr. Chairman, how much I appreciate as a freshman Member of the House your patience and forbearance in allowing me to go ahead and proceed with this testimony. It is appreciated very much.

MR. PASSMAN. I want to say to the distinguished gentleman that you have made an important contribution in the examination. The questions that you have asked and the answers that you have received are worth a great deal not only to the committee but will be of value to the Congress and to the country.